Learn C
on the Mac

DAVE MARK

Apress®

Learn C on the Mac

Copyright © 2009 by Dave Mark

ISBN-13 (paperback): 978-1-4302-1809-8

ISBN-13 (electronic): 978-1-4302-1810-4

Printed and bound in the United States of America 9 8 7 6 5 4 3 2

Lead Editor: Clay Andres
Technical Reviewer: Kevin O'Malley
Editorial Board: Clay Andres, Steve Anglin, Mark Beckner, Ewan Buckingham, Tony Campbell, Gary Cornell, Jonathan Gennick, Michelle Lowman, Matthew Moodie, Jeffrey Pepper, Frank Pohlmann, Ben Renow-Clarke, Dominic Shakeshaft, Matt Wade, Tom Welsh
Project Manager: Beth Christmas
Copy Editor: Heather Lang
Associate Production Director: Kari Brooks-Copony
Production Editor: Laura Esterman
Compositor/Artist/Interior Designer: Diana Van Winkle
Proofreader: Liz Welch
Indexer: Toma Mulligan
Cover Designer: Kurt Krames
Manufacturing Director: Tom Debolski

Distributed to the book trade worldwide by Springer-Verlag New York, Inc., 233 Spring Street, 6th Floor, New York, NY 10013. Phone 1-800-SPRINGER, fax 201-348-4505, e-mail orders-ny@springer-sbm.com, or visit http://www.springeronline.com.

For information on translations, please contact Apress directly at 2855 Telegraph Avenue, Suite 600, Berkeley, CA 94705. Phone 510-549-5930, fax 510-549-5939, e-mail info@apress.com, or visit http://www.apress.com.

Apress and friends of ED books may be purchased in bulk for academic, corporate, or promotional use. eBook versions and licenses are also available for most titles. For more information, reference our Special Bulk Sales–eBook Licensing web page at http://www.apress.com/info/bulksales.

The source code for this book is available to readers at http://www.apress.com.

To my incredible family, D³KR4FR

Contents at a Glance

Contents

About the Author

 **Dave Mark** has been writing about the Mac for the past 20 years. His books include the *Macintosh Programming Primer* series (Addison-Wesley 1992), *Beginning iPhone Development* (Apress 2009), and the bestselling previous editions of this book. Dave loves the water and spends as much time as possible on it, in it, or near it. He lives with his wife and three children in Virginia.

About the
Technical Reviewer

Kevin O'Malley is a software engineer and author whose articles have appeared on the Apple Developer Connection, O'Reilly MacDevCenter, and Dr. Dobb's Journal web sites, as well as in *The Perl Journal* and *IEEE Internet Computing*. He is the author of *Programming Mac OS X: A Guide for UNIX Developers* (Manning Publications 2003). He worked at the University of Michigan's Artificial Intelligence laboratory for ten years as a software engineer. Kevin was also an adjunct lecturer in the University of Michigan's Department of Electrical Engineering and Computer Science, where he taught two programming courses. He currently works at Google in Mountain View, California.

Acknowledgments

This book could not have been written without the support of my wonderful family. Deneen, Daniel, Kelley, and Ryan, thank you all for everything you've done for me. I truly am a lucky man.

Many, many thanks to the fine folks at Apress. My friend Clay Andres started this ball rolling by bringing me over to Apress. Dominic Shakeshaft listened to my complaints with a gracious smile and great British charm. Beth Christmas, my esteemed project manager, pushed when I needed pushing and kept me going when I was flagging. My production editor, Laura Esterman, magically managed me across multiple books and kept me from getting things hopelessly tangled. To Heather Lang, copy editor extraordinaire, I am very lucky to have you as an editor. To Grace Wong and the production team, thank you with all my heart; it's a great pleasure to work with you. Thanks to Kari-Brooks Copony, who pulled together this gorgeous interior design, and to Diana Van Winkle for all the hard work of pouring a confused set of Word files into this very finished product. Pete Aylward assembled the marketing message and got it out to the world. To all the folks at Apress, thank you, thank you, thank you!

A very special shout out goes to Kevin O'Malley, my incredibly talented tech reviewer. Kevin made many important technical contributions to this book, helping me scrub the prose and the sample code to ensure that it followed the C standard to the letter. Any divergence from the standard is on me. Kevin, I owe you big time, buddy!

Finally, thanks to my friends and colleagues Jeff LaMarche, Dave Wooldridge, Todd Hitt, and David Sobsey for your patience as I've taken time away from our projects to finish this book. I'll say it again—I am indeed a very lucky man.

Preface

One of the best decisions I ever made was back in 1979 when I hooked up with my buddy Tom Swartz and learned C. At first, C was just a meaningless scribble of curly brackets, semicolons, and parentheses. Fortunately for me, Tom was a C guru, and with him looking over my shoulder, I learned C quickly.

Now it's your turn.

This time, I'll be looking over *your* shoulder as you learn C. My goal is to present every aspect of C the way I would have liked it explained to me. I've saved up all the questions I had as I learned the language and tried to answer them here.

Learning to program in C will open a wide range of opportunities for you. C is a tremendously popular programming language and is the basis for Java, C++, and Objective-C. Whether you want to start your own software company or just write programs for your own enjoyment, you will discover that C programming is its own reward. Most of all, C programming is fun.

I hope you enjoy this book. If you have any suggestions or corrections, I'd love to hear from you. In the meantime, turn the page, and let's get started!

Chapter 1

Welcome Aboard

Welcome! Chances are, you are reading this because you love the Mac. And not only do you love the Mac, but you also love the idea of learning how to design and develop your very own Mac programs.

You've definitely come to the right place.

This book assumes that you know how to use your Mac. That's it. You don't need to know anything about programming, not one little bit. We'll start off with the basics, and each step we take will be a small one to make sure that you have no problem following along.

This book will focus on the basics of programming. At the same time, you'll learn C, one of the most widely used programming languages in the world. And once you know C, you'll have a leg up on learning programming languages like Objective-C, C++, and Java—all of which are based on C. If you are going to write code these days, odds are good you'll be writing it in one of these languages.

Once you get through *Learn C on the Mac*, you'll be ready to move on to object-oriented programming and Objective-C, the official programming language of Mac OS X. Not to worry; in this book, we'll take small steps, so nobody gets lost. You can definitely do this!

Who Is This Book For?

When I wrote the very first edition of *Learn C on the Macintosh* back in 1991, I was writing with college students in mind. After all, in college was where I really learned to program. It seems I was way off. My first clue that I had underestimated my audience was when I started getting e-mails from fifth graders who were making their way through the book. Fifth graders! And not just one but lots of nine-, ten-, and eleven-year-old kids were digging in and learning to program. Cool! And the best part of all was when these kids started sending me actual shipping products that they created. You can't imagine how proud I was and still am.

Over the years, I've heard from soccer moms, hobbyists, even folks who were using the Mac for the very first time, all of whom made their way through *Learn C on the Macintosh* and came out the other end, proud, strong, and full of knowledge.

So what do you need to know to get started? Although learning C by just reading a book is possible, you'll get the most out of this book if you run each example program as you encounter it. To do this, you'll need a Mac running Mac OS X (preferably version 10.5 or later) and an Internet connection. You'll need the Internet connection to download the free tools Apple has graciously provided for anyone interested in programming the Mac and to download the programs that go along with this book.

Again, if you know nothing about programming, don't worry. The first few chapters of this book will bring you up to speed. If you have some programming experience (or even a lot), you might want to skim the first few chapters, and then dig right into the C fundamentals that start in Chapter 3.

The Lay of the Land

Here's a quick tour of what's to come in this book:

- Chapter 2 takes you to Apple's web site, so you can download the free tools we'll use throughout this book.

- Chapter 3 starts you off with the basics of building a simple program.

- Chapter 4 shows you how to embed a series of programming statements into a reusable function, something you can call again and again.

- Chapter 5 adds variables and operators into the mix, bringing the power of mathematical expressions into your programs.

- Chapter 6 introduces the concept of flow control, using constructs like `if`, `else`, `do`, and `while` to control the direction your program takes.

- Chapter 7 covers pointers and parameters, two concepts that will add a dramatic new level of power to your programs.

- Chapter 8 extends the simple data types used in the first half of the book, adding the ability to work with more complex data types like arrays and text strings.

- Chapter 9 takes this concept one step further, adding the ability to design your own custom data structures.

- Chapter 10 shows you how to save your program's data and read it back in again by introducing the concept of the data file.

- Chapter 11 covers a variety of advanced topics—typecasting, unions, recursion, binary trees, and much more.

- Finally, Chapter 12 wraps things up and points you to the next step on your journey.

Ready to get started? Let's go!

Chapter 2

Go Get the Tools!

before we dig into the specifics of programming, you'll need to download a special set of tools from Apple's web site. The good news is that these tools are absolutely *free*. And, more importantly, Apple's tools give you everything you'll need to create world-class Mac programs, whether they be written in C, Objective-C, Java, or even C++.

To gain access to these tools, go to Apple's web site and sign up as a member of the Apple Developer Connection (ADC) program. The ADC web site offers an incredible wealth of information designed to help programmers build applications for the Mac and for the iPod Touch and iPhone.

Here's the web address to the front page of the ADC site:

```
http://developer.apple.com
```

You'll want to bookmark this page in your browser so you can refer to it later. In fact, you might want to create a *Learn C on the Mac* bookmark folder in your browser just for web sites I mention in this book.

Don't let the sheer volume of information on this site overwhelm you. Over time, that information will start to make a lot more sense. For now, let's get in, get the tools, and get out—no need to linger just yet.

Create an ADC Account

Before Apple will let you download the tools, you'll first need to join ADC's iPhone Developer Program or Mac Developer Program. Both are free to join. Since not everyone has an iPhone just yet, let's stick with the Mac Developer Program.

On the front page of the ADC web site, click the button that says *Visit Mac Dev Center* or type this URL into your browser:

`http://developer.apple.com/mac/`

The Mac Dev Center is the part of ADC dedicated to all things related to Mac programming. Look for the link that says *sign-up*. You'll find it in the very first paragraph of text on the page, as shown in Figure 2-1. The link will take you to a sign-up page, where you'll fill out a form and agree to the ADC terms and conditions.

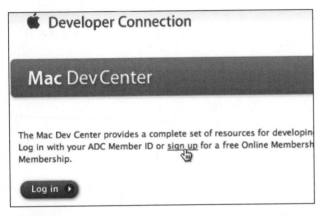

Figure 2-1. *Click the sign-up link on the Mac Dev Center front page.*

Once you complete the sign-up process, make a note of your Apple ID and password. These will come in incredibly useful. You'll use them to log in each time you come back to the Mac Dev Center. You'll also be able to use your Apple ID in other areas of the Apple web site, including Apple's online store.

Download the Tools

Once you have your Apple ID, go back to the Mac Dev Center front page (`http://developer.apple.com/mac/`).

If you are not already logged in, click the *Log in* button shown in Figure 2-1. Enter your Apple ID and password, and you'll be logged in and brought back to the Mac Dev Center front page. But this time, you'll have access to a variety of Mac Dev Center resources. Most importantly, you'll now be able to download Xcode, Apple's suite of programming tools.

Take a look at Figure 2-2: notice the cursor pointing to the *Xcode* link. At the time of this writing, version 3.1 was the latest and greatest version of Xcode. Don't worry if the version number is greater than 3.1. The project files that go along with this book will be updated to run with the latest version of Xcode.

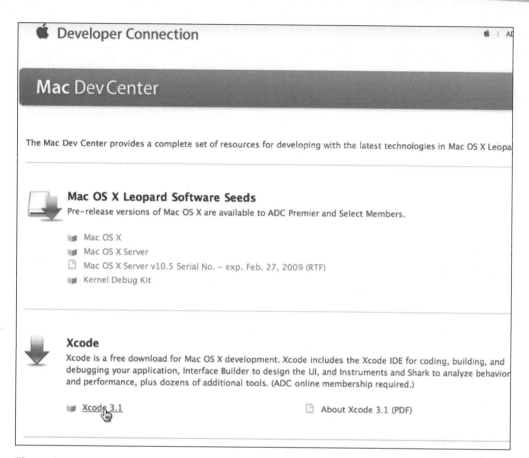

Figure 2-2. *Once you're logged in to the Mac Dev Center site, find the link to the Xcode download page.*

Before you click the Xcode download link, make sure you have plenty of space available on your hard drive. The download file takes up more than a gigabyte (GB) of hard drive space. And you'll need space to unpack the file and still more space for your programming projects. I would make sure you have at least 3GB of extra space on your drive.

CAUTION

It is always a good policy to leave 10 percent of your hard drive empty. That gives Mac OS X room to do its behind-the-scenes maneuvering, with plenty of room to spare. If that 3GB you are saving for Xcode will eat into your 10 percent empty space, consider moving some files off to another drive.

Once you've ensured that you have enough hard drive space, click the Xcode link. A few seconds later, your browser will start downloading the Xcode *.dmg* file. A *.dmg* file is a disk image, sort of like a virtual hard drive. You'll see how to open your *.dmg* file in a moment.

It's a good idea to check the status of your download, to make sure the download has actually started and to get a sense of how long it will take. Your web browser should have a download window. In Safari, you open the download window by selecting **Downloads** from the **Window** menu or by pressing ⌥⌘L. My download-in-progress is shown in Figure 2-3. Note the magnifying glass icon on the right side of the *Downloads* window. Click this icon once your download is complete to open a Finder window containing your *.dmg* file. Click the icon, and let's install the tools.

Figure 2-3. *Safari's download window showing the Xcode download. Note the magnifying glass icon on the right; it will reveal the .dmg file in the Finder.*

Installing the Tools

Once your *.dmg* file download is complete, double-click the file in the Finder. The Finder will open the *.dmg* file (see Figure 2-4) and mount the file on your desktop, just as if it were a hard drive.

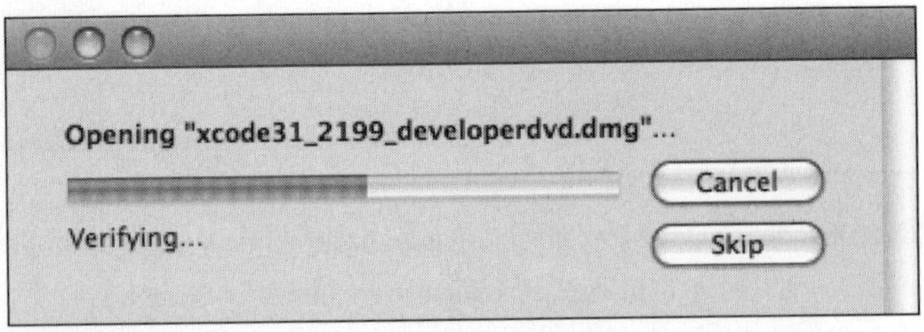

Figure 2-4. *The Finder is opening and mounting our .dmg file.*

As you can see in Figure 2-5, the *.dmg* file will be mounted as a volume named *Xcode Tools*. Click *Xcode Tools*, and double-click the icon labeled *XcodeTools.mpkg*. *XcodeTools.mpkg* is the actual installer.

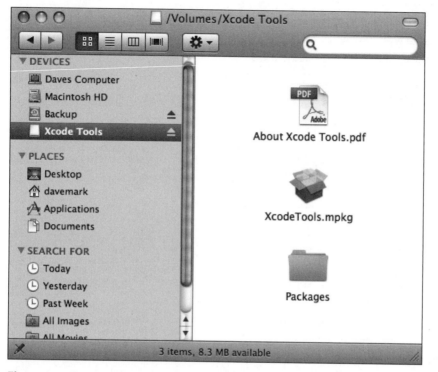

Figure 2-5. *The .dmg file mounted as the volume named Xcode Tools*

Once the installer launches, follow the instructions. In general, when given a choice, use the default settings. In other words, don't make any changes; just click the continue button. You won't be able to install Xcode on any drive other than your boot drive. Keep going until the installer tells you the tools are installed. This will take a few minutes.

NOTE

Once the installer is finished installing the tools, eject the *Xcode Tools* volume, just as you would any other volume. One way is to click the eject button to the right of the *Xcode Tools* entry in the Finder. Once the volume is ejected, it will disappear from the Finder. Once you are certain that the tools were installed properly, you might also want to delete the *.dmg* file from your downloads folder, just to save some hard drive space.

Take Your Tools for a Test Drive

Now that you've installed the tools, let's explore. The first thing to note is the new *Developer* folder at the top level of your hard drive. Go ahead and take a look. It is at the same level as your *Applications* folder. As you make your way down your programming path, you will spend a *lot* of time in the *Developer* folder.

TIP

Unix folks have created a very efficient system for describing where files live. Files and folders at the top level of your hard drive start with a slash character "/", which is followed by the file or folder name. Thus, we might refer to */Applications* or */Developer*. To dive deeper, add another slash and another file or folder name. For example, inside the *Applications* folder is a *Utilities* subfolder, and inside that is an application named Terminal. Unix folks would refer to the Terminal application using this path: */Applications/Utilities/Terminal*.

Get the idea?

The tools package you just installed came with its own set of applications. They live inside their own *Applications* folder within the *Developer* folder. Unix folks refer to this folder as */Developer/Applications*. We'll use this Unix path naming convention throughout this book, because it works really well.

TIP

To get to the */Developer* folder using the Finder, click the icon for your main drive. Unless you renamed it, it will have the name *Macintosh HD*.

In the Finder, navigate into */Developer/Applications*. Inside that folder, you'll find several subfolders along with a number of applications. The most important of these applications is the one named Xcode.

As you'll learn throughout this book, Xcode is a program that helps you organize and build your own programs. Technically, Xcode is known as an **integrated development environment** (IDE). An IDE is a comprehensive, all-in-one, Swiss Army knife for programmers. IDEs typically feature a sophisticated source code editor (for writing your programs) and a variety of tools for building, running, testing, and analyzing your programs. As IDEs go, Xcode is quite a good one.

If you are new to programming, don't let this detail overwhelm you. As you make your way through this book, you'll learn how to use Xcode to create, build, and run a ton of programs.

All this will be old hat to you very soon. For the moment, our goal is to run Xcode, create a test program, and run the test program, just to verify that we have installed Xcode properly.

Double-click the Xcode icon.

The Xcode Welcome Screen

When you launch Xcode for the very first time, a welcome screen appears, similar to the one shown in Figure 2-6. The welcome screen acts as a front end for lots of useful information that Apple provides. Click around, and check out what's there. Don't worry; you won't hurt anything, and it's good to get a sense of the range of materials available.

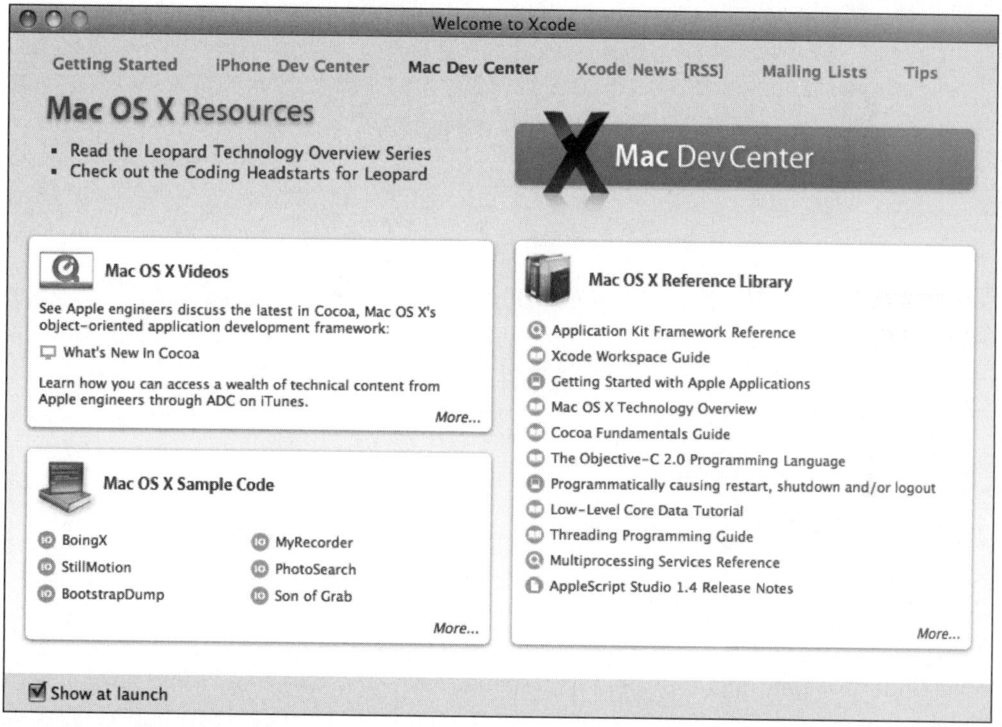

Figure 2-6. *Xcode's welcome screen*

As you get used to working with Xcode, you might get tired of seeing this welcome screen. No problem! To get rid of the welcome screen, uncheck the *Show at launch* check box in the lower-left corner of the window.

Creating Your First Xcode Project

Xcode organizes all the files you use to build a specific program using something called a **project file**. The project file is an organization center for all the information related to your project. The project file does *not* hold the resources that make up your **project**. Instead, it knows where everything lives on your hard drive and makes it easy to edit your project elements and combine all the pieces into a running program. Again, don't worry about the details. For now, just follow along, and by the end of this book, you'll feel very comfortable using Xcode.

Let's create a new project, just to make sure Xcode is installed properly.

Select **New Project...** from the **File** menu. Xcode will bring up a new window asking you to select the project type that you want to create. As you can see in Figure 2-7, there are a *lot* of different project types. The left side of the window lets you choose between iPhone OS and Mac OS X. In this book, we'll be creating projects designed to run on the Mac, so we'll focus on the Mac OS X project types.

NOTE

In case you're new to programming, OS stands for **operating system.** Your operating system is the program running on your computer, iPhone, or iPod that manages all the device's activities.

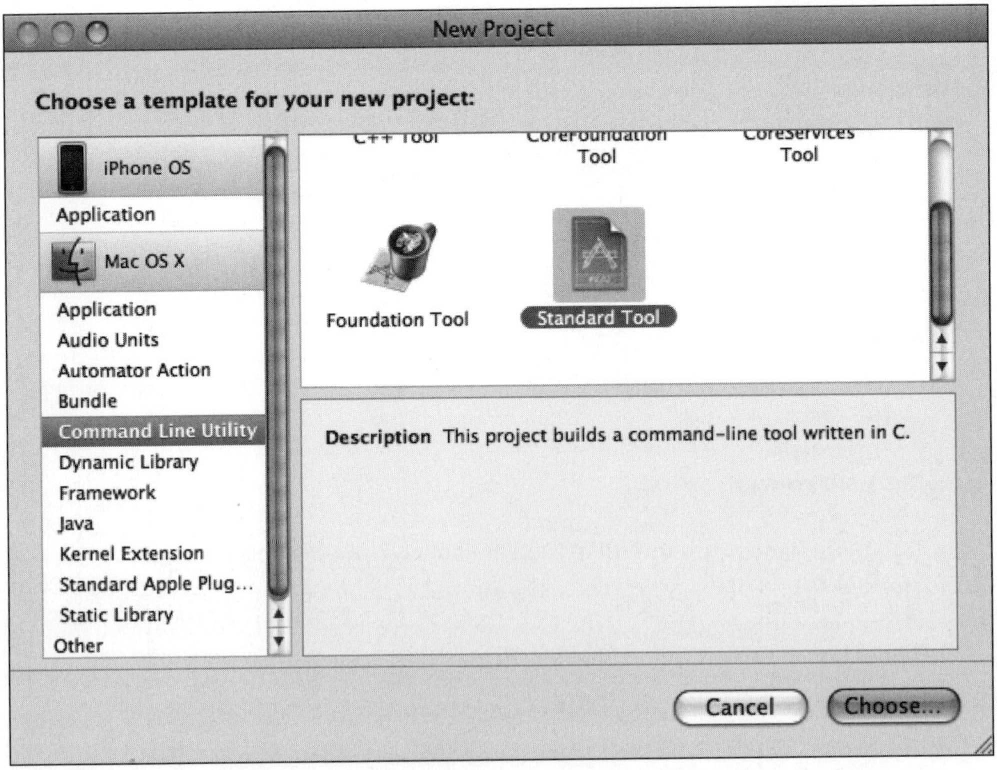

Figure 2-7. *Xcode prompting you to determine what type of new project you want to create*

The programs in this book will all make use of the command line utility template. Basically, a command line utility is a program that runs in a text window, without taking advantage of Mac gadgets like windows, buttons, scroll bars, and the like. Though all those graphical gadgets are fun to work with, and you *will* eventually want to add them to your programs, the basics of programming are best explained without adding all that complexity.

Click the text that says *Command Line Utility* in the left-hand pane of the *New Project* window. Then, in the upper-right pane, click the *Standard Tool* icon. Now click the *Choose…* button.

Saving Your New Project

The next step is to decide where to save our new project file. When you clicked the *Choose…* button, Xcode prompted you to select the name of your new project and to select the folder in which to save your new project. Start by navigating over to your *Documents* folder. Now click the *New Folder* button, and name your new folder *Learn C Projects*. Navigate into the *Learn C Projects* folder, and type **hello** in the *Save As* field (see Figure 2-8).

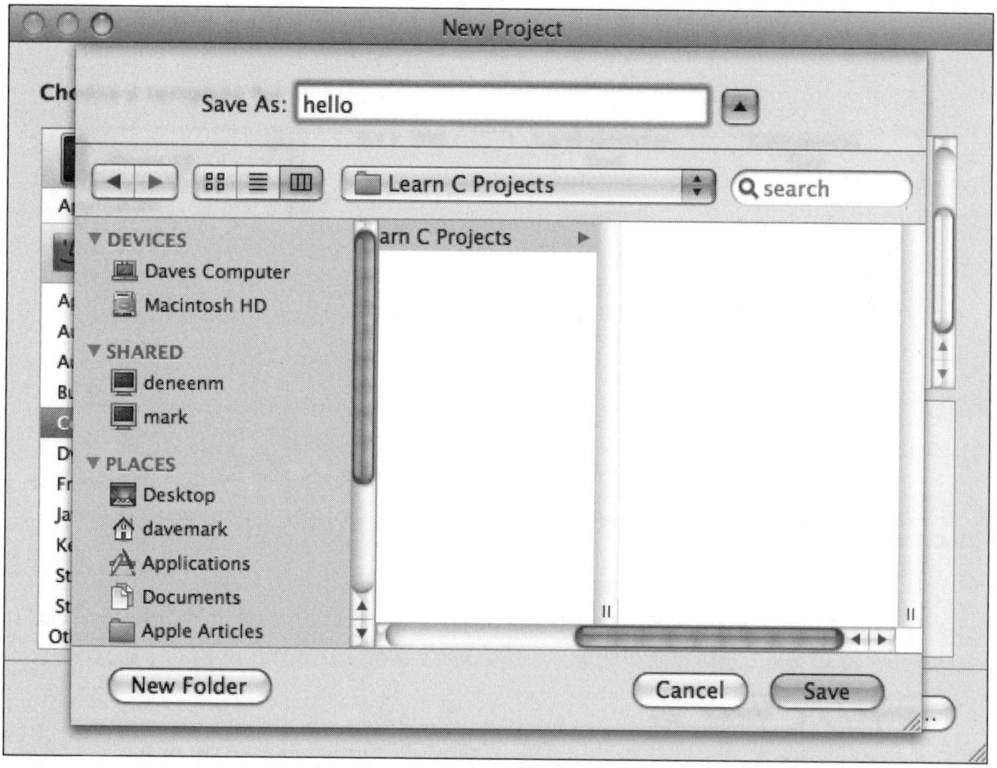

Figure 2-8. *Where should you save your new project? Click the Choose… button to select a destination, and name your new project hello.*

Now click the *Save* button. This creates a new folder named *hello*, creates a new project file, and saves the project file and its related resources within this folder.

Running the Project

The most noticeable thing that happened when you clicked the *Save* button is the appearance of the new project window (see Figure 2-9). Your project window is jam-packed with all sorts of buttons, controls, and text. Don't worry about all that stuff. Over time, you'll become quite comfortable with everything you see. For now, you only need to know that this project window is your first sign that Xcode is installed properly.

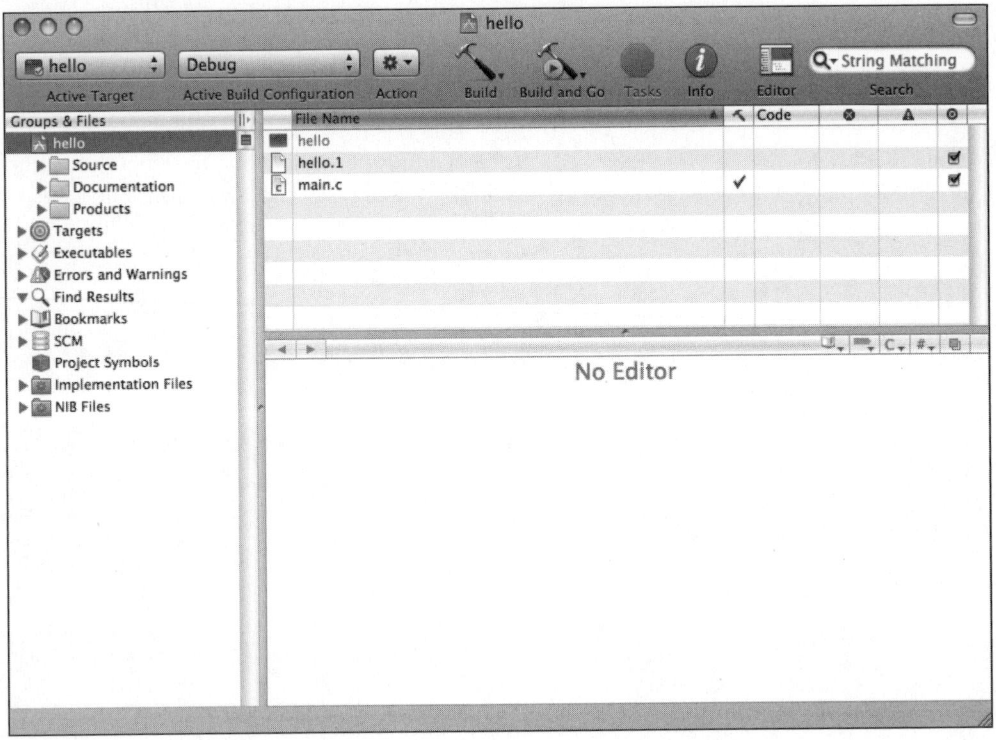

Figure 2-9. *Your new project window*

Your First Program

We have just created a new Xcode project. Like all the programs in this book, this project is completely text based—there are no buttons, scroll bars, icons, and so on. All the action will happen in a simple scrolling text window known as the console window. Before we take our program for a test run, let's open the console window.

Select **Console** from Xcode's **Run** menu. A blank console window will appear (see Figure 2-10).

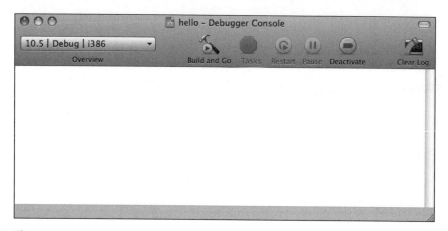

Figure 2-10. *The blank console window, before we run our program*

As you can see, the body of the console window is blank. Let's run our program and see what happens.

Select **Build and Run** from the **Build** menu. If the console window disappears, bring it to the front by again selecting **Console** from Xcode's **Run** menu.

Our text program puts a time stamp in the console window, telling us exactly when our program started running. It next displays the text *Hello, World!* followed by an exit status message, and then exits gracefully (see Figure 2-11). We didn't have to do anything to the project to tell the program what to do. When Xcode creates a new C project, this program is what comes right out of the box.

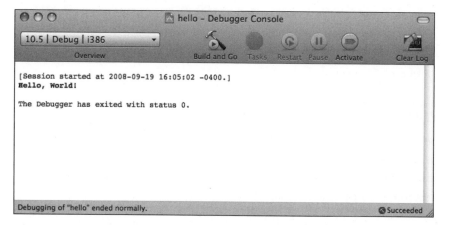

Figure 2-11. *The console window, showing the text produced when we ran our program*

ading the Book Projects

one last thing in this chapter before we can move on: download all the sample projects that go along with this book. You'll find them all on the Apress web site. This URL will take you to the main web page for *Learn C on the Mac*:

```
http://www.apress.com/book/view/9781430218098
```

In the column on the left side of this web page, you'll see a section called *Book Details* and, below that, a section called *Book Extras*. In the *Book Extras* section, you'll find a link labeled *Source Code*. Click that link. A file called *Learn C Projects.zip* will download to your hard drive.

Locate the file *Learn C Projects.zip* in your downloads folder and double-click it. The file will unzip itself and leave you with a new folder named *Learn C Projects*. That, my friend, contains the keys to the kingdom, the collected projects from the entire book. Drag the folder someplace safe. If you like, once you've placed *Learn C Projects* in its new home, you can drag it from its new location to the sidebar in a Finder window to make it a bit easier to get to.

Let's Move On

Well, that's about it for this chapter. You've accomplished a lot. You've joined ADC, logged in, downloaded the Xcode installer, installed Xcode, created a new project, and built and run your very first program. Awesome! I'd say that calls for a nice, cool beverage of your choice and a well-deserved round of applause.

Feel free to quit Xcode if you like. We'll fire it up again in the next chapter. See you there!

Chapter 3

Programming Basics

efore we dig into C programming specifics, we'll spend a few minutes discussing the basics of programming: Why write a computer program? How do computer programs work? We'll answer these questions and look at all of the elements that come together to create a computer program, such as source code, a compiler, and the computer itself.

If you've already done some programming, skim through this chapter. If you feel comfortable with the material, skip ahead to Chapter 4. Most of the issues covered in this chapter will be independent of the C language.

Programming

Why write a computer program? There are many reasons. Some programs are written in direct response to a problem too complex to solve by hand. For example, you might write a program to calculate the constant π to 5,000 decimal places or to determine the precise moment to fire the boosters that will safely land the Mars Rover.

Other programs are written as performance aids, allowing you to perform a regular task more efficiently. You might write a program to help you balance your checkbook, keep track of your baseball card collection, or lay out this month's issue of *Dinosaur Today*.

Whatever their purpose, each of these examples shares a common theme. They are all examples of the art of programming. Your goal in reading this book is to learn how to use the C programming language to create programs of your own. Before we get into C, however, let's take a minute to look at some other ways to solve your programming problems.

Some Alternatives to C

As mentioned in Chapter 1, C is one of the most popular programming languages around. There's very little you can't do in C (or in some variant of C), once you know how. On the other hand, a C program is not necessarily the best solution to every programming problem.

For example, suppose you are trying to build a database to track your company's inventory. Rather than writing a custom C program to solve your problem, you might be able to use an off-the-shelf package like FileMaker Pro or perhaps a Unix-based solution like MySQL or PostgreSQL to construct your database. The programmers who created these packages solved most of the knotty database-management problems you'd face if you tried to write your program from scratch. The lesson here is, before you tackle a programming problem, examine all the alternatives. You might find one that will save you time and money or that will prove to be a better solution to your problem.

Some problems can be solved using the Mac's built-in scripting language, AppleScript. Just like C, AppleScript is a programming language. Typically, you'd use AppleScript to control other applications. For example, you might create an AppleScript script that gets your daily calendar from iCal, formats it just the way you like it using TextEdit, and then prints out the results. Or, perhaps, you might write a script that launches Safari and opens each of your bookmarked news sites in a separate window. If you can use existing applications to do what you need, chances are good you can use AppleScript to get the job done.

Some applications feature their own proprietary scripting language. For instance, Microsoft Excel lets you write programs that operate on the cells within a spreadsheet. Some word processing programs let you write scripts that control just about every word processing feature in existence. Though proprietary scripting languages can be quite useful, they aren't much help outside their intended environments. You wouldn't find much use for the Excel scripting language outside Excel, for example.

What About Objective-C, C++, and Java?

There is a constant debate as to which programming language is the best one to learn first. Naturally, the C++ people think that C++ is by far the best language to start with. Java and Objective-C people feel the same way about Java and Objective-C. But the truth is, each of those languages is based on C. And if you learn C first, you'll have a huge leg up on learning any of them. And when the next C-based languages hit the streets, you'll have a leg up on that one, as well.

In a nutshell, C is the best language to start with because many other languages use the vast majority of C's syntax and structure. Objective-C, C++, and Java each start with C and add in their own specific forms for adding objects to your programs. Learning C first is like learning to walk before you learn how to run. If you learn C first, you'll have an excellent foundation on which to base your future programming education.

TAKING APPLESCRIPT FOR A TEST DRIVE

Want to mess with AppleScript? Everything you need to do just that is already on your hard drive. Look in your *Applications* folder for an *AppleScript* subfolder (that's */Applications/AppleScript* in programmer language). Inside the *AppleScript* subfolder, you'll find an application named Script Editor that lets you create and run AppleScript scripts.

To try your hand at scripting, launch TextEdit (it's also in the *Applications* folder), and type a few lines of text into the text editing window that appears, as shown in the following image:

Next, launch Script Editor. Type in the following script, and click the *Run* button:

```
tell application "TextEdit"
    get the fifth word of front document
end tell
```

If all goes well, the fifth word from the TextEdit window should appear in the results pane at the bottom of the Script Editor window, as shown in the following image:

What's the Best Language for Programming the Mac or iPhone?

All the programs in this book will run in the console, a scrolling text window that is part of Xcode. If you would like to build applications that feature the Mac look-and-feel with buttons, scroll bars, and windows, you'll need to finish this book, then learn Objective-C, and then learn Cocoa.

Objective-C is a programming language, like C, but it's designed to work with objects. Objects are blocks of code that represent parts of your program, such as a scrolling window, an image, or a menu. Cocoa is a vast collection of objects that represent all elements of the Mac experience. Objective-C and Cocoa were designed to work together. Learn C, Objective-C, and Cocoa, and you will have everything you need to develop even the most complex Macintosh applications.

Learn C on the Mac is the beginning of a series of books that will teach you how to build professional Mac and iPhone applications. Once you've finished this book, you'll want to dig into *Learn Objective-C on the Mac* by Mark Dalrymple and Scott Knaster (Apress 2009). It was designed as a sequel to *Learn C* and does a great job taking you from C to Objective-C.

Learn Cocoa on the Mac was written by Dave Mark (hey, that's me!) and Jeff LaMarche (Apress 2009). It completes the cycle, giving you everything you need to build your own scrollable, clickable Mac applications.

If you are interested in building applications that run on the iPhone or iPod Touch, check out *Beginning iPhone Development* by Dave Mark (yes, me again) and Jeff LaMarche (Apress 2009). *Beginning iPhone Development* was also written as a sequel to *Learn Objective*-C. Instead of focusing on Cocoa, though, *Beginning iPhone Development* focuses on Cocoa Touch, the object collection designed for iPhone and iPod Touch.

So, first, finish this book, and then make your way through *Learn Objective-C on the Mac*. If Mac application design is your goal, next pick up a copy of *Learn Cocoa on the Mac*. If the iPhone is your thing, pick up *Beginning iPhone Development*.

And that's the road map. Oh, one more thing. You can find each of these books on the Apress web site at http://www.apress.com.

The Programming Process

In Chapter 2, you installed the Mac developer tools and went through the process of creating a project, which you then built and ran. Let's take a look at the programming process in a bit more detail.

Source Code

No matter their purpose, most computer programs start as **source code**. Your source code will consist of a sequence of instructions that tells the computer what to do. Source code is written in a specific programming language, such as C. Each programming language has a specific set of rules that defines what is and isn't legal in that language.

Your mission in reading this book is to learn how to create useful, efficient, and, best of all, legal C source code.

If you were programming using everyday English, your source code might look like this:

```
Hi, Computer!
Do me a favor. Take the numbers from 1 to 10,
add them together, then tell me the sum.
```

If you wanted to run this program, you'd need a programming tool that understood source code written in English. Since Xcode doesn't understand English but does understand C, let's look at a C program that does the same thing:

```c
#include <stdio.h>

int main (int argc, const char * argv[]) {
    int    number, sum;

    sum = 0;

    for ( number=1; number<=10; number++ ) {
        sum += number;
    }

    printf( "The sum of the numbers from 1 to 10 is %d.", sum );

    return 0;
}
```

If this program doesn't mean anything to you, don't panic. Just keep reading. By the time you finish reading this book, you'll be writing C code like a pro.

In case you were wondering, here's what appeared in the console window when we ran this program:

```
The sum of the numbers from 1 to 10 is 55.
```

Want to try this out for yourself? In Chapter 2, you downloaded the project files for the book from the Apress web site. Open the *Learn C Projects* folder on your hard drive; next, open the folder called *03.01 - sample*, and double-click the file named *sample.xcodeproj* to open the project in Xcode.

Figure 3-1 shows the project window associated with *sample.xcodeproj*. The project window is a complex beast, full of incredibly useful tools to help with our programming pursuits. The most important part of the project window, at least for the moment, is the editing pane, the area that allows us to edit our source code.

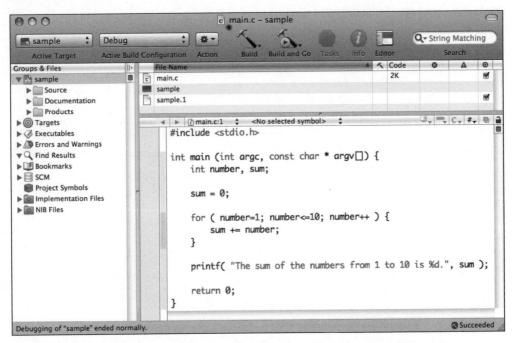

Figure 3-1. *An Xcode project window, showing some source code in the editing pane*

Open the console window by selecting **Console** from the **Run** menu or by typing ⇧⌘R. Now run the program by selecting **Build and Run** from the **Build** menu or by typing ⌘R.

The program should build and then run, and the text I showed you previously should appear in the console, albeit surrounded by some other text, like the date and an exit message. You can ignore the extra bits and revel in the fact that your program works!

OK, enough reveling. Let's get back to the programming process.

Compiling Your Source Code

Once your source code is written, your next job is to hand it off to a **compiler**. The compiler translates your C source code into instructions that make sense to your computer. These instructions are known as **machine language** or **object code**. Source code is for you; machine language/object code is for your computer. You write the source code using an **editor**, and then the compiler translates your source code into a machine-readable form.

NOTE

Don't let the terminology bog you down. Read the rest of this chapter, just to get a basic sense of the programming process, and then move on to Chapter 4. I'll lay out everything step-by-step for you, so you won't get lost.

Think of the process of building and running your program as a three-stage process. First, Xcode **compiles** all your source code into object code. Next, all the object code in your project is **linked** together by a program called a **linker** to form your application. That linked application is what actually **runs** on your computer.

Take a look at Figure 3-2. This project contains two source code files, one named *main.c* and another named *extras.c*, as well as an object file named *lib.o*. Sometimes, you'll find yourself making use of some code that others have already compiled. Perhaps they want to share their code but do not want to show you their source code. Or, perhaps, you built a **library** of code that you'll use again and again and don't want to recompile each time you use the code. By **precompiling** the library into object code and adding the object code into your project, you can save some time.

As it turns out, a library called the *C standard library* comes with Xcode and every other C development environment in the universe. Hmm, I guess that's why they call it "standard." The C standard library comes packed with an incredible number of useful programming bits and pieces that we can use in our own programs. We'll talk about those bits and pieces as we make use of them throughout the book.

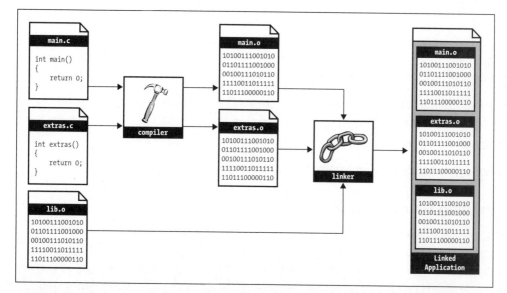

Figure 3-2. *Building your application. First, your source code is compiled, and then your object code is linked. The linked application is ready to run.*

As you can see in Figure 3-2, Xcode starts by compiling *main.c* and *extras.c* into object code. Next, all three object files are linked together by the linker into a runnable application. The programs in this book were all designed to run in the console window. As you make your way through the rest of the books in this series, you'll learn how to add the rest of the pieces necessary to create applications that can be run from the Finder. For now, Xcode's console will do just fine.

What's Next?

At this point, don't worry too much about the details. The basic concept to remember from this chapter is how your C programs run: They start life as source code and then get converted to object code by the compiler. Finally, all the object code gets linked together to form your runnable application.

Chapter 4

C Basics: Functions

*e*very programming language is designed to follow strict rules that define the language's source code structure. The C programming language is no different. These next few chapters will explore the syntax of C.

Chapter 3 discussed some fundamental programming topics, including the process of translating source code into machine code through a tool called the compiler. This chapter focuses on one of the primary building blocks of C programming, the function.

C Functions

C programs are made up of functions. A **function** is a chunk of source code that accomplishes a specific task. You might write a function that adds together a list of numbers or one that calculates the radius of a given circle. Here's an example:

```c
int SayHello( void ) {
    printf( "Hello!!!\n" );
}
```

This function, named SayHello(), does one thing. It calls another function, named printf(), that prints a message in a special scrolling text window known as the **console window** or just plain **console**.

Technically, the function printf() sends its output to something called **standard output** and Xcode redirects standard output to the console window. You'll learn more about standard output in Chapter 10, when we discuss the process of working with files. For the moment, just think of printf() as a function that sends information to the console.

<u>NOTE</u>

> Throughout this book, we'll designate a function by placing a pair of parentheses after its name. This will help distinguish between variable names and function names. For example, the name doTask refers to a variable (variables are covered in Chapter 5), while doTask() refers to a function.

The Function Definition

Functions start off with a **function declaration**, in this case:

```
int SayHello( void )
```

A function declaration consists of a **return type**, the function name, and a pair of parentheses wrapped around a **parameter list**. We'll talk about the return type and parameter list later. For now, the important thing is to be able to recognize a function declaration and be able to pick out the function's name from within the declaration.

Following the declaration comes the **body** of the function. The body is always placed between a pair of curly braces: { and }. These braces are known in programming circles as left curly and right curly. Here's the body of SayHello():

```
{
    printf( "Hello!!!\n" );
}
```

The body of a function consists of a series of **statement**s. The simplest statements are typically followed by a semicolon (;). If you think of a program as a detailed set of instructions for your computer, a statement is one specific instruction. The printf() featured in the body of SayHello() is a statement. It instructs the computer to display some text in the console window.

As you make your way through this book, you'll learn C's rules for creating efficient, compilable statements.

Creating efficient statements will make your programs run faster with less chance of error. The more you learn about programming (and the more time you spend at your craft), the more efficient you'll make your code.

Syntax Errors and Algorithms

When you ask the compiler to compile your source code, the compiler does its best to translate your source code into object code. Every so often, the compiler will hit a line of source code that it just doesn't understand. When this happens, the compiler reports the problem to you. It does not complete the compile. The compiler will not let you run your program until every line of source code compiles.

As you learn C, you'll find yourself making two types of mistakes. The simplest type, called a **syntax error**, prevents the program from compiling. The syntax of a language is the set of rules that defines what is or is not legal. A well-formed compiler will only compile code that properly follows the C language syntax, as defined by the official C standard. Many syntax errors are the result of a mistyped letter, or typo. Another common syntax error occurs when you forget the semicolon at the end of a statement.

Syntax errors are usually fairly easy to fix. If the compiler doesn't tell you exactly what you need to fix, it will usually tell you where in your code the syntax error occurred and give you enough information to spot and repair the error.

The second type of mistake is a **semantic error**, or a flaw in your program's algorithm. An **algorithm** is the approach used to solve a problem. You use algorithms all the time. For example, here's an algorithm for sorting your mail:

1. Start by taking the mail out of the mailbox.

2. If there's no mail, you're done! Go watch TV.

3. Take a piece of mail out of the pile.

4. If it's junk mail, throw it away, and go back to step 2.

5. If it's a bill, put it with the other bills, and go back to step 2.

6. If it's not a bill and not junk mail, read it, and go back to step 2.

This algorithm completely describes the process of sorting through your mail. Notice that the algorithm works, even if you didn't get any mail. Notice also that the algorithm always ends up at step 2, with the TV on.

Figure 4-1 shows a pictorial representation of the mail-sorting algorithm, commonly known as a **flow chart**. Much as you might use an outline to prepare for writing an essay or term paper, you might use a flow chart to flesh out a program's algorithm before you actually start writing the program. Here's how this works.

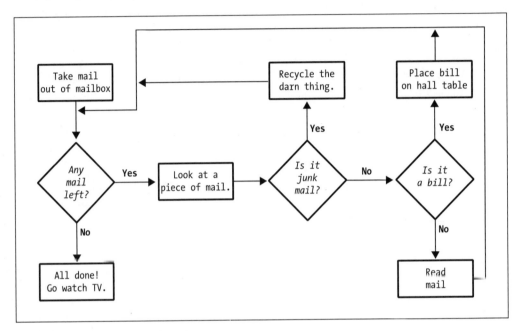

Figure 4-1. *The mail-sorting flow chart*

This flow chart uses two types of boxes. The rectangular box portrays an action, such as taking mail out of the mailbox or recycling the junk mail. Once you've taken the action, follow the arrow leading out of the rectangle to go on to the next step in the sequence.

Each diamond-shaped box poses a yes/no question. Unlike their rectangular counterparts, diamond-shaped boxes have two arrows leading out of them. One shows the path to take if the answer to the question inside the box is yes; the other shows the path to take if the answer is no. Follow the flow chart through, comparing it to the algorithm described previously.

In the C world, a well-designed algorithm results in a well-behaved program. On the other hand, a poorly designed algorithm can lead to unpredictable results. Suppose, for example, you wanted to write a program that added three numbers together, printing the sum at the end. If you accidentally printed one of the numbers instead of the sum of the numbers, your program would still compile and run. The result of the program would be in error, however (you printed one of the numbers instead of the sum), because of a flaw in your program's algorithm.

The efficiency of your source code is a direct result of good algorithm design. Keep the concept of algorithm in mind as you work your way through the examples in this book.

Calling a Function

In Chapter 2, you ran a test program to make sure Xcode (your programming software) was installed properly. The test program sat in a file called *main.c* and consisted of a single function, called main(). As a refresher, here's the source code from *main.c*:

```c
#include <stdio.h>

int main (int argc, const char * argv[]) {
    // insert code here...
    printf( "Hello, World!\n" );
    return 0;
}
```

At first blush, even this starter program can seem intimidating, but no worries, mate. There's really only one line in this code that you really need to focus on at this point in the book, and that's this function call:

```c
    printf( "Hello, World!\n" );
```

Though this program has lots of complicated-looking elements all around, at its heart is a single function call. As far as all the other dangly bits, you can read the "Five Easy Pieces" sidebar, or just ignore them and know that we'll get to them as we go along.

So what does "calling a function" really mean? Basically, whenever your source code calls a function, each of the statements in the *called* function is executed before the next statement of the *calling* function is executed.

Confused? Look at Figure 4-2. In this example, main() starts with a call to the function MyFunction(). This call to MyFunction() will cause each of the statements inside MyFunction() to be executed. Once the last statement in MyFunction() is executed, control is returned to main(). Next, main() calls AnotherFunction(). Once the last statement in AnotherFunction() is executed, control is again returned to main(), and main() can then exit with a return code of 0. When main() exits, your program exits. Returning a value of 0 tells whatever program launched your program that all is OK and that you are exiting normally.

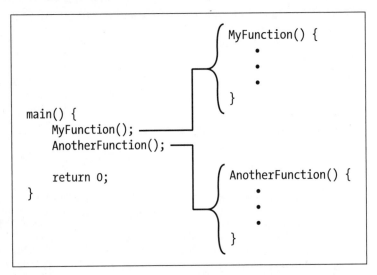

Figure 4-2. *main() calls MyFunction(). All the statements in MyFunction() are executed. Once MyFunction() returns, main() then calls AnotherFunction().*

Every C program you write will have a main() function. Your program will start running with the first line in main() and, unless something unusual happens, end with the last line in main(). Along the way, main() may call other functions which may, in turn, call other functions and so on.

FIVE EASY PIECES

The source code in *main.c* can be broken into five basic pieces. Here's the first piece:

```
#include <stdio.h>
```

In C, any line that starts off with a pound sign (#) is known as a **preprocessor directive**, an instruction that asks the compiler to do something special. This particular directive is called a **#include** (pronounced "pound include"). It asks the compiler to include code from another file on your hard drive as if that code was in this file in the first place. A #include file is also known as a **header file** or just plain **header**. As it turns out, the file *stdio.h* contains all kinds of goodies that we'll use throughout the book. Just ignore this line for now.

Here's the second piece:

```
int main (int argc, const char * argv[]) {
}
```

As we discussed a bit earlier, this is the function declaration for the function named main(). The curly braces surround the body of the function.

The third piece of this puzzle is this line:

```
// insert code here...
```

Any time the compiler encounters two slashes (//) in a row, it ignores the slashes and anything else on that line. This line of code is called a **comment**. Its only purpose is to document your code and to help make clear what's going on at this point in the program. Comments are a good thing.

The fourth piece is the call to the function printf(), which we'll focus on in a bit:

```
printf( "Hello, World!\n" );
```

The fifth and final piece of our program is this line of code:

```
return 0;
```

A return statement in a function tells the compiler that you are done with this function and you want to return. In this case, you want the function to return a value of 0.

Again, don't get hung up on the specifics. It'll all become clear as you go.

A Brief History of C

Before we dive deep into our discussion of functions, a bit of background on the evolution of the C language is in order.

Way back when, in the early 1970s, a group of programmers at AT&T's research arm, Bell Laboratories, created the first C compiler. Two of the programmers on that team, Brian Kernighan and Dennis Ritchie, wrote a book that described the rules a well-formed C program must follow. That book was called *The C Programming Language* and became the de facto standard reference for all C programmers. The book was fondly referred to as *K&R*, named for the initials of the authors' last names.

During the 1980s, the American National Standards Institute (**ANSI**) worked to establish a more formal, national standard for the C programming language. This standard was formally ratified in 1989 and became known as **ANSI C**. The new standard was also commonly referred to as **C89**. A new version of *K&R* was published in 1988 based on the updated ANSI C standard.

In 1990, the *Organisation Internationale de Normalization*, also known as the International Organization for Standardization (ISO), adopted the C89 standard. This new version became known as **ISO C** or **C90**. ISO C evolved over time. In 1999, the ANSI adopted the current ISO C standard, which became known as **C99**. At the time of this writing, C99 is the current standard for the C programming language.

NOTE

Keep in mind that the ISO folks continue to work on improving the language. Interested in following along? Here's a link to the official home of the ISO C working group: `http://www.open-std.org/jtc1/sc22/wg14/`.

The following link is from the preceding web page and shows the work being done on C since that standard was adopted: `http://www.open-std.org/jtc1/sc22/wg14/www/standards.html#9899`.

As I stated earlier, the syntax of a language gives programmers a set of strict rules that must be followed if their code is to compile without error. For example, ISO C tells you when you can and can't use a semicolon. ISO C tells you to use a pair of curly braces to surround the body of each function. You get the idea. The greatest benefit to having an international standard for C is portability. With a minimum of tinkering, you can get an ISO C program written on one computer up and running on another computer. When you finish with this book, you'll be able to program in C on any computer that has an ISO C compiler.

The Standard Library

One element of the ISO C standard that relates directly to our discussion of functions is the **Standard Library**. The Standard Library is a set of functions available to every ISO C programmer. As you may have guessed, the `printf()` function you've seen in our sample source code is part of the Standard Library, as are tons of other great functions. You'll learn some of the more popular ones as you make your way through this book. Once you get comfortable with the Standard Library functions presented here, dig through some of the Standard Library documentation that you'll find on the Web, just to get a sense of what else is in there.

A number of great sites discuss the Standard Library. One of my favorite resources on the net is Wikipedia (`http://www.wikipedia.org`), an open-content, collaborative encyclopedia. If you've never played with Wikipedia, here's an excellent link to get you started:

```
http://en.wikipedia.org/wiki/ANSI_C_standard_
library
```

This page is a terrific way to get to know the Standard Library. There's a lot of interesting information here, but the best part is the table titled *C Standard Library headers* on the right side of the page, as shown in Figure 4-3. It contains a link to each of the Standard Library `#include` files. Each link takes you to a page that describes the functions included in that particular header file.

For example, click the *stdio.h* link. Wow, there sure are a ton of functions in this header file. If you scroll down a bit, you'll find a link to a page that describes the Standard Library function `printf()`. Follow that link, and you'll come to a page that contains just about everything you could ever want to know about `printf()`.

Yeah, it's a bit techie, but it's an invaluable reference resource once you start developing your own code or if you encounter a function in this book and want to know more.

C Standard Library headers

- assert.h
- complex.h
- ctype.h
- errno.h
- fenv.h
- float.h
- inttypes.h
- iso646.h
- limits.h
- locale.h
- math.h
- setjmp.h
- signal.h
- stdarg.h
- stdbool.h
- stddef.h
- stdint.h
- stdio.h
- stdlib.h
- string.h
- tgmath.h
- time.h
- wchar.h
- wctype.h

Figure 4-3. *This table of links on the Wikipedia page for the C Standard Library lists the Standard Library #include files. Click one of the links, and you'll be taken to a page that describes all the Standard Library functions covered by that #include file.*

Another great page (also referenced at the bottom of the Wikipedia page) is the detailed C Standard Library reference maintained by our friends at the University of Tasmania:

`http://www.infosys.utas.edu.au/info/documentation/C/CStdLib.html`

Enjoy!

Exploring Unix and Your Mac's Built-In Manual

One more thing is worth mentioning before we head back to functionville. Your Mac comes with an incredible built-in resource, just perfect for experimenting with C and learning about the Standard Library—the Terminal application. Terminal is found in */Applications/ Utilities*. In the Finder, you can use the shortcut ⇧⌘U to bring up the *Utilities* folder. Once there, double-click the *Terminal* application to launch it. You should see something similar to Figure 4-4. Don't worry if your Terminal window looks a bit different than mine. That's perfectly normal.

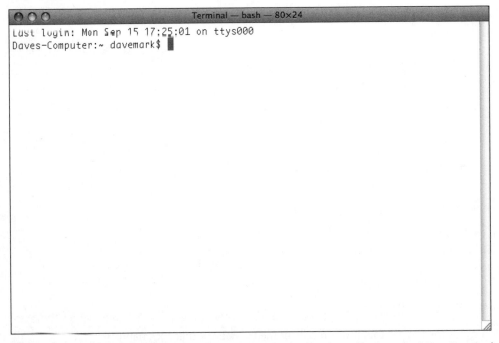

Figure 4-4. *The Terminal window, as it appears when the application is first launched. Your Terminal window may look slightly different—no worries if it does.*

The Terminal application allows us to communicate with the Mac's operating system a variant of the Unix operating system. If you've never heard of Unix, don't worry. You spend your entire life without touching Unix, and you can still create incredibly wonderful and complex C applications. That said, if you are a little bit curious, I'll sprinkle a bit of Unix goodness here and there throughout this book.

The Unix operating system was developed by a group of programmers at AT&T's Bell Laboratories in 1969. This was the same group that would go on to develop the C programming language. An **operating system**, or **OS**, is a program that runs on a computer, typically at startup, and is responsible for managing the computers resources and coordinating the computer's activities. One way to think of this is that the operating system sits in between your applications and your actual computer.

In the Terminal window shown in Figure 4-4, you can see two lines of text. The first one is a welcome message that includes the date and time of your last login, or Terminal session. The second line is called the **command prompt**. Here's the command prompt from my Terminal window:

```
Daves-Computer:~ davemark$
```

My command prompt tells me what directory I am currently looking at. It's my computer name, followed by a colon, followed by the name of the directory on that computer, followed by a dollar sign ($). My computer name is Daves-Computer. My current directory is ~davemark. In the Unix universe, ~xxx is the home directory of the user named xxx. So ~davemark is the home directory of the user named davemark. Unless your user name happens to be davemark, your command prompt will likely be slightly different.

Let's type a simple Unix command. Type the command *ls*, followed by a carriage return. The ls command asks Unix to list the files and folders in the current directory. Here's what I saw when I pressed Return:

```
Daves-Computer:~ davemark$ ls
Applications    Documents    Library    Music       Public
Desktop         Downloads    Movies     Pictures    Sites
Daves-Computer:~ davemark$
```

As you can see, Unix listed nine different folders in my home directory, followed by the same prompt, showing me that it was ready for me to type another command.

This next command is going to give us access to a set of **manual pages** built into every copy of Unix. Type the command *man printf*, followed by a carriage return. man is a program specifically designed to open a manual page. The word after man tells man which manual page to display.

If all goes well, Terminal will clear its window and list the first page of its printf manual page. Use the up and down arrow keys to scroll through the printf man page. You can also press the spacebar to move down a screen at a time.

When you are done reading the printf man page, press the q key, and the man program will quit ("q" for "quit," get it?). Want to learn more about man? Any guesses how you could bring up the manual page for man itself?

You guessed it! Type the command *man man*. This asks man to bring up its own man page. Pretty cool.

Press q to exit the man man page. Try typing the command *man stdio*, followed by a carriage return. This man page describes functions that make up the stdio part of the Standard Library.

Between the Wikipedia links and the built-in manuals, you've got some great resource material you can use to learn more about the Standard Library. As you make your way through the book, you'll encounter more Standard Library functions. Take the time to read about each one. Get a sense of what each function can and can't do. Get comfortable with the Standard Library documentation.

When you are done playing with Terminal, select **Quit Terminal** from the **Terminal** menu or just type ⌘Q.

Now let's get back to functionville.

Same Program, Two Functions

As you start writing your own programs, you'll find yourself designing many individual functions. You might need a function that puts a form up on the screen for the user to fill out. You might need a function that takes a list of numbers as input, providing the average of those numbers in return. Whatever your needs, you will definitely be creating a lot of functions. Let's see how it's done.

Our first program contained a function named main() that passed the text string "Hello, world!\n" to printf(). Our next program, *hello2*, captures that functionality in a new function, named SayHello().

You've probably been wondering why the characters "\n" keep appearing at the end of all our text strings. Don't worry; nothing's wrong with your copy of the book. The "\n" is perfectly normal. It tells `printf()` to move the cursor to the beginning of the next line in the text window, sort of like pressing the Return key in a text editor.

The sequence "\n" is frequently referred to as a **newline character**, a **carriage return**, or just plain **return**. By including a return at the end of a `printf()`, we know that the next line we print will appear at the beginning of the next line in the text window.

The hello2 Project

In the Finder, open the *Learn C Projects* folder. Open the subfolder named *04.01 - hello2*, and double-click the project file *hello2.xcodeproj*. A project window with the title *hello2* will appear, as shown in Figure 4-5.

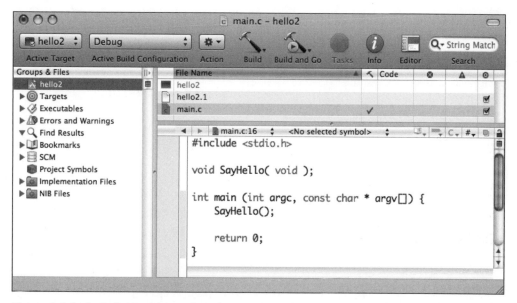

Figure 4-5. *In the hello2 project window, the area on the top is called the toolbar. The area to the lower left is called the Groups & Files pane. The area on the right, just below the toolbar, is called the detail pane. The area below that is called the editing pane.*

The area with the gray background on the top of the project window is called the **toolbar**. The toolbar contains a variety of menus that allow you to customize your project and buttons that help you control your project, as well as a search field.

The area below the toolbar is divided into a series of panes. A **pane** is a subarea of a window. The area to the left is called the ***Groups & Files* pane**. The *Groups & Files* pane lists all the files and resources associated with your project, organized in a variety of ways.

Take a look at Figure 4-6. Notice the gray triangle to the left of the very first item in the *Groups & Files* pane. Just like its Finder counterpart, this is called a **disclosure triangle**. Click it, and the disclosure triangle turns 90 degrees and reveals the items below it. Click it again, and it turns back, hiding its subitems again.

The very first item in the *Groups & Files* pane has the same name as the project, in this case, *hello2*. As you can see in Figure 4-6, this item is divided into three subitems: *Source*, *Documentation*, and *Products*. *Source* is where you'll find all the source code for your project. In our project, we only have a single file, *main.c*. Later in the book, we'll explore projects with more than one source code file.

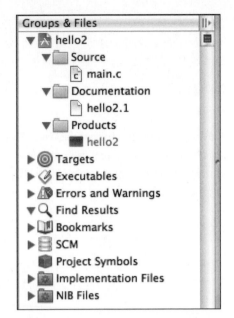

Figure 4-6. *This is the Groups & Files pane of the hello2 project window. Note the disclosure triangle to the left of the very first item. Click the triangle, and the subitems are revealed. Click again, and the subitems are hidden.*

Documentation is where the man pages that describe your project live. We're not going to get into the process of creating man pages in this book. If you are interested in learning more, go into Terminal, and type the command *man mdoc*.

Products are the fruits of your labor, your executables. In this book, all of our programs are text based and will run just fine in the console window, so we won't make use of anything that appears here.

TIP

Want to learn more about the rest of the items in the *Groups & Files* pane? Apple has an excellent tutorial on their web site. Here's a link: `http://developer.apple.com/documentation/ DeveloperTools/Conceptual/XcodeWorkspace/100-The_Project_Window/ chapter_3_section_2.html`.

Turn your attention back to Figure 4-5. The area on the right, just below the toolbar, is called the **detail pane**. Select an item in the *Groups & Files* pane, and the selected items (and any subitems) will be detailed in the detail pane.

The area below the detail pane is called the **editing pane**. Select a source code file in the *Groups & Files* or detail pane, and its contents will be displayed in the editing pane.

Notice the project window shown in Figure 4-7. In this one, the editing pane is missing. If this happens to you, you can easily bring the editing pane back into view. Locate the small dot at the bottom of the window. In Figure 4-7, the dot is just to the left of the cursor. Click the dot and drag straight up. Your editing pane should reappear. Ta-da!

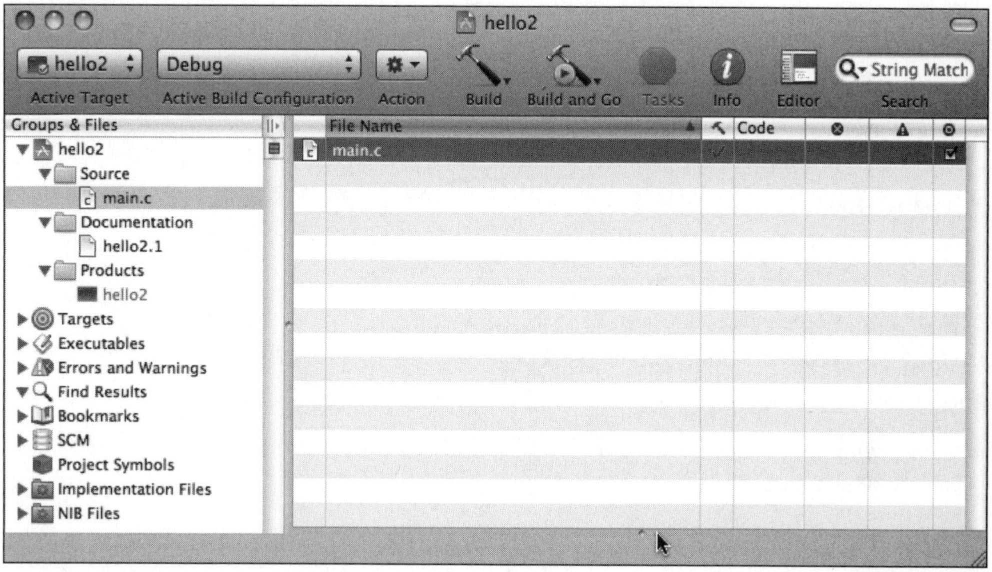

Figure 4-7. *The hello2 project window, with the editing pane hidden. To bring the editing pane into view, click the dot near the bottom of the window, just to the left of the cursor, and drag up.*

Another way to bring the editing pane back is to double-click the dot at the bottom of the window. You can also click the icon labeled *Editor* on the right side of the toolbar. Finally, if you double-click any file in the *Groups & Files* or detail pane, the appropriate editor for that file type is launched. If you double-click *main.c*, for example, Xcode will open a new editing window so you have a bit more room to edit your source code.

Let's get back to our project.

The hello2 Source Code

Here's the source code from *main.c*:

```c
#include <stdio.h>

void SayHello( void );

int main (int argc, const char * argv[]) {
    SayHello();

    return 0;
}


void SayHello( void ) {
    printf( "Hello, world!\n" );
}
```

Let's walk through this line by line. hello2 starts off with this line of source code:

```c
#include <stdio.h>
```

You'll find this line (or a slight variation) at the beginning of each one of the programs in this book. It tells the compiler to include the source code from the file *stdio.h* as it compiles *main.c*. *stdio.h* contains information we'll need if we are going to call `printf()` in this source code file. You'll see the `#include` preprocessor directive used throughout this book. Get used to seeing this line of code at the top of each of our source code files.

The line following `#include` is blank. This is completely cool. Since the C compiler ignores all blank lines, you can use them to make your code a little more readable. I like to leave two blank lines between each of my functions.

This line of code appears next:

```c
void SayHello( void );
```

While this line might look like a function definition, don't be fooled! If this were a function definition, it would not end with a semicolon, and it would be followed by a left curly ({) and the rest of the function. This line is known as a **function prototype** or **function declaration**. You'll include a function prototype for every function, other than `main()`, in your source code file.

To understand why, it helps to know that a compiler reads your source code file from the beginning to the end, a line at a time. By placing a complete list of function prototypes at the beginning of the file, you give the compiler a preview of the functions it is about to compile. The compiler uses this information to make sure that calls to these functions are made correctly.

NOTE

This will make a lot more sense to you once we get into the subject of parameters in Chapter 7. For now, get used to seeing function prototypes at the beginning of all your source code files.

Next comes the function `main()`. The first thing `main()` does is call the function SayHello():

```
int main (int argc, const char * argv[]) {
    SayHello();
```

At this point, the lines of the function `SayHello()` get run. When `SayHello()` is finished, `main()` can move on to its next line of code. The keyword `return` tells the compiler to return from the current function, without executing the remainder of the function. We'll talk about `return` later on. Until then, the only place you'll see this line is at the end of `main()`.

```
        return 0;
}
```

Following `main()` is another pair of blank lines, followed by the function `SayHello()`. SayHello() prints the string "Hello, world!", followed by a return, in a window, and then returns control to `main()`.

```
void SayHello( void ) {
    printf( "Hello, world!\n" );
}
```

Let's step back for a second and compare our first program to *hello2*. In our first program, `main()` called `printf()` directly. In hello2, `main()` calls a function that then calls `printf()`. This extra layer demonstrates a basic C programming technique, taking code from one function and using it to create a new function. This example took this line of code:

```
printf( "Hello, world!\n" );
```

and used it to create a new function called `SayHello()`. This function is now available for use by the rest of the program. Every time we call the function `SayHello()`, it's as if we executed the line of code:

```
printf( "Hello, world!\n" );
```

SayHello() may be a simple function, but it demonstrates an important concept. Wrapping a chunk of code in a single function is a powerful technique. Suppose you create an extremely complex function, say, 100 lines of code in length. Now, suppose you call this function in five different places in your program. With 100 lines of code, plus the five function calls, you are essentially achieving 500 lines' worth of functionality. That's a pretty good return on your investment!

Let's watch hello2 in action.

Running hello2

In Xcode, bring up the console window by selecting **Console** from the **Run** menu or by pressing ⇧⌘R. Now ask Xcode to compile your source code, link all the object code together, and then run the resulting executable. As you've already seen, Xcode can do all that with one command. Select **Build and Run** from Xcode's **Build** menu or type ⌘R.

You'll see a window similar to the one shown in Figure 4-8. Gee, this looks just like the output from Chapter 2's test program. Of course, that was the point. Even though we embedded our printf() inside the function SayHello(), hello2 produced the same results.

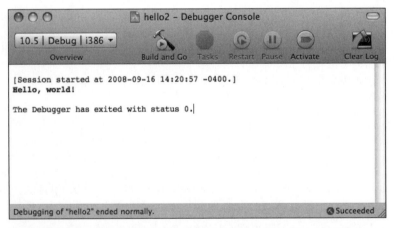

Figure 4-8. *These are the results of running hello2. Notice that this console output looks just like the result of running Chapter 2's test program. We used a different programming technique to get the same result.*

Before we move on to our next program, let's revisit a little terminology we first touched on at the beginning of the chapter. The window that appeared when we ran hello2 is referred to as the console window or just plain console. There are a number of Standard Library functions designed to send text to the console window. The text that appears in the console window is known as **output**. After you run a program, you're likely to check the output that appears in the console to make sure your program ran correctly.

Let's Do That Again, Again, Again

Imagine what would happen if you changed hello2's version of `main()` so that it read as follows:

```c
int main (int argc, const char * argv[]) {
    SayHello();
    SayHello();
    SayHello();

    return 0;
}
```

What's different? In this version, we've added two more calls to `SayHello()`. Can you picture what the console will look like after we run this new version?

To find out, close the hello2 project window, and then select **Open...** from Xcode's **File** menu. Note that as soon as you close the project window, Xcode will close all the other project-related windows automatically.

When Xcode prompts you to open a project, navigate into the *Learn C Projects* folder and then into the *04.02 - hello3* subdirectory, and open the *hello3.xcodeproj* project file.

When you run hello3, the console window shown in Figure 4-9 will appear. Take a look at the output. Does it make sense to you? Each call to `SayHello()` generates the text "Hello, world!" followed by a carriage return.

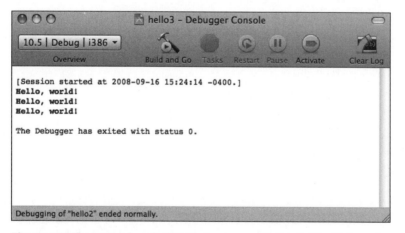

Figure 4-9. *The output from hello3. The program calls* SayHello() *three times. Can you tell from the output?*

ing Some Errors

n to the next chapter, let's see how the compiler responds to errors in our hello3 project window, select *main.c* so the source code appears in the ...g pane. Recall that you can also double-click *main.c* to make the file appear in its own window. Either method is fine.

In the source code window, find the line of source code containing the SayHello() function definition. Note that the **definition** of a function is where you actually provide the function body. A function **declaration** does *not* include curly braces. A function definition *does* include curly braces. Got it? Good! The line should read

```
void SayHello( void ) {
```

Click in the line, so the blinking cursor appears just before the left curly brace at the end of the line. Now type a semicolon so that the line now reads like this:

```
void SayHello( void ) ;{
```

Here's the entire file, showing the tiny change you just made:

```
#include <stdio.h>

void SayHello( void );

int main (int argc, const char * argv[]) {
    SayHello();
    SayHello();
    SayHello();

    return 0;
}


void SayHello( void ) ;{
    printf( "Hello, world!\n" );
}
```

Keep in mind that you only added a single semicolon to the source code. Let's give it a try. Select **Build and Run** from Xcode's **Build** menu or press ⌘R. Xcode knows that you changed your source code since the last time it was compiled, and it will try to recompile *main.c*. The *Build Results* window will appear, listing a single error:

```
Error: syntax error before '{' token
```

If you click that error, the section of source code where the error occurred is shown in the bottom half of the *Build Results* window. Figure 4-10 shows what this looks like.

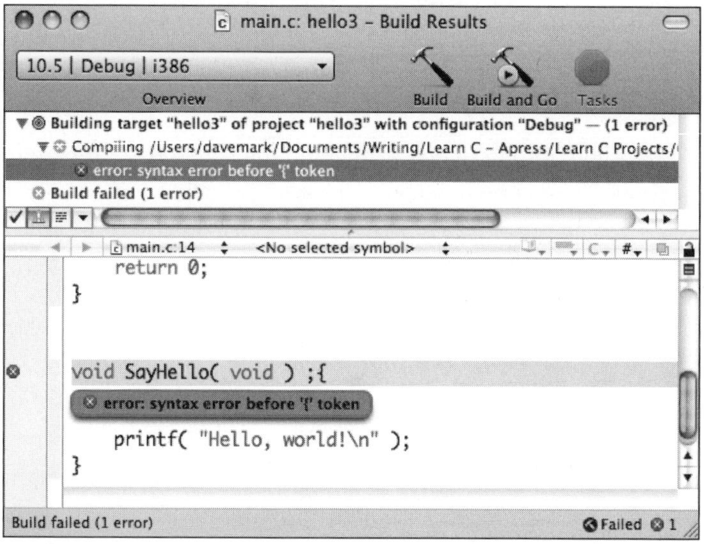

Figure 4-10. *The Build Results window lists the error on top and shows the error in place at the bottom.*

Sometimes, the compiler will give you a perfectly precise message that exactly describes the error it encountered, as it did in this case. At other times, the compiler acts like my crazy Aunt Ferlipedy. Here's an example.

Delete the semicolon you just added. To verify that you did this correctly, build and run your program. It should run just fine.

Next, find the `main()` function definition:

```
int main (int argc, const char * argv[]) {
```

Add a semicolon just before the left curly brace at the end of the line, just as you did earlier, in the definition of `SayHello()`. Here's what the line looks like now:

```
int main (int argc, const char * argv[]) ;{
```

Try to build again. This time, the compiler got so confused by the extra semicolon, it reported four errors instead of just one, and threw in four warnings to boot (see Figure 4-11). Notice, however, that the very first error message gives you a pretty good idea of what is going on. It complains about a syntax error before the left curly brace (*before '{' token*). The compiler is reading your source code and making its way down *main.c* when it encounters what it thinks is a function definition. But then, just when it expects an open curly brace, it finds a semicolon. It thinks, "Hrm. That's not right. Better report an error."

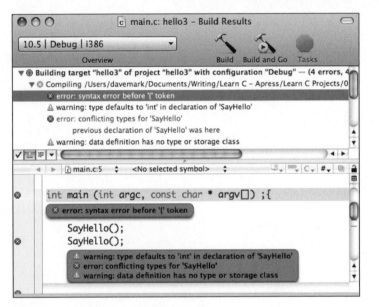

Figure 4-11. *This time, the Build Results window lists four errors and four warnings, all because of a little semicolon.*

In the build window, if you double-click the first error line (the line that says *error: syntax error before '{' token*), Xcode will take you to the offending line in the *main.c* editing window. In general, when you encounter an error compiling your code, you'll double-click the error message, figure out what's wrong, fix it, and then move on to the next error. Sometimes, I fix one error and immediately recompile, just on the off chance that this one error actually was the cause of all the other error message, as is the case with our errant semicolon.

Go back to your *main.c* editing window. Delete the extra semicolon, and then select **Build and Run** from the **Build** menu. Xcode will recompile your code and rerun the program, proving that you have indeed fixed the error. Good.

C Is Case Sensitive

Many different types of errors are possible in C programming. One of the most common results from the fact that C is a **case-sensitive** language. In a case-sensitive language, there is a big difference between lowercase and uppercase letters, which means you can't refer to printf() as Printf() or even PRINTF().

Figure 4-12 shows the warning message you'll get if you change your call of printf() to PRINTF(). Basically, this message is telling you that Xcode couldn't find a function named PRINTF() and was unable to link the program. In this case, the compiler did its job, but since no PRINTF() function could be found, the build ultimately failed. To fix this problem, just change PRINTF() back to printf() and rebuild.

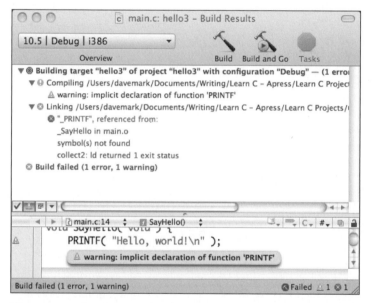

Figure 4-12. *The error and warning messages you get when you change printf() to PRINTF().*

What's Next?

Congratulations! You've made it through basic training. You know how to open a project, how to compile your code, and even how to cause an error message or two. You've learned about the most important function: main(). You've also learned about printf() and the Standard Library.

Now you're ready to dig into the stuff that gives a C program life: variables and operators.

CHAPTER 4 EXERCISE

Open the project *hello2.xcodeproj*, and edit *main.c* as instructed in each step. Then, describe the error that results:

1. Change the line:

   SayHello();

   to

   SayHello(;

2. Change things back. Now, change the following line:

   ```
   int main (int argc, const char * argv[])
   ```

   to

   ```
   int MAIN (int argc, const char * argv[])
   ```

3. Change things back. Now, delete the left curly brace after the line:

   ```
   int main (int argc, const char * argv[])
   ```

4. Change things back. Now, delete the semicolon at the end of this line:

   ```
   printf( "Hello, world!\n" );
   ```

   so it reads

   ```
   printf( "Hello, world!\n" )
   ```

Chapter 5

C Basics: Variables and Operators

*a*t this point, you should feel pretty comfortable using Xcode. You should know how to open a project and how to edit a project's source code. You should also feel comfortable running a project and (heaven forbid) fixing any syntax errors that may have occurred along the way.

On the programming side, you should recognize a function when you see one. When you think of a function, you should first think of `main()`, the function that gets called to start your program. You should remember that functions are made up of statements.

With these things in mind, we're ready to explore the foundation of C programming: **variables** and **operators**. Variables and operators are the building blocks you'll use to construct your program's statements.

An Introduction to Variables

A large part of the programming process involves working with data. You might need to add together a column of numbers or sort a list of names alphabetically. The tricky part of this process is representing your data in a program, which is where variables come in.

Variables can be thought of as containers for your program's data. Imagine a table with three containers sitting on it. Each container represents a different variable. One container is labeled cup1, one labeled cup2, and the third cup3. Now, imagine you have three pieces of paper. Write a number on each piece of paper and place one piece inside each of the three containers. Figure 5-1 shows a picture of what this might look like.

Figure 5-1. *Three cups, each one labeled and each with its own value. Each cup represents a different variable.*

Figure 5-2. *A fourth container containing the sum of the other three containers. This container represents a variable named sum with a value of 11.*

Now imagine asking a friend to reach into each cup, pull out the number in each one, and add the three values together. You can ask your friend to place the sum of the three values in a fourth container created just for this purpose. The fourth container is labeled sum and can be seen in Figure 5-2.

This is exactly how variables work. Variables are containers for your program's data. You create a variable and place a value in it. You then ask the computer to do something with the value in your variable. You can ask the computer to add three variables together, placing the result in a fourth variable. You can even ask the computer to take the value in a variable, multiply it by two, and place the result back into the original variable.

Getting back to our example, now imagine that you changed the values in cup1, cup2, and cup3. Once again, you could call on your friend to add the three values, updating the value in the container sum. You've reused the same variables, using the same formula, to achieve a different result. Here's the C version of this formula:

```
sum = cup1 + cup2 + cup3;
```

Every time you execute this line of source code, you place the sum of the variables cup1, cup2, and cup3 into the variable named sum. At this point, it's not important to understand exactly how this line of C source code works. What *is* important is to understand the basic idea behind variables. Each variable in your program is like a container with a value in it. This chapter will teach you how to create your own variables and how to place a value in a variable.

Working with Variables

Variables come in a variety of flavors, called **types**. A variable's type determines the type of data that can be stored in that variable. You determine a variable's type when you create the variable (we'll discuss creating variables in just a second). Some variable types are useful for working with numbers. Other variable types are designed to work with text. In this chapter, we'll work strictly with variables of one type, a numerical type called int (eventually, we'll get into other variable types). A variable of type int can hold a numerical value, such as 27 or –589.

Working with variables is a two-stage process. First you *create* a variable; then you *use* the variable. In C, you create a variable by **declaring** it. Declaring a variable tells the compiler, "Create a variable for me. I need a container to place a piece of data in." When you declare a variable, you have to specify the variable's type as well as its name. In our earlier example, we created four containers. Each container had a label. In the C world, this would be the same as creating four variables with the names cup1, cup2, cup3, and sum. In C, if we want to use the value stored in a variable, we use the variable's name. I'll show you how to do this later in the chapter.

Here's an example of a variable declaration:

```
int     myVariable;
```

This declaration tells the compiler to create a variable of type int (remember, ints are useful for working with numbers) with the name myVariable. The type of the variable (in this case, int) is extremely important. As you'll see, variable type determines the type and range of values a variable can be assigned.

Variable Names

Here are a few rules to follow when you create your own variable names:

- Variable names must always start with an uppercase or lowercase letter (A, B, . . . , Z or a, b, . . . , z) or with an underscore (_).

- The remainder of the variable name must be made up of uppercase or lowercase letters, numbers (0, 1, . . . , 9), or underscores.

These two rules yield variable names like myVariable, THIS_NUMBER, VaRiAbLe_1, and A1234_4321. Note that a C variable may never include a space or a character like an ampersand (&) or asterisk (*). These rules *must* be followed.

However, these rules do leave a fair amount of room for inventiveness. Over the years, different groups of programmers came up with additional guidelines (also known as **conventions** or **style guides**) that made variable names more consistent and a bit easier to read.

As an example of this, Unix programmers tended to use all lowercase letters in their variable names. When a variable name consisted of more than one word, the words were separated by an underscore. This yielded variable names like my_variable or number_of_puppies.

Another popular convention stems from a programming language named Smalltalk. Instead of limiting all variable names to lower case and separating words with an underscore, Smalltalk used a convention known as **InterCap**, where all the words in a variable or function name are stuck together. Rather than include a special, separating character, each new word added to the first word starts with a capital letter. For example, instead of number_of_puppies, you'd use numberOfPuppies. Instead of my_variable, you'd use myVariable. Function names follow the same convention, but start with a capital letter, giving us function names such as SmellTheFlowers() or HowMuchChangeYouGot().

Which convention should you use? For now, we'll follow the InterCap Smalltalk convention described in the previous paragraph. But as you make your way through the programming universe, you'll encounter different naming conventions that vary with each programming environment you encounter.

As mentioned in Chapter 4, C is a case-sensitive language. The compiler will cough out an error if you sometimes refer to myVariable and other times refer to myvariable. Adopt a variable naming convention and stick with it. Be consistent!

The Size of a Type

When you declare a variable, the compiler reserves a section of memory for the exclusive use of that variable. When you assign a value to a variable, you are actually modifying the variable's dedicated memory to reflect that value. The number of bytes assigned to a variable is determined by the variable's type. You should check your compiler's documentation to see how many bytes go along with each of the standard C types.

The Xcode compiler assigns 4 bytes to each int. Later in the book, in Chapter 8, we'll write a program that explores the size of a variety of C data types.

The variable declaration

```
int    myInt;
```

reserves 4 bytes of memory for the exclusive use of the variable myInt. If you later assign a value to myInt, that value is stored in the 4 bytes allocated for myInt. If you ever refer to myInt's value, you'll be referring to the value stored in myInt's 4 bytes.

If your compiler used 2-byte ints, the preceding declaration would allocate 2 bytes of memory for the exclusive use of myInt. As you'll see, it is important to know the size of the types you are dealing with.

Why is the size of a type important? The size of a type determines the range of values that type can handle. As you might expect, a type that's 4 bytes in size can hold a wider range of values than a type that's only 1 byte in size. Let's discuss how all this works.

Bytes and Bits

Each byte of computer memory is made up of 8 **bits**. Each **bit** has a value of either 1 or 0. Figure 5-3 shows a byte holding the value 00101011. The value 00101011 is said to be the **binary** representation of the value of the byte. Look closer at Figure 5-3. Notice that each bit is numbered (the bit numbers are above each bit in the figure), with bit 0 on the extreme right side to bit 7 on the extreme left. This is a standard bit-numbering scheme used in most computers.

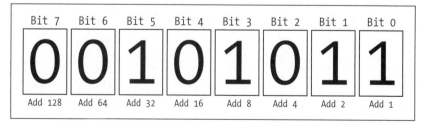

Figure 5-3. *A byte holding the binary value 00101011. Note that the rightmost bit is bit 0, and the leftmost bit is bit 7. Each bit contributes to the total value of the byte, if the bit is set to 1.*

Notice also the labels that appear beneath each bit in the figure ("Add 1," "Add 2," etc.). These labels are the key to binary numbers. Memorize them (it's easy—each bit is worth twice the value of its right neighbor). These labels are used to calculate the value of the entire byte. Here's how it works:

- Start with a value of 0.

- For each bit with a value of 1, add the label value below the bit.

That's all there is to it! In the byte pictured in Figure 5-3, you'd calculate the byte's value by adding 1 + 2 + 8 + 32 = 43. Where did we get the 1, 2, 8, and 32? They're the bottom labels of the only bits with a value of 1. Try another one. What's the value of the byte pictured in Figure 5-4?

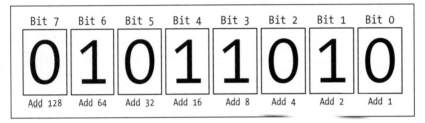

Figure 5-4. *What's the value of this byte? Remember, only the bits set to 1 contribute to the value of the byte.*

Easy, right? 2 + 8 + 16 + 64 = 90. Right! How about the byte in Figure 5.5?

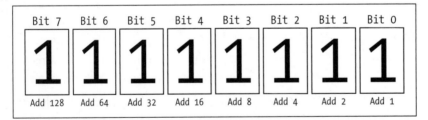

Figure 5-5. *What's the value of this byte? Note that this byte holds the largest value a byte can hold.*

This is an interesting one: 1 + 2 + 4 + 8 + 16 + 32 + 64 + 128 = 255. This example demonstrates the largest value that can fit in a single byte. Why? Because every bit is turned on. We've added everything we can add to the value of the byte.

The smallest value a byte can have is 0 (00000000). Since a byte can range in value from 0 to 255, a byte can have 256 possible values.

TWO'S COMPLEMENT NOTATION

Actually, the byte calculation approach in the "Bytes and Bits" section is just one of several ways to represent a number using binary. This approach is fine if you want to represent integers that are always greater than or equal to zero (known as **unsigned** integers). Computers use a different technique, known as **two's complement notation**, when they want to represent integers that might be either negative or positive.

To represent a negative number using two's complement notation:

1. Start with the binary representation of the positive version of the number.

2. Complement all the bits (turn the ones into zeros and the zeros into ones).

3. Add one to the result.

For example, the binary notation for the number 9 is 00001001. To represent −9 in two's complement notation, flip the bits (11110110) and then add 1. The two's complement for −9 is 11110110 + 1 = 11110111.

The binary notation for the number 2 is 00000010. The two's complement for −2 would be 11111101 + 1 = 11111110. Notice that in binary addition, when you add 01 + 01, you get 10. Just as in regular addition, you carry the 1 to the next column.

Don't worry about the details of binary representation and arithmetic. What's important to remember is that the computer uses one notation for positive-only numbers and a different notation for numbers that can be positive or negative. Both notations allow a byte to take on one of 256 different values. The positives-only scheme allows values ranging from 0 to 255. The two's complement scheme (see the "Two's Complement Notation" sidebar) allows a byte to take on values ranging from −128 to 127. Note that both of these ranges contain exactly 256 values.

Going from 1 Byte to 2 Bytes

So far, you've discovered that 1 byte (8 bits) of memory can hold one of $2^8 = 256$ possible values. By extension, 2 bytes (16 bits) of memory can hold one of $2^{16} = 65,536$ possible values. If the 2 bytes are **unsigned** (never allowed to hold a negative value), they can hold values ranging from 0 to 65,535. If the 2 bytes are **signed** (allowed to hold both positive and negative values), they can hold values ranging from −32,768 to 32,767.

A 4-byte int can hold $2^{32} = 4,294,967,296$ possible values. Wow! A signed 4-byte int can hold values ranging from −2,147,483,648 to 2,147,483,647, while an unsigned 4-byte int can hold values from 0 to 4,294,967,295.

To declare a variable as unsigned, precede its declaration with the unsigned qualifier. Here's an example:

```
unsigned int    myInt;
```

Now that you've defined the type of variable your program will use (in this case, `int`), you can assign a value to your variable.

Operators

One way to assign a value to a variable is with the **assignment operator**, which looks like the equals symbol (=). An **operator** is a special character (or set of characters) that represents a specific computer operation. The assignment operator tells the computer to compute the value of the right side of the = and assign that value to the left side of the =. Take a look at this line of source code:

```
myInt = 237;
```

This statement causes the value 237 to be placed in the memory allocated for `myInt`. In this line of code, `myInt` is known as an **l-value** ("l-value" stands for "left-value"), because it appears on the *left* side of the = operator. A variable makes a fine l-value. A number (like 237) makes a terrible l-value. Why? Because values are copied *from the right* side *to the left* side of the = operator. In this line of code

```
237 = myInt;
```

you are asking the compiler to copy the value in `myInt` to the number 237. Since you can't change the value of a number, the compiler will report an error when it encounters this line of code (most likely, the error message will say something about an "invalid lvalue in assignment"). Go ahead; try this yourself.

> **NOTE**
>
> As we just illustrated, you can use numerical **constants** (such as 237) directly in your code. In the programming world, these constants are called **literals**.

Look at this example:

```
#include <stdio.h>

int main (int argc, const char * argv[]) {
    int        myInt, anotherInt;

    myInt = 503;
    anotherInt = myInt;

    return 0;
}
```

Notice that we've declared two variables in this program. One way to declare multiple variables is the way we did here, separating the variables by a comma (,). There's no limit to the number of variables you can declare using this method.

We could have declared these variables using two separate declaration lines:

```
int     myInt;
int     anotherInt;
```

Either way is fine. As you'll see, C is an extremely flexible language. Let's look at some other operators.

The +, -, ++, and -- Operators

The addition (+) and subtraction (-) operators each take two values and reduce them to a single value. An operator that operates on two values is said to be a **binary** operator. An operator that operates on one value is said to be a **unary** operator. A value operated on by an operator is said to be an **operand**.

For example, this statement

```
myInt = 5 + 3;
```

will first resolve the right side of the = operator by adding the numbers 5 and 3 together. Once that's done, the resulting value (8) is assigned to the variable on the left side of the = operator. This statement assigns the value 8 to the variable myInt. Assigning a value to a variable means copying the value into the memory allocated to that variable.

Here's another example:

```
myInt = 10;
anotherInt = 12 - myInt;
```

The first statement assigns the value 10 to myInt. The second statement subtracts 10 from 12 to get 2, and then assigns the value 2 to anotherInt.

The increment (++) and decrement (--) operators operate on a single value only. ++ **increments** (raises) the value by 1, and -- **decrements** (lowers) the value by 1. Take a look:

```
myInt = 10;
myInt++;
```

The first statement assigns myInt a value of 10. The second statement changes myInt's value from 10 to 11. Here's another example:

```
myInt = 10;
--myInt;
```

This time the second line of code left `myInt` with a value of 9. You may have noticed that the first example showed the `++` operator following `myInt`, while the second example showed the `--` operator preceding `myInt`.

The position of the `++` and `--` operators determines when their operation is performed in relation to the rest of the statement. Placing the operator on the right side of a variable or expression (**postfix notation**) tells the compiler to resolve all values before performing the increment (or decrement) operation. Placing the operator on the left side of the variable (**prefix notation**) tells the compiler to increment (or decrement) first, then continue evaluation. Confused? The following examples should make this point clear:

```
myInt = 10;
anotherInt = myInt--;
```

The first statement assigns `myInt` a value of 10. In the second statement, the `--` operator is on `myInt`'s right side. This use of postfix notation tells the compiler to assign `myInt`'s value to `anotherInt` before decrementing `myInt`. This example leaves `myInt` with a value of 9 and `anotherInt` with a value of 10.

Here's the same example, written using prefix notation:

```
myInt = 10;
anotherInt = --myInt;
```

This time, the `--` operator is on the left side of `myInt`. In this case, the value of `myInt` is decremented before being assigned to `anotherInt`. The result? `myInt` and `anotherInt` are both left with a value of 9.

> **NOTE**
>
> The uses of prefix and postfix notation shows both a strength and a weakness of the C language. On the plus side, C allows you to accomplish a lot in a small amount of code. In our examples, we changed the value of two different variables in a single statement. C is powerful.
>
> On the downside, C code written in this fashion can be extremely cryptic and difficult to read for even the most seasoned C programmer. Write your code carefully.

The += and -= Operators

In C, you can place the same variable on both the left and right sides of an assignment statement. For example, the following statement increases the value of `myInt` by 10:

```
myInt = myInt + 10;
```

The same results can be achieved using the += operator. In other words,

```
myInt += 10;
```

is the same as

```
myInt = myInt + 10;
```

In the same way, the -= operator can be used to decrement the value of a variable. The statement

```
myInt -= 10;
```

decrements the value of myInt by 10.

The *, /, *=, and /= Operators

The multiplication (*) and division (/) operators each take two values and reduce them to a single value, much the same as the + and - operators do. The following statement

```
myInt = 3 * 5;
```

multiplies 3 and 5, leaving myInt with a value of 15. This statement

```
myInt = 5 / 2;
```

divides 5 by 2, and assuming myInt is declared as an int (or any other type designed to hold whole numbers), assigns the integral (truncated) result to myInt. The number 5 divided by 2 is 2.5. Since myInt can only hold whole numbers, the value 2.5 is truncated and the value 2 is assigned to myInt.

NOTE

Math alert! Numbers like –37, 0, and 22 are known as **whole numbers** or **integers**. Numbers like 3.14159, 2.5, and .0001 are known as **fractional** or **floating point numbers**.

The *= and /= operators work much the same as their += and -= counterparts. The statement

```
myInt *= 10;
```

is identical to the statement

```
myInt = myInt * 10;
```

Similarly, this statement

```
myInt /= 10;
```

is identical to this one:

```
myInt = myInt / 10;
```

> **NOTE**
>
> The / operator doesn't perform its truncation automatically. The accuracy of the result is limited by the data type of the operands. As an example, if the division is performed using ints, the result will be an int and is truncated to an integer value.
>
> Several data types (such as float) support floating point division using the / operator. We'll get to them later in this book.

To wrap up this discussion, it is worth mentioning that most C programmers prefer the shortcut version of each of the operators we just covered. For example, most C programmers would use

```
myInt++;
myInt /= 2;
```

instead of

```
myInt = myInt + 1;
myInt = myInt / 2;
```

Both chunks of code will accomplish the same result. Use what you think will be easiest for you to read late at night, with lots of caffeine coursing through your system, and a steady stream of e-mails coming in from a client or boss demanding that you finish this project immediately—'cause that's when your coding choices will matter most.

Using Parentheses

Sometimes the expressions you create can be evaluated in several ways. Here's an example:

```
myInt = 5 + 3 * 2;
```

You can add 5 + 3 and then multiply the result by 2 (giving you 16). Alternatively, you can multiply 3 by 2 and add 5 to the result (giving you 11). Which is correct?

C has a set of built-in rules for resolving the order of operators. As it turns out, the * operator has a higher precedence than the + operator, so the multiplication will be performed first, yielding a result of 11.

Though it helps to understand the relative precedence of the C operators, keeping track of them all is hard. That's why the C gods gave us parentheses! Use parentheses in pairs to define the order in which you want your operators performed. The following statement

```
myInt = ( 5 + 3 ) * 2;
```

will leave `myInt` with a value of 16. This statement

```
myInt = 5 + ( 3 * 2 );
```

will leave `myInt` with a value of 11. You can use more than one set of parentheses in a statement, as long as they occur in pairs—one left parenthesis associated with each right parenthesis. The statement

```
myInt = ( ( 5 + 3 ) * 2 );
```

will leave `myInt` with a value of 16.

Operator Precedence

In the previous section, I referred to C's built-in rules for resolving operator precedence. If you have a question about which operator has a higher precedence, look it up in the chart in Table 5-1. Here's how the table works.

Table 5-1. *The Relative Precedence of C's Built-In Operators*

Operators by Precedence	Order
$->$, . , $++^{postfix}$, $--^{postfix}$	Left to right
$*^{pointer}$, $\&^{address\ of}$, $+^{unary}$, $-^{unary}$, ! , ~ , $++^{prefix}$, $--^{prefix}$, sizeof	Right to left
Typecast	Right to left
$*^{multiply}$, / , %	Left to right
$+^{binary}$, $-^{binary}$	Left to right
$<<^{left\text{-}shift}$, $>>^{right\text{-}shift}$	Left to right
> , >= , < , <=	Left to right
== , !=	Left to right
$\&^{bitwise\text{-}and}$	Left to right
^	Left to right
|	Left to right
&&	Left to right
||	Left to right
?:	Right to left
= , += , -= , *= , /= , %= , >>= , <<= , &= , |= , ^=	Right to left
,	Left to right

The higher an operator is in the chart, the higher its precedence. For example, suppose you are trying to predict the result of this line of code:

```
myInt = 5 * 3 + 7;
```

First, look up the operator * in Table 5-1. Hmm, this one seems to be in the chart twice, once with label "pointer" and once with the label "multiply." You can tell just by looking at this line of code that we want the multiply version. The compiler is pretty smart. Just like you, it can tell that this is the multiply version of *.

OK, now look up +. Yup, it's in there twice also, once as unary and once as binary. A unary + or – is the sign that appears before a number, like +147 or –32768. In our line of code, the + operator has two operands, so clearly binary + is the one we want.

Now that you've figured out which operator is which, you can see that the multiply * is higher up on the chart than the binary +, and thus has a higher precedence. This means that the * will get evaluated before the +, as if the expression were written as

```
myInt = (5 * 3) + 7;
```

So far so good. Now, what about the following line of code?

```
myInt = 27 * 6 % 5;
```

Both of these operators are on the fourth line in the chart. Which one gets evaluated first? If both operators under consideration are on the same line in the chart, the order of evaluation is determined by the entry in the chart's rightmost column. In this case, the operators are evaluated from left to right. In the current example, * will get evaluated before %, as if the line of code were written

```
myInt = (27 * 6) % 5;
```

What about this line of code?

```
myInt = 27 % 6 * 5;
```

In this case, the % will get evaluated before the *, as if the line of code were written

```
myInt = (27 % 6) * 5;
```

Of course, you can avoid this exercise altogether with a judicious sprinkling of parentheses. As you look through the chart, you'll definitely notice some operators that you haven't learned about yet. As you read through this book and encounter new operators, check back with Table 5-1 to see where they fit in.

Sample Programs

So far in this chapter, we've discussed variables (mostly of type `int`) and operators (mostly mathematical). The program examples on the following pages combine variables and operators into useful C statements. We'll also learn a bit more about our friend from the Standard Library, the `printf()` function.

Opening operator.xcodeproj

Our next program, operator, provides a testing ground for some of the operators covered in the previous sections. *main.c* declares a variable (`myInt`) and uses a series of statements to change the value of the variable. By including a `printf()` after each of these statements, *main.c* makes it easy to follow the variable, step by step, as its value changes.

In Xcode, close any project windows that may be open. In the Finder, locate the *Learn C Projects* folder and the *05.01 - operator* subfolder, and double-click the file *operator.xcodeproj*. The operator project window should appear (see Figure 5-6).

NOTE

Recall that you can double-click the source code file name to open a new editing window, or you can click the *Editor* toolbar icon to open an editing pane within the project window.

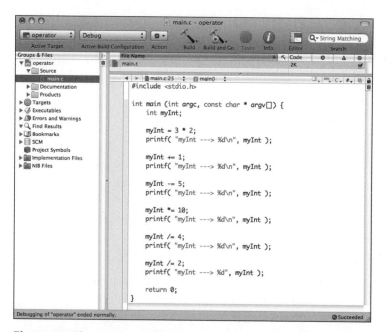

Figure 5-6. *The operator project window (note that the window has been rearranged a bit to show all of main.c)*

Run operator by selecting **Build and Run** from the **Build** menu. Xcode will compile *main.c*, and then link and run the program. Compare your output to that shown in Figure 5-7. They should be about the same.

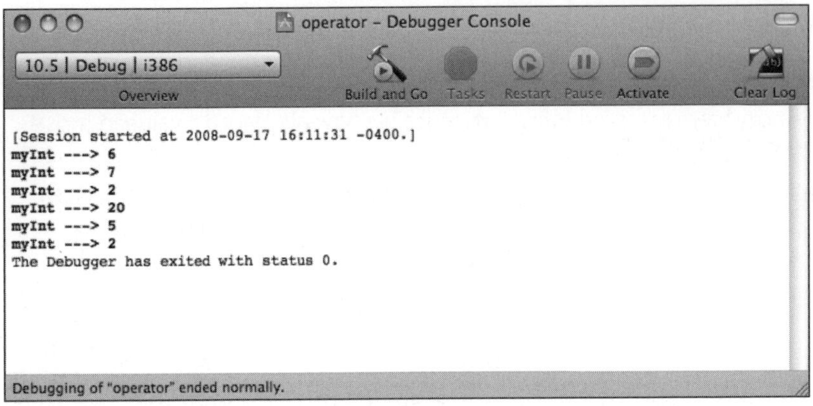

Figure 5-7. *This picture of the console window shows the output from running our operator project.*

Stepping Through the operator Source Code

Let's take a look at the operator project's source code. In Xcode, bring *main.c* in an editing window.

main.c starts off with our usual #include of *stdio.h*. This gives us access to printf().

```
#include <stdio.h>
```

main() starts out by defining an int named myInt:

```
int main (int argc, const char * argv[]) {
    int    myInt;
```

NOTE

Earlier I used the phrase "declaring a variable" and now I'm using the term "defining." What's the difference? A variable *declaration* is any statement that specifies a variable's name and type. The line int myInt; certainly does that. A variable *definition* is a declaration that causes memory to be allocated for the variable. Since the previous statement does cause memory to be allocated for myInt, it does qualify as a definition. Later in the book, you'll see some declarations that don't qualify as definitions. For now, just remember, a variable definition causes memory to be allocated.

At this point in the program (after `myInt` has been declared but before any value has been assigned to it), `myInt` is said to be **uninitialized**. In computerese, **initialization** refers to the process of establishing a variable's value for the first time. A variable that has been declared, but that has not had a value assigned to it, is said to be **uninitialized**. You **initialize** a variable the first time you assign a value to it.

Since `myInt` was declared to be of type `int`, and since Xcode is currently set to use 4-byte `int`s, 4 bytes of memory were reserved for `myInt`. Since we haven't placed a value in those 4 bytes yet, they could contain any value at all. Some compilers place a value of 0 in a newly allocated variable, but others do not. The key is not to depend on a variable being preset to some specific value. If you want a variable to contain a specific value, assign the value to the variable yourself!

NOTE

In Chapter 7, you'll learn about global variables. Global variables are always set to 0 by the compiler. All the variables used in this chapter are local variables, not global variables. Local variables are not guaranteed to be initialized by the compiler.

The next line of code uses the `*` operator to assign a value of 6 to `myInt`. Following that, we use `printf()` to display the value of `myInt` in the console window.

```
myInt = 3 * 2;
printf( "myInt ---> %d\n", myInt );
```

The code between `printf()`'s left and right parentheses is known as an **argument list**. The **arguments** in an argument list are automatically provided to the function you are calling (in this case, `printf()`). The receiving function can use the arguments passed to it to determine its next course of action.

Interestingly, when you define or declare a function, the elements between the parentheses that correspond to the argument list are known as **parameters**.

You'll learn more about parameters in Chapter 7. For the moment, let's talk about `printf()` and the arguments used by this Standard Library function.

The first argument passed to `printf()` defines what will be drawn in the console window. The simplest call to `printf()` uses a quoted text string as its only argument. A quoted text string consists of a pair of double-quote characters (") with zero or more characters between them. For example, this call of `printf()`:

```
printf( "Hello!" );
```

will draw the characters He11o! in the console window. Notice that the double-quote characters are not part of the text string.

In a slightly more complex scenario, you can request that printf() draw a variable's value in the midst of the quoted string. In the case of an int, do this by embedding the two characters %d within the first argument and by passing the int as a second argument. printf() will replace the %d with the value of the int.

In these two lines of code, we first set myInt to 6, use printf() to print the value of myInt in the console window.

```
myInt = 3 * 2;
printf( "myInt ---> %d\n", myInt );
```

This code produces this line of output in the console window:

```
myInt ---> 6
```

The two characters \n in the first argument represent a carriage return and tell printf() to move the cursor to the beginning of the next line before it prints any more characters. If we deleted all of the \n characters from the program, all the output would appear on a single line in the console window. Give it a try. Just remember to put them back in when you are done playing.

NOTE

> The %d in the first argument is known as a **format specifier**. It specifies the type of the argument to be included in the string to be printed. The d in the format specifier tells printf() that you are printing an integer variable.

You can place any number of % specifications in the first argument, as long as you follow the first argument by the appropriate number of variables. Here's another example:

```
int    var1, var2;

var1 = 5;
var2 = 10;
printf( "var1 = %d\n\nvar2 = %d\n", var1, var2 );
```

This chunk of code will draw this text in the console window:

```
var1 = 5

var2 = 10
```

Notice the blank line between the two lines of output. It was caused by the \n\n in the first `printf()` argument. The first carriage return placed the cursor at the beginning of the next console line (directly under the v in var1). The second carriage return moved the cursor down one more line, leaving a blank line in its path.

Let's get back to our source code. The next line of *main.c* increments `myInt` from 6 to 7, and prints the new value in the console window.

```
myInt += 1;
printf( "myInt ---> %d\n", myInt );
```

The next line decrements `myInt` by 5 and prints its new value of 2 in the console window:

```
myInt -= 5;
printf( "myInt ---> %d\n", myInt );
```

Next, `myInt` is multiplied by 10, and its new value of 20 is printed in the console window:

```
myInt *= 10;
printf( "myInt ---> %d\n", myInt );
```

After that, `myInt` is divided by 4, resulting in a new value of 5:

```
myInt /= 4;
printf( "myInt ---> %d\n", myInt );
```

Finally, `myInt` is divided by 2. Since 5 divided by 2 is 2.5 (not a whole number), a truncation is performed, and `myInt` is left with a value of 2:

```
myInt /= 2;
printf( "myInt ---> %d\n", myInt );

    return 0;
}
```

Opening postfix.xcode

Our next program demonstrates the difference between postfix and prefix notation (recall the ++ and -- operators defined earlier in the chapter?) If you have a project open in Xcode, close it. In the Finder, go into the *Learn C Projects* folder and then into the *05.02 - postfix* subfolder, and double-click the project file *postfix.xcodeproj*.

Take a look at the source code in the file *main.c*, and try to predict the result of the two `printf()` calls before you run the program. There's extra ice cream for everyone if you get this right. Careful, this one's tricky.

Once your guesses are locked in, select **Build and Run** from the **Build** menu. How'd you do? Compare your two guesses with the output in Figure 5-8. Let's look at the source code.

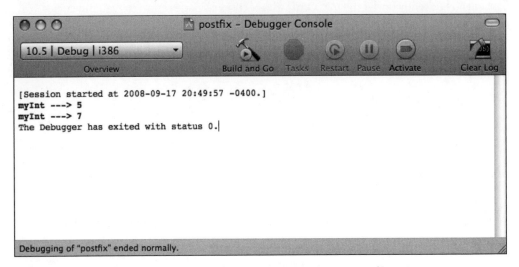

Figure 5-8. *The output generated by postfix. Is this the output you expected?*

Stepping Through the postfix Source Code

The first half of *main.c* is pretty straightforward. The variable myInt is defined to be of type int. Then, myInt is assigned a value of 5. Next comes the tricky part.

```
#include <stdio.h>

int main (int argc, const char * argv[]) {
    int    myInt;

    myInt = 5;
```

The first call to printf() actually has a statement embedded in it. This is another great feature of the C language. Where there's room for a variable, there's room for an entire statement. Sometimes, performing two actions within the same line of code is convenient. For example, this line of code

```
printf( "myInt ---> %d\n", myInt = myInt * 3 );
```

first triples the value of myInt, and then passes the result (the tripled value of myInt) on to printf(). The same could have been accomplished using two lines of code:

```
myInt = myInt * 3;
printf( "myInt ---> %d\n", myInt );
```

In general, when the compiler encounters an assignment statement where it expects a variable, it first completes the assignment, and then passes on the result of the assignment as if it were a variable. Let's see this technique in action.

In *main.c*, our friend the postfix operator emerges again. Just prior to the two calls of printf(), myInt has a value of 5. The first of the two printf()'s increments the value of myInt using postfix notation:

```
    printf( "myInt ---> %d\n", myInt++ );
```

The use of postfix notation means that the value of myInt will be passed on to printf() before myInt is incremented. Therefore, the first printf() will accord myInt a value of 5. However, when the statement is finished, myInt will have a value of 6.

The second printf() acts in a more rational (and preferable) manner. The prefix notation guarantees that myInt will be incremented (from 6 to 7) before its value is passed on to printf().

```
    printf( "myInt ---> %d", ++myInt );

    return 0;
}
```

BREAKING THE PRINTF() INTO TWO STATEMENTS

Can you break each of these printf()s into two separate statements? Give it a try; then, read on.

The first printf() looks like this:

```
printf( "myInt ---> %d\n", myInt++ );
```

Here's the two-statement version:

```
printf( "myInt ---> %d\n", myInt );
myInt++;
```

Notice that the statement incrementing myInt was placed after the printf(). Do you see why? The postfix notation makes this necessary. Run through both versions, and verify this for yourself.

The second printf() looks like this:

```
printf( "myInt ---> %d\n", ++myInt );
```

Here's the two-statement version:

```
++myInt;
printf( "myInt ---> %d\n", myInt );
```

This time the statement incrementing myInt came before the printf(). This time, it's the prefix notation that makes this necessary. Again, go through both versions, and verify this for yourself.

The purpose of demonstrating the complexity of the postfix and prefix operators is twofold. On one hand, it's extremely important that you understand exactly how these operators work from all angles. This will allow you to write code that works and will aid you in making sense of other programmers' code.

On the other hand, embedding prefix and postfix operators within function arguments may save you lines of code but, as you can see, may prove a bit confusing. So what's a coder to do? Put clarity before brevity. Make sure your code is readable. After all, you will likely have to go back and edit it at some point. Readable code is *much* easier to maintain. As long as your code is correct, the compiler will do the same thing with it. So write for the programmer, not the machine.

Backslash Combinations

The last program in this chapter, slasher, demonstrates several different **backslash combinations**. A backslash combination combines a backslash character (\) and a second character to produce a specific result when the combination is printed in the console window. One backslash combination you've seen a lot of in this book is \n, which produces a new line in the console.

C allows you to embed any number of backslash combinations in a text string. For example, this line of code:

```
printf( "Hello\n\nGoodbye" );
```

produces the following output in the console window:

```
Hello

Goodbye
```

The single blank line between Hello and Goodbye was caused by the two \n characters. The first \n would have caused the console to put Goodbye on the line immediately below Hello. The second \n moved the Goodbye down one more line.

There are a number of backslash combinations. Let's discuss a few of the most interesting ones:

- \r causes the cursor to move to the beginning of the *same* line. This allows you to draw some text and then overwrite the same text.

- \b is a backspace character. Using it has the same effect as pressing the Delete key while you are typing: it erases the last character typed.

- \\ allows you to place a backslash character in a string. Think about this for a moment. If you simply embedded a backslash character in your string, the compiler would attempt to combine the backslash with the very next character, producing some unpredictable results. Unpredictable is bad.

- \" allows you to place a quote character in a string. When the compiler first sees a double-quote character in your code, it assumes you are starting a text string. It keeps reading, reading, reading, until it encounters a second, matching double-quote character. The second quote tells the compiler that it has reached the end of the string. So how do you place a quote character inside a string without ending the string? Easy. Use the \" where you want the quote to appear.

- \t allows you to place a tab in a string.

Support for Backslash Combinations

Backslash combinations stem from the olden days, where all programs ran on video displays with a fixed number of rows and columns. The backslash combinations helped programmers overcome the limitations of these displays, giving them a bit more control. As computers evolved, many of these backslash combinations became unnecessary. Over time, many development environments stopped supporting all but the most basic of these.

To see this yourself, we'll run our next program, slasher, using the Terminal application that you used in Chapter 4. The Terminal application implements a classic console window that supports all the well-known backslash combinations, just like an old video display terminal. We'll use the built in Unix tools that you installed when you installed Xcode at the beginning of the book to compile the program as well.

NOTE

After you are done playing with the Unix version of slasher, take the Xcode version for a spin. You'll find it in the *Learn C Projects* folder, in the *05.03 - slasher* subdirectory.

Running slasher

In the Finder, go to the *Learn C Projects* folder and into the *05.03 – slasher* subdirectory, and double-click the file named *slasher*. The Terminal application will launch, and a new window will appear, similar to the one shown in Figure 5-9.

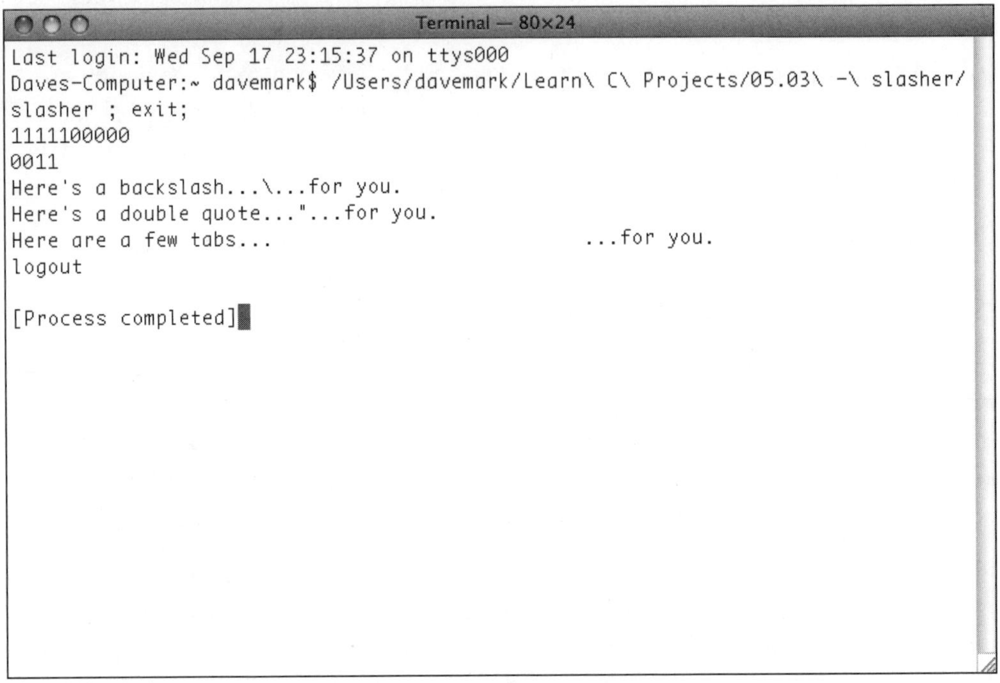

```
●●●                          Terminal — 80×24
Last login: Wed Sep 17 23:15:37 on ttys000
Daves-Computer:~ davemark$ /Users/davemark/Learn\ C\ Projects/05.03\ -\ slasher/
slasher ; exit;
1111100000
0011
Here's a backslash...\...for you.
Here's a double quote..."...for you.
Here are a few tabs...                          ...for you.
logout

[Process completed]█
```

Figure 5-9. *Running slasher using the Terminal application. Don't worry if the first few lines look a bit different on your Terminal window.*

You can ignore the first few lines of text in the Terminal window. The key lines of output to pay attention to are these five:

```
1111100000
0011
Here's a backslash...\...for you.
Here's a double quote..."...for you.
Here are a few tabs...                          ...for you.
```

As we step through the source code, you'll see a series of six `printf()`s, each of which corresponds to one of these lines of output. Once we finish going through the source code, we'll take a shot at compiling the source using the Unix compiler and the Terminal, instead of using Xcode.

Stepping Through the slasher Source Code

main.c consists of a series of `printf()`s, each of which demonstrates a different backslash combination. The first `printf()` prints a series of ten zeros, followed by the characters \r (also known as the backslash combination \r). The \r backslash combination generates a carriage return without a line feed, leaving the cursor at the beginning of the current line (unlike \n, which leaves the cursor at the beginning of the next line down).

```
#include <stdio.h>

int main (int argc, const char * argv[]) {
    printf( "0000000000\r" );
```

The next `printf()` prints five ones over the first five zeros, as if someone had printed the text string "1111100000". The \n at the end of this `printf()` moves the cursor to the beginning of the next line in the console window.

```
    printf( "11111\n" );
```

The next `printf()` demonstrates \b, the backspace backslash combination. \b tells `printf()` to back up one character so that the next character printed replaces the last character printed. This `printf()` sends out four zeros, backspaces over the last two, then prints two ones. The result is as if you had printed the string "0011".

```
    printf( "0000\b\b11\n" );
```

The \ can also be used to cancel a character's special meaning within a quoted string. For example, the backslash combination \\ generates a single \ character. The difference is, this \ loses its special backslash powers. It doesn't affect the character immediately following it.

The backslash combination \" generates a double-quote character ("), taking away the special meaning of the double quote. As I said earlier, without the \ before it, the " character would mark the end of the quoted string. The backslash allows you to include quotation marks inside a quoted string.

The backslash combinations \\ and \" are demonstrated in the next two `printf()`s:

```
    printf( "Here's a backslash...\\...for you.\n" );
    printf( "Here's a double quote...\"...for you.\n" );
```

The \t combination generates a single tab character. The Terminal window has a tab stop every eight spaces. Here's a `printf()` example:

```
    printf( "Here's a few tabs...\t\t\t\t...for you.\n" );

    return 0;
}
```

Building slasher the Unix Way

This section is completely optional. You can skip it entirely, or scan it to follow along, or do every darned step along the way. We're going to use Terminal to compile the slasher source code into a runnable Unix application. In effect, we're going to rebuild the slasher application that you just ran.

In your home directory, create a new folder called *slasher*. Your home directory is the directory with the house icon, named with your login name. For example, my home directory is in the *Users* folder and is called *davemark*.

Next, locate the folder containing the slasher project. You'll find it in the *Learn C Projects* directory, in the *05.03 - slasher* subdirectory. Inside that folder, you'll find a file named *main.c*, which contains the slasher source code. Use the Finder to drag a copy of *main.c* into the new *slasher* folder you created in your home directory.

If Terminal is running, open a new window by selecting **New Window** from the **Shell** menu. If Terminal is *not* running, launch it. You'll find it in the *Applications* folder, in the *Utilities* subfolder.

At this point, you should have a *slasher* folder in your home folder containing a copy of *slasher*'s *main.c* file and a new Terminal window, which looks like the one shown in Figure 5-10.

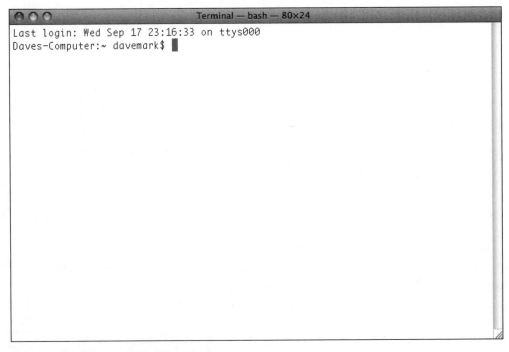

Figure 5-10. *A brand-new Terminal window*

We're now going to type some Unix commands into the Terminal window. Our first goal is to make sure we can see the new *slasher* folder we just created in our home directory. Type this command, followed by a carriage return:

```
cd ~
```

Note that there is a space in between the `cd` and the tilde character (~). This command tells Unix to change your directory (cd) to the home directory—in Unix-speak, the tilde directory is always your home directory.

Next, you'll type this command

```
ls
```

followed by a carriage return. This command asks Unix to list all the visible files in the current directory, which, in this case, is your home directory. Here's the list I got:

```
Desktop     Library    Music      Public      slasher
Documents   Movies     Pictures   Sites
```

Note that our newly created *slasher* directory is in this list. If you don't see *slasher* in your list, chances are good that you created the directory in the wrong place. Go find the folder and drag it into your home directory. Then, go back to Terminal, and do another `ls`.

Next, let's go into the *slasher* directory and make sure the *main.c* file is there. Issue these two commands:

```
cd slasher
ls
```

Remember to type a carriage return after each command. The first command changes directories to the *slasher* directory. The second command lists the visible files in that directory. Here's the result of my `ls`:

```
main.c
```

If your *slasher* directory is empty, you did not successfully copy *main.c* into the *slasher* folder you created. Go fix that.

Once `ls` shows *main.c* in the *slasher* directory, you are ready to do a compile. Type this command:

```
cc -o slasher main.c
```

Be sure to end it with a carriage return. You've just asked Unix to compile the C code in the file *main.c* and link the resulting object code into an executable file named *slasher*. The -o tells the cc command that you want to name the output, the word slasher tells it the name to use. If you left -o slasher out of the command, cc would put the output in a file named a.out.

Which Compiler Did You Run?

In the Unix world, cc is a **command**, and -o slasher is a **switch** that modifies the command. The command cc asks Unix to find and run the C compiler. Interestingly, you can have multiple C compilers installed on your computer. All Unix users have a search path associated with their accounts that Unix uses to find programs they ask it to run. Try this command:

which cc

Here's the result I got when I typed this command:

/usr/bin/cc

The command which asks Unix to search its search path and tell me which version of the cc command it will execute if I just type cc. Let's ask for a little more detail. Type this command:

ls -l /usr/bin/cc

The -l switch stands for long and asks the ls command to do a bit longer listing than usual. Here's what I got in response:

lrwxr-xr-x 1 root wheel 7 Sep 5 08:39 /usr/bin/cc -> gcc-4.0

To learn more about the ls command, type the command *man ls* in the Terminal window. For now, the important piece of information to pull from this is that the cc command will run the GCC 4.0 compiler. "GCC" stands for GNU compiler collection, which has been adopted by most Unix systems as their standard compiler.

GNU and about GCC are definitely worth learning more about. Today's homework assignment is to read through these two web pages; you will be a better programmer for it:

http://en.wikipedia.org/wiki/GNU_Compiler_Collection
http://en.wikipedia.org/wiki/GNU

The most important thing to pull from this discussion is this: as you make your way through the programs in this book, you are using GCC 4.0 to compile your code. Or, if you are from the future, at least you know how to find out which version of GCC you are running. Your compiler version might not mean anything to you now, but as your programming skills mature and your programming projects become more complex, this information will become important to you.

Running the Unix Version of slasher

Before we got sidetracked, we had just used `cc` to compile *main.c* and name the resulting executable *slasher*.

To see the results of your compile, do another `ls`. You should see these two files:

```
main.c  slasher
```

Notice that a new file named *slasher* has been created. You can run this program by typing the following command:

```
./slasher
```

Note the `./` before the word `slasher`. This tells Unix to run the *slasher* in the current directory, as opposed to some other file named *slasher* that might be elsewhere in its search path.

Here's the output I saw when I ran my copy of slasher:

```
1111100000
0011
Here's a backslash...\...for you.
Here's a double quote..."...for you.
Here are a few tabs...                    ...for you.
```

Feel free to quit Terminal. Your work here is done.

And that wraps up the sample programs for this chapter. Before we move on, however, I'd like to talk to you about something personal—your coding habits.

Sprucing Up Your Code

You are now in the middle of your C learning curve. You've learned about variables, types, functions, and bytes. You've learned about an important part of the Standard Library, the function `printf()`. At this point in the learning process, programmers start developing their coding habits.

Coding habits are the little things programmers do that make their code a little bit different (and hopefully better!) than anyone else's. Before you get too set in your ways, here are a few coding habits you can, and should, add to your arsenal.

Source Code Spacing

You may have noticed the tabs, spaces, and blank lines scattered throughout the sample programs. These are known in C as **white space**. With a few exceptions, white space is ignored by C compilers. Believe it or not, as far as the C compiler goes, this program:

```
#include <stdio.h>
int main (int argc,
const char * argv[])
                                                    {

    int myInt;myInt


=
5
;
printf("myInt=",myInt);}
```

is equivalent to this program:

```
#include <stdio.h>


int main (int argc, const char * argv[]) {
    int myInt;

    myInt = 5;
    printf( "myInt =", myInt );
}
```

The C compiler doesn't care if you put five statements per line or if you put 20 carriage returns between your statements and your semicolons. One thing the compiler won't let you do is place white space in the middle of a word, such as a variable or function name. For example, this line of code won't compile:

```
my  Int = 5;
```

Instead of a single variable named myInt, the compiler sees two items, one named my and the other named Int. Too much white space can confuse the compiler.

Too little white space can also confuse the compiler. For example, this line of code won't compile:

```
intmyInt;
```

The compiler needs at least one piece of white space to tell it where the type ends and where the variable begins. On the other hand, as you've already seen, this line compiles just fine:

```
myInt=5;
```

Since a variable name can't contain the character =, the compiler has no problem telling where the variable ends and where the operator begins.

As long as your code compiles properly, you're free to develop your own white-space style. Here are a few hints:

- Place a blank line between your variable declarations and the rest of your function's code. Also, use blank lines to group related lines of code.

- Sprinkle single spaces throughout a statement. Compare this line:

```
printf("myInt=",myInt);
```

with this line:

```
printf( "myInt =", myInt );
```

The spaces make the second line easier to read.

- When in doubt, use parentheses. Compare this line:

```
myInt=var1+2*var2+4;
```

with this line:

```
myInt = var1 + (2*var2) + 4;
```

What a difference parentheses and spaces make!

- Always start variable names with a lowercase letter, using an uppercase letter at the start of each subsequent word in the name. This yields variable names such as `myVar`, `areWeDone`, and `employeeName`.

- Always start function names with an uppercase letter, using an uppercase letter at the start of each subsequent word in the name. This yields function names such as `DoSomeWork()`, `HoldThese()`, and `DealTheCards()`.

These hints are merely suggestions. Use a set of standards that make sense for you and the people with whom you work. The object here is to make your code as readable as possible.

Comment Your Code

One of the most critical elements in the creation of a computer program is clear and comprehensive documentation. When you deliver your award-winning graphics package to your customers, you'll want to have two sets of documentation. One set is for your customers, who'll need a clear set of instructions that guide them through your wonderful new creation. The other set of documentation consists of the comments you'll weave throughout your code. Source code comments act as a sort of narrative, guiding a reader through your code. You'll include comments that describe how your code works, what makes it special, and what to look out for when changing it.

Well-commented code includes a comment at the beginning of each function that describes the function, the function arguments, and the function's variables. Sprinkling individual comments among your source code statements to explain the role each line plays in your program's algorithm is also a good idea. In addition, you should include a block of comments that describe your program's overall approach, solutions used, key concepts, any information that will help someone maintaining your code in the future to wrap their head around your project.

How do you add a comment to your source code? Let's take a look.

All C compilers recognize the sequence /* as the start of a comment and will ignore all characters until they hit the sequence */ (the end-of-comment characters). In addition, all C99-compliant compilers support the use of // to mark a single-line comment. All characters from // onward on the current line will be ignored.

Here's some commented code:

```c
int main (int argc, const char * argv[]) {
    int    numPieces; // Number of pieces of pie left

    numPieces = 8;     // We started with 8 pieces

    numPieces--;       // Peter had a piece
    numPieces--;       // Quagmire had a piece
    numPieces -= 2;    // Cleveland had two pieces!!
    numPieces -= 4;    // Joe had the rest!!!

    printf( "Slices left = %d", numPieces );
                    /* How about
                       some cake
                       instead?   */
    return 0;
}
```

Notice that, although most of the comments fit on the same line, the last comment was split between three lines. The preceding code will compile just fine.

Although this example is relatively trivial, at times, you will want to comment out a large block of code. You could put // at the beginning of every line of code, but who wants to do that 100 times? Instead, put /* just before the offending code and */ just after. This works just fine, as long as the code to be commented out does not contain the characters */. If so, you'll need to do a tiny bit of editing to keep your comment going.

Since each of the programs in this book is examined in detail, line by line, the comments were left out. This was done to make the examples as simple as possible. In this instance, do as I say, not as I do. Comment your code. No excuses!

The Curly Brace Controversy

There are two generally accepted styles for placing curly braces in your code. The first style is the one we've been using:

```
int main (int argc, const char * argv[]) {
    printf( "Hello, world!" );

    return 0;
}
```

The second style places the opening curly brace on its own line:

```
int main (int argc, const char * argv[])
{
    printf( "Hello, world!" );

    return 0;
}
```

Personally, I prefer the second form. Here are the advantages to this approach: I think it makes your code look a bit cleaner and that your eye can more easily find the matching closing brace that matches an opening brace.

The downside to this approach is that it adds an extra line of code to every block of code in which it is used. This means you see less code per screenful of code listing.

Experiment with both bracing styles to see which one works best for you. In this book, I've adopted the first style (left curly at the end of the line of code) for two reasons: One, this is the default bracing style used by Xcode and most of Apple's sample code. And two, Xcode makes finding matching braces and parentheses magically simple. When you type a closing curly brace or parenthesis, Xcode will highlight and blink the matching opening brace or parenthesis. This is hugely helpful and fun to watch, too. Give it a try.

What's Next?

This chapter introduced the concepts of variables and operators, tied together in C statements and separated by semicolons. We looked at several examples, each of which made heavy use of the Standard Library function printf(). You learned about the console window, quoted strings, and backslash combinations.

Chapter 6 will increase our programming options significantly, introducing you to C control structures such as the for loop and the if statement. Get ready to expand your C-programming horizons. See you in Chapter 6.

CHAPTER 5 EXERCISES

1. Find the error in each of the following code fragments:

   a. `printf( Hello, world );`

   b. `int    myInt  myOtherInt;`

   c. `myInt =+ 3;`

   d. `printf("myInt = %d" );`

   e. `printf("myInt = ", myInt );`

   f. `printf("myInt = %d\", myInt );`

   g. `myInt + 3 = myInt;`

   h.
   ```
   int main (int argc, const char * argv[]) {
        int   myInt;
        myInt = 3;
        anotherInt = myInt;

        return 0;
   }
   ```

2. Compute the value of `myInt` after each code fragment is executed:

   a.
   ```
   myInt = 5;
   myInt *= (3+4) * 2;
   ```

   b.
   ```
   myInt = 2;
   myInt *= ( (3*4) / 2 ) - 9;
   ```

   c.
   ```
   myInt = 2;
   myInt /= 5;
   myInt--;
   ```

   d.
   ```
   myInt = 25;
   myInt /= 3 * 2;
   ```

   e.
   ```
   myInt = (3*4*5) / 9;
   myInt -= (3+4) * 2;
   ```

   f.
   ```
   myInt = 5;
   printf( "myInt = %d", myInt = 2 );
   ```

   g.
   ```
   myInt = 5;
   myInt = (3+4) * 2;
   ```

   h.
   ```
   myInt = 1;
   myInt /= (3+4) / 6;
   ```

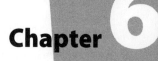

Controlling Your Program's Flow

So far, you've learned quite a bit about the C language. You know about functions (especially one named `main()`), which are made up of statements, each of which is terminated by a semicolon. You know about variables, which have a name and a type. Up to this point, you've dealt with variables of type `int`.

You also know about operators, such as =, +, and +=. You've learned about postfix and prefix notation and the importance of writing clear, easy-to-understand code. You've learned about the Standard Library, a set of functions that comes as standard equipment with every C programming environment. You've also learned about `printf()`, an invaluable component of the Standard Library.

Finally, you've learned a few housekeeping techniques to keep your code fresh, sparkling, and readable. Comment your code, because your memory isn't perfect, and insert some white space to keep your code from getting too cramped.

Next up on the panel? Learning how to control your program's flow.

Flow Control

The programs we've written so far have all consisted of a straightforward series of statements, one right after the other. Every statement is executed in the order it occurred. **Flow control** is the ability to control the order in which your program's statements are executed. The C language provides several keywords you can use in your program to control your program's flow. One of these is the `if` keyword.

The if Statement

The if keyword allows you to choose among several options in your program. In English, you might say something like this:

```
If it's raining outside I'll bring my umbrella;
otherwise I won't.
```

In this sentence, you're using if to choose between two options. Depending on the weather, you'll do one of two things: you'll bring your umbrella, or you won't bring your umbrella. C's if statement gives you this same flexibility. Here's an example:

```c
#include <stdio.h>

int main (int argc, const char * argv[]) {
    int     myInt;

    myInt = 5;

    if ( myInt == 0 )
        printf( "myInt is equal to zero." );
    else
        printf( "myInt is not equal to zero." );

    return 0;
}
```

This program declares myInt to be of type int and sets the value of myInt to 5. Next, we use the if statement to test whether myInt is equal to 0. If myInt is equal to 0 (which we know is not true), we'll print one string. Otherwise, we'll print a different string. As expected, this program prints the string "myInt is not equal to zero".

if statements come two ways. The first, known as plain old if, fits this pattern:

```c
if ( expression )
    statement
```

An if statement will always consist of the word "if," a left parenthesis, an expression, a right parenthesis, and a statement (I'll define both "expression" and "statement" in a minute). This first form of if executes the statement if the expression in parentheses is true. An English example of the plain if might be

```
If it's raining outside, I'll bring my umbrella.
```

Notice that this statement only tells us what will happen if it's raining outside. No particular action will be taken if it is not raining.

The second form of `if`, known as `if-else`, fits this pattern:

```
if ( expression )
    statement
else
    statement
```

An `if-else` statement will always consist of the word "if," a left parenthesis, an expression, a right parenthesis, a statement, the word "else," and a second statement. This form of `if` executes the first statement if the expression is true and executes the second statement if the expression is false. An English example of an `if-else` statement might be

```
If it's raining outside, I'll bring my umbrella,
otherwise I won't.
```

Notice that this example tells us what will happen if it is raining outside (I'll bring my umbrella) and if it isn't raining outside (I won't bring my umbrella). The example programs presented later in the chapter demonstrate the proper use of both `if` and `if-else`.

Our next step is to define the terms "expression" and "statement."

A SAFER FORM OF IF

Here's a cool safety tip. The previous chunk of code started its `if` statement with

```
if ( myInt == 0 )
```

The following take on this `if` statement is a bit safer:

```
if ( 0 == myInt )
```

Can you see why the second version would be safer? Here's a hint. A very common mistake made by C programmers, even expert C programmers, is to type = when they mean to type ==. In this example, that would lead to an `if` that looked like this:

```
if ( myInt = 0 )
```

This `if` will first assign the value of 0 to the variable `myInt`, not at all what you intended. Even worse, this code will compile, so the compiler won't be able to clue you in to your mistake by reporting an error. If you used the second form of `if`, your mistake would look like this:

```
if ( 0 = myInt )
```

The compiler will catch this mistake, since you can't assign a new value to 0. Some programmers just hate the way this looks. Others love it and embrace this form for its safety. You are the programmer; you make the call.

Expressions

In C, an **expression** is anything that has a value. For example, a variable is a type of expression, since variables always have a value. Even uninitialized variables have a value—we just don't know what the value is! Uninitialized variables are said to be **undefined**. The following are all examples of expressions:

- `myInt + 3`

- `( myInt + anotherInt ) * 4`

- `myInt++`

An assignment statement is also an expression. Can you guess the value of an assignment statement? Think back to Chapter 5. Remember when we included an assignment statement as a parameter to `printf()`? The value of an assignment statement is the value of its left side. Check out the following code fragment:

```
myInt = 5;
myInt += 3;
```

Both of these statements qualify as expressions. The value of the first expression is 5. The value of the second expression is 8 (because we added three to `myInt`'s previous value).

Literals can also be used as expressions. The number "8" has a value. Guess what? Its value is 8. All expressions, no matter what their type, have a numerical value.

NOTE

Technically, there is an exception to the rule that all expressions have a numerical value. The expression `(void)0` has no value. In fact, any value or variable cast to type `void` has no value.

Umm, but Dave, what's a cast? What is type `void`?

We'll get to both of these topics later in this book. For the moment, when you see `void`, think "no value."

True Expressions

Earlier, we defined the `if` statement as follows:

```
if ( expression )
    statement
```

We then said the statement gets executed if the expression is true. Let's look at C's concept of truth.

Everyone has an intuitive understanding of the difference between true and false. I think we'd all agree that the statement

```
5 equals 3
```

is false. We'd also agree that the following statement is true:

```
5 and 3 are both greater than 0
```

This intuitive grasp of true and false carries over into the C language. In the case of C, however, both true and false have numerical values. Here's how it works.

In C, any expression that has a value of 0 is said to be false. Any expression with a value other than 0 is said to be true. As stated earlier, an if statement's statement gets executed if its expression is true. To put this more accurately, an if statement's statement gets executed if (and only if) its expression has a value other than 0.

Here's an example:

```
myInt = 27;

if ( myInt )
    printf( "myInt is not equal to 0" );
```

The if statement in this piece of code first tests the value of myInt. Since myInt is not equal to 0, the printf() gets executed.

Comparative Operators

C expressions have a special set of operators, called **comparative operators**. Comparative operators compare their left sides with their right sides and produce a value of either 1 or 0, depending on the relationship of the two sides.

For example, the operator == determines whether the expression on the left is equal in value to the expression on the right. The expression

```
myInt == 5
```

evaluates to 1 if myInt is equal to 5 and to 0 if myInt is not equal to 5. Here's an example of the == operator at work:

```
if ( myInt == 5 )
    printf( "myInt is equal to 5" );
```

If myInt is equal to 5, the expression myInt == 5 evaluates to 1, and printf() gets called. If myInt isn't equal to 5, the expression evaluates to 0, and the printf() is skipped. Just remember, the key to triggering an `if` statement is an expression that resolves to a value other than 0.

Table 6-1 shows some of the other comparative operators. You'll see some of these operators in the example programs later in the chapter.

Table 6-1. *Comparative Operators*

Operator	Resolves to 1 if . . .
==	Left side is equal to right
<=	Left side is less than or equal to right
>=	Left side is greater than or equal to right
<	Left side is less than right
>	Left side is greater than right
!=	Left side is not equal to right

Logical Operators

The C standard provides a pair of constants that really come in handy when dealing with our next set of operators. The constant `true` has a value of 1, while the constant `false` has a value of 0. Both of these constants are defined in the include file `<stdbool.h>`. You can use these constants in your programs to make them a little easier to read. Read on, and you'll see why.

NOTE

In addition to `true` and `false`, most C environments also provide the constants TRUE and FALSE (with values of 1 and 0 respectively). Don't be fooled. `true` and `false` are part of the C standard; TRUE and FALSE are not.

The members of our next set of operators are known, collectively, as **logical operators**. The set of logical operators is modeled on the mathematical concept of truth tables. If you don't know much about truth tables (or are just frightened by mathematics in general), don't panic. Everything you need to know is outlined in the next few paragraphs.

NOTE

Truth tables are part of a branch of mathematics known as Boolean algebra, named for George Boole, the man who developed it in the late 1830s. The term **Boolean** has come to mean a variable that can take one of two values. Bits are Boolean; they can take on the value 0 or 1.

The first of the set of logical operators is the ! operator, which is commonly referred to as the NOT operator. For example, !A is pronounced "not A."

The ! operator turns true into false and false into true. Table 6-2 shows the truth table for the ! operator. In this table, T stands for true, which has the value 1, and F stands for false, which has the value 0. The letter "A" in the table represents an expression. If the expression A is true, applying the ! operator to A yields the value false. If the expression A is false, applying the ! operator to A yields the value true.

Table 6-2. *Truth Table for the ! Operator*

A	!A
T	F
F	T

Here's a piece of code that demonstrates the ! operator:

```
bool     myFirstBool, mySecondBool;

myFirstBool = false;
mySecondBool = ! myFirstBool;
```

The first thing you'll notice about this chunk of code is the new data type, bool. A bool can hold either a 0 or a 1. That's it. bools are perfect for working with logical operators. Our example starts by declaring two bools. We assign the value false to the first bool, and then use the ! operator to turn the false into a true and assign it to the second bool.

NOTE

bool is not a built-in C data type. It is a macro created using the #define mechanism to provide a prettier version of its underlying type, _Bool. The file <stdbool.h> gives you access to true and false and contains the definition of bool. We'll get into macros and #define in Chapter 8.

Take another look at Table 6-2. The ! operator converts true into false and false into true. What this really means is that ! converts 1 to 0 and 0 to 1, which comes in handy when you are working with an if statement's expression, like this one:

```
if ( mySecondBool )
    printf( "mySecondBool must be true" );
```

The previous chunk of code translated mySecondBool from false to true, which is the same thing as saying that mySecondBool has a value of 1. Either way, mySecondBool will cause the if to fire, and the printf() will get executed.

Take a look at this piece of code:

```
if ( ! mySecondBool )
    printf( "mySecondBool must be false" );
```

This `printf()` will get executed if `mySecondInt` is `false`. Do you see why? If `mySecondBool` is `false`, then `!mySecondInt` must be `true`.

The `!` operator is a **unary** operator. Unary operators operate on a single expression. The other two logical operators, `&&` and `||`, are **binary** operators. Binary operators, such as the `==` operator presented earlier, operate on two expressions, one on the left side and one on the right side of the operator.

The `&&` operator is commonly referred to as the **logical and** operator. The result of an `&&` operation is `true` if, and only if, both the left side and the right side are `true`. Here's an example:

```
bool    hasCar, hasTimeToGiveRide;

hasCar = true;
hasTimeToGiveRide = true;

if ( hasCar && hasTimeToGiveRide )
    printf( "Hop in - I'll give you a ride!\n" );
else
    printf( "I have no car, no time, or no car and no time!\n" );
```

This example uses two variables. One indicates whether the program has a car, the other whether the program has time to give us a ride to the mall. All philosophical issues aside (can a program have a car?), the question of the moment is, which of the two `printf()`'s will fire? Since both sides of the `&&` were set to `true`, the first `printf()` will be called. If either one (or both) of the variables were set to `false`, the second `printf()` would be called. Another way to think of this is that we'll only get a ride to the mall if our friendly program has a car *and* has time to give us a ride. If either of these is not true, we're not getting a ride. By the way, notice the use here of the second form of `if`, the `if-else` statement.

The `||` operator is commonly referred to as the **logical or** operator. The result of a `||` operation is `true` if the left side, the right side, or both sides of the `||` are `true`. Put another way, the result of a `||` is `false` if, and only if, both the left side and the right side of the `||` are `false`. Here's an example:

```
bool    nothingElseOn, newEpisode;

nothingElseOn = true;
newEpisode = true;
```

```
if ( newEpisode || nothingElseOn )
    printf( "Let's watch Family Guy!\n" );
else
    printf( "Something else is on or I've seen this one.\n" );
```

This example uses two variables to decide whether or not we should watch *Family Guy*. One variable indicates whether anything else is on right now, and the other tells you whether this episode is a rerun. If this is a brand-new episode *or* if nothing else is on, we'll watch *Family Guy*.

Here's a slight twist on the previous example:

```
int    nothingElseOn, itsARerun;

nothingElseOn = true;
itsARerun = false;

if ( (! itsARerun) || nothingElseOn )
    printf( "Let's watch Family Guy!\n" );
else
    printf( "Something else is on or I've seen this one.\n" );
```

This time, we've replaced the variable newEpisode with its exact opposite, itsARerun. Look at the logic that drives the if statement. Now we're combining itsARerun with the ! operator. Before, we cared whether the episode was a newEpisode. This time, we are concerned that the episode is not a rerun. See the difference?

Both the && and the || operators are summarized in the table in Table 6-3. Note that A&&B is only true if A and B are both true. A||B is true if A, B, or both are true.

Table 6-3. *Truth Table for the && and || Operators*

A	B	A && B	A || B
T	T	T	T
T	F	F	T
F	T	F	T
F	F	F	F

NOTE

On most keyboards, you type an & (ampersand) character by holding down the Shift key and typing a 7. You type a | character by holding down the Shift key and typing a \ (backslash). Don't confuse the | with the letter L or I, or with the ! character.

truthTester.xcodeproj

If you look in the folder *Learn C Projects*, you'll find a subfolder named *06.01 – truthTester* that contains a project that implements the three examples we just went through. Launch the project *truthTester.xcodeproj*. Take a look at the source code in *main.c*. Play with the code. Take turns changing the variables from `true` to `false` and back again. Use this code to get a good feel for the `!`, `&&`, and `||` operators.

You might also try commenting out the line `#include <stdbool.h>` toward the top of the file. To do this, just insert the characters `//` at the very beginning of the line. When you compile, you'll get a number of errors complaining that `bool`, `true`, and `false` are undeclared. Remember this! As you write your own programs, be sure to `#include <stdbool.h>` if you want to use `bool`, `true`, and `false`.

Compound Expressions

All of the examples presented so far have consisted of relatively simple expressions. Here's an example that combines several different operators:

```
int    myInt;

myInt = 7;

if ( (myInt >= 1) && (myInt <= 10) )
    printf( "myInt is between 1 and 10" );
else
    printf( "myInt is not between 1 and 10" );
```

This example tests whether a variable is in the range between 1 and 10. The key here is the expression that lies between the `if` statement's parentheses:

```
(myInt >= 1) && (myInt <= 10)
```

This expression uses the `&&` operator to combine two smaller expressions. Notice that the two smaller expressions were each surrounded by parentheses to avoid any ambiguity. If we left out the parentheses, like so:

```
myInt >= 1 && myInt <= 10
```

the expression might not be interpreted as we intended. Once again, use parentheses for safe computing.

Statements

At the beginning of the chapter, we defined the if statement as follows:

```
if ( expression )
    statement
```

We've covered expressions pretty thoroughly. Now, we'll turn our attention to the statement.

At this point in this book, you probably have a pretty intuitive model of the statement. You'd probably agree that this:

```
myInt = 7;
```

is a statement. But is the following one statement or two?

```
if ( isCold )
    printf( "Put on your sweater!" );
```

Actually, the previous code fragment is a statement within another statement: printf() is one statement residing within a larger statement, the if statement.

The ability to break your code out into individual statements is not a critical skill. Getting your code to compile, however, *is* critical. As new types of statements are introduced (like the if and if-else introduced in this chapter) pay attention to the statement syntax. And pay special attention to the examples. Where do the semicolons go? What distinguishes this type of statement from all other types?

As you build up your repertoire of statement types, you'll find yourself using one type of statement within another. That's perfectly acceptable in C. In fact, every time you create an if statement, you'll use at least two statements, one within the other. Take a look at this example:

```
if ( myVar >= 1 )
    if ( myVar <= 10 )
        printf( "myVar is between 1 and 10" );
```

This example used an if statement as the statement for another if statement. This example calls the printf() if both if expressions are true; that is, if myVar is greater than or equal to 1 and less than or equal to 10. You could have accomplished the same result with this piece of code:

```
if ( ( myVar >= 1 ) && ( myVar <= 10 ) )
        printf( "myVar is between 1 and 10" );
```

The second piece of code is a little easier to read. There are times, however, when the method demonstrated in the first piece of code is preferred. Take a look at this example:

```
if ( myVar != 0 )
    if ( ( 1 / myVar ) < 1 )
        printf( "myVar is in range" );
```

One thing you don't want to do in C is divide a number by zero. Any number divided by zero is infinity, and infinity is a foreign concept to the C language. If your program ever tries to divide a number by zero, the compiler will likely report a "division by zero" warning and your program is likely to exit prematurely, reporting a "floating point exception." The first expression in this example tests to make sure myVar is not equal to zero. If myVar is equal to zero, the second expression won't even be evaluated! The sole purpose of the first if is to make sure the second if never tries to divide by zero. Make sure you understand this point. Imagine what would happen if we wrote the code this way:

```
if ( (myVar != 0) && ((1 / myVar) < 1) )
        printf( "myVar is in range" );
```

As it turns out, if the left half of the && operator evaluates to false, the right half of the expression will never be evaluated and the entire expression will evaluate to false. Why? Because if the left operand is false, it doesn't matter what the right operand is—true or false, the expression will evaluate to false. Be aware of this as you construct your expressions.

NOTE

> The approach of not evaluating the remainder of an expression if the evaluation of the first portion of the expression determines the value of the expression is known as **short circuit evaluation** or **minimal evaluation**.

The Curly Braces

Earlier in this book, you learned about the curly braces ({}) that surround the body of every function. These braces also play an important role in statement construction. Just as parentheses can be used to group terms of an expression together, curly braces can be used to group multiple statements together. Here's an example:

```
onYourBack = TRUE;

if ( onYourBack ) {
    printf( "Flipping over" );
    onYourBack = FALSE;
}
```

In the example, if onYourBack is true, both of the statements in curly braces will be executed. A pair of curly braces can be used to combine any number of statements into a single superstatement, also known as a **block**. You can use this technique anywhere a statement is called for.

Curly braces can be used to organize your code, much as you'd use parentheses to ensure that an expression is evaluated properly. This concept is especially appropriate when dealing with nested statements. Consider this code, for example:

```
if ( myInt >= 0 )
    if ( myInt <= 10 )
        printf( "myInt is between 0 and 10.\n" );
else
    printf( "myInt is negative.\n" ); /* <---Error!!! */
```

Do you see the problem with this code? Which if does the else belong to? As written (and as formatted), the else looks like it belongs to the first if. That is, if myInt is greater than or equal to 0, the second if is executed; otherwise, the second printf() is executed. Is this right?

Nope. As it turns out, an else belongs to the if closest to it (the second if, in this case). Here's a slight rewrite:

```
if ( myInt >= 0 )
    if ( myInt <= 10 )
        printf( "myInt is between 0 and 10.\n" );
    else
        printf( "myInt is not between 0 and 10.\n" );
```

One point here is that formatting is nice, but it won't fool the compiler. More importantly, this example shows how easy it is to make a mistake. Check out this version of the code:

```
if ( myInt >= 0 ) {
    if ( myInt <= 10 )
        printf( "myInt is between 0 and 10.\n" );
}
else
    printf( "myInt is negative.\n" );
```

Do you see how the curly braces help? In a sense, they act to hide the second if inside the first if statement. There is no chance for the else to connect to the hidden if.

No one I know ever got fired for using too many parentheses or too many curly braces.

Where to Place the Semicolon

So far, the statements you've seen fall into two categories: simple statements and compound statements. Function calls, such as calls to printf(), and assignment statements are called **simple statements**. Always place a semicolon at the end of a simple statement, even if it is broken over several lines, like this:

```
printf( "%d%d%d%d", var1,
                    var2,
                    var3,
                    var4 );
```

Statements made up of several parts, including, possibly, other statements, are called **compound statements**. Compound statements obey some pretty strict rules of syntax. The if statement, for example, always looks like this:

```
if ( expression )
    statement
```

Notice that there are no semicolons in this definition. The statement part of the if can be a simple statement or a compound statement. If the statement is simple, follow the semicolon rules for simple statements and place a semicolon at the end of the statement. If the statement is compound, follow the semicolon rules for that particular type of statement.

Notice that using curly braces, or curlies, to build a superstatement or block out of smaller statements does not require the addition of a semicolon.

The Loneliest Statement

Guess what? A single semicolon qualifies as a statement, albeit a somewhat lonely one. For example, this code fragment

```
if ( bored )
    ;
```

is a legitimate (and thoroughly useless) if statement. If bored is true, the semicolon statement gets executed. The semicolon by itself doesn't do anything but fill the bill where a statement is needed. There are times where the semicolon by itself is exactly what you need.

The while Statement

The if statement uses the value of an expression to decide whether to execute or skip over a statement. If the statement is executed, it is executed just once. Another type of statement, the while statement, repeatedly executes a statement as long as a specified expression is true. The while statement follows this pattern:

```
while ( expression )
    statement
```

The while statement is also known as the **while loop**, because once the statement is executed, the while loops back to reevaluate the expression. Here's an example of the while loop in action:

```
int    i;

i=0;

while ( ++i < 3 )
    printf( "Looping: %d\n", i );

printf( "We are past the while loop." );
```

This example starts by declaring a variable, i, to be of type int. i is then initialized to 0. Next comes the while loop. The first thing the while loop does is evaluate its expression. The while loop's expression is

```
++i < 3
```

Before this expression is evaluated, i has a value of 0. The prefix notation used in the expression (++i) increments the value of i to 1 before the remainder of the expression is evaluated. The evaluation of the expression results in true, since 1 is less than 3. Since the expression is true, the while loop's statement, a single printf() is executed. Here's the output after the first pass through the loop:

```
Looping: 1
```

Next, the while loops back and reevaluates its expression. Once again, the prefix notation increments i, this time to a value of 2. Since 2 is less than 3, the expression evaluates to true, and the printf() is executed again. Here's the output after the second pass through the loop:

```
Looping: 1
Looping: 2
```

Once the second printf() completes, it's back to the top of the loop to reevaluate the expression. Will this never end? Once again, i is incremented, this time to a value of 3. Aha! This time, the expression evaluates to false, since 3 is not less than 3. Once the expression evaluates to false, the while loop ends, and control passes to the next statement, the second printf() in our example:

```
printf( "We are past the while loop." );
```

The while loop was driven by three factors: **initialization**, **modification**, and **termination**. Initialization is any code that affects the loop but occurs before the loop is entered. In our example, the critical initialization occurred when the variable i was set to 0.

COUNTER VARIABLE NAMING

Frequently, you'll use a variable in a loop that changes value each time through the loop. In our example, the variable i was incremented by one each time through the loop. The first time through the loop, i had a value of 1. The second time, i had a value of 2. Variables that maintain a value based on the number of times through a loop are known as **counters**.

In the interest of clarity, some programmers use names like counter or loopCounter. The nice thing about names like i, j, and k is that they don't get in the way, as they don't take up a lot of space on the line. On the other hand, your goal should be to make your code as readable as possible, so it would seem that a name like counter would be better than the uninformative i, j, or k.

One popular compromise holds that the closer a variable's use is to its declaration, the shorter its name can be.

Once again, pick a style you are comfortable with, and stick with it!

Modification is any code within the loop that changes the value of the loop's expression. In our example, the modification occurred within the expression itself when the counter, i, was incremented.

Termination is any condition that causes the loop to terminate. In our example, termination occurs when the expression has a value of false. This occurs when the counter, i, has a value that is not less than 3. Take a look at this example:

```
int    i;

i=1;

while ( i < 3 ) {
    printf( "Looping: %d\n", i );
    i++;
}

printf( "We are past the while loop." );
```

This example produces the same results as the previous example. This time, however, the Initialization and modification conditions have changed slightly. In this example, i starts with a value of 1 instead of 0. In the previous example, the ++ operator was used to increment i at the very *top of the loop*. This example modifies i at the *bottom of the loop*.

Both of these examples show different ways to accomplish the same end. The phrase "there's more than one way to eat an Oreo" sums up the situation perfectly. There will always be more than one solution to any programming problem. Don't be afraid to do things your own way. Just make sure your code works properly and is easy to read.

The for Statement

Nestled inside the C language, right next to the while statement, is the for statement. The for statement is similar to the while statement, following the basic model of initialization, modification, and termination. Here's the pattern for a for statement:

```
for ( expression1 ; expression2 ; expression3 )
    statement
```

The first expression represents the for statement's initialization. Typically, this expression consists of an assignment statement, setting the initial value of a counter variable. This first expression is evaluated once, at the beginning of the loop.

The second expression is identical in function to the expression in a while statement, providing the termination condition for the loop. This expression is evaluated each time through the loop, before the statement is executed.

Finally, the third expression provides the modification portion of the for statement. This expression is evaluated at the bottom of the loop, immediately following execution of the statement.

Note that all three of these expressions are optional and may be left out entirely. For example, here's a for loop that leaves out all three expressions:

```
for ( ; ; )
    DoSomethingForever();
```

Since this loop has no terminating expression, it is known as an **infinite loop**. Infinite loops are generally considered bad form and should be avoided like the plague!

The for loop can also be described in terms of a while loop:

```
expression1;
while ( expression2 ){
    statement
    expression3;
}
```

Here's an example of a for loop:

```
int    i;

for ( i = 1; i < 3; i++ )
    printf( "Looping: %d\n", i );

printf( "We are past the for loop." );
```

This example is identical in functionality to the while loops presented earlier. Note the three expressions on the first line of the for loop. Before the loop is entered, the first expression is evaluated (remember, assignment statements make great expressions):

```
i = 1
```

Once the expression is evaluated, i has a value of 1. We are now ready to enter the loop. At the top of each pass through the loop, the second expression is evaluated:

```
i < 3
```

If the expression evaluates to true, the loop continues. Since i is less than 3, we can proceed. Next, the statement is executed:

```
printf( "Looping: %d\n", i );
```

Here's the first line of output:

```
Looping: 1
```

Having reached the bottom of the loop, the for evaluates its third expression:

```
i++
```

This changes the value of i to 2. We go back to the top of the loop and evaluate the termination expression:

```
i < 3
```

Since i is still less than 3, the loop continues. Once again, `printf()` does its thing. The console window looks like this:

```
Looping: 1
Looping: 2
```

Next, the for statement evaluates expression3, incrementing the value of i to 3:

```
i++
```

Again, we go back to the top of the loop, and evaluate the termination expression:

```
i < 3
```

Lo and behold! Since i is no longer less than 3, the loop ends and the second `printf()` in our example is executed:

```
printf( "We are past the for loop." );
```

As was the case with `while`, for can take full advantage of a pair of curly braces:

```
for ( i = 0; i < 10; i++ ) {
    DoThis();
    DoThat();
    DanceALittleJig();
}
```

In addition, both `while` and `for` can take advantage of the loneliest statement, the lone semicolon:

```
for ( i = 0; i < 1000; i++ )
    ;
```

The preceding example does nothing 1,000 times. Actually, the example does take some time to execute. The initialization expression is evaluated once, and the modification and termination expressions are each evaluated 1,000 times. Here's a `while` version of the loneliest loop:

```
i = 0;

while ( i++ < 1000 )
    ;
```

NOTE

Some compilers will eliminate a loop containing only the semicolon and just set i to its terminating value (the value it would have if the loop executed normally). This is an example of **code optimization**. The nice thing about code optimization is that it can make your code run faster and more efficiently. The downside is that an optimization pass on your code can sometimes cause unwanted side effects, like eliminating the while loop just discussed. Some people turn optimization off during development for this reason.

Getting to know your compiler's optimization capabilities and tendencies is a good idea. Read the documentation!

loopTester.xcodeproj

Interestingly, there is an important difference between the for and while loops you just saw. Take a minute to look back and try to predict the value of i the first time through each loop and after each loop terminates. Were the results the same for the while and for loops? Hmm . . . you might want to take another look.

Here's a sample program that should clarify the difference between these two loops. Look in the folder *Learn C Projects*, inside the subfolder named *06.02 - loopTester*, and open the project *loopTester.xcodeproj*. loopTester implements a while loop and two slightly different for loops. Run the project. Your output should look like that shown in Figure 6-1.

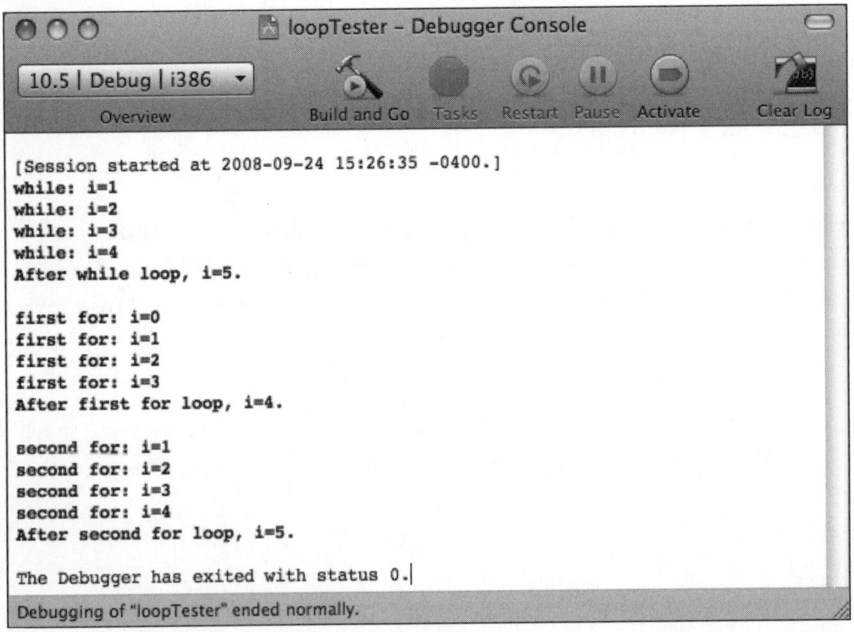

Figure 6-1. *The output from loopTester, showing the results from a while loop and two slightly different for loops*

loopTester starts off with the standard #include. main() defines a counter variable i and sets i to 0:

```
#include <stdio.h>

int main (int argc, const char * argv[]) {
    int    i;

    i = 0;
```

main() then enters a while loop:

```
    while ( i++ < 4 )
        printf( "while: i=%d\n", i );
```

The loop executes four times, resulting in this output:

```
while: i=1
while: i=2
while: i=3
while: i=4
```

Do you see why? If not, go through the loop yourself, calculating the value for i each time through the loop. Remember, since we are using postfix notation (i++), i gets incremented *after* the test is made to see if it is less than 4. The test and the increment happen at the top of the loop, before the loop is entered.

Once the loop completes, we print the value of i again:

```
    printf( "After while loop, i=%d.\n\n", i );
```

Here's the result:

```
After while loop, i=5.
```

Here's how we got that value. The last time through the loop (with i equal to 4), we go back to the top of the while loop, test to see if i is less than 4 (it no longer is), and then do the increment of i, bumping it from 4 to 5.

OK, one loop down, two to go. This next loop looks like it should accomplish the same thing. The difference is that we don't do the increment of i until the bottom of the loop, after we've been through the loop once already.

```
    for ( i = 0; i < 4; i++ )
        printf( "first for: i=%d\n", i );
```

As you can see by the output, i ranges from 0 to 3 instead of from 1 to 4.

```
first for: i=0
first for: i=1
first for: i=2
first for: i=3
```

Once we drop out of the for loop, we again print the value of i:

```
    printf( "After first for loop, i=%d.\n\n", i );
```

Here's the result:

```
After first for loop, i=4.
```

This time, the while loop ranged i from 1 to 4, leaving i with a value of 5 at the end of the loop. The for loop ranged i from 0 to 3, leaving i with a value of 4 at the end of the loop. So how do we fix the for loop so it works the same way as the while loop? Take a look:

```
    for ( i = 1; i <= 4; i++ )
        printf( "second for: i=%d\n", i );
```

This for loop started i at 1 instead of 0. It tests to see if i is *less than or equal to* 4 instead of just less than 4. We could also have used the terminating expression i < 5 instead. Either one will work. As proof, here's the output from this loop:

```
second for: i=1
second for: i=2
second for: i=3
second for: i=4
```

Once again, we print the value of i at the end of the loop:

```
    printf( "After second for loop, i=%d.\n", i );

    return 0;
}
```

Here's the last piece of output:

```
After second for loop, i=5.
```

This second for loop is the functional equivalent to the while loop. Take some time to play with this code. You might try to modify the while loop to match the first for loop.

By far, the while and for statements are the most common types of C loops. For completeness, however, we'll cover the remaining loop, a little-used gem called the do statement.

The do Statement

The do statement is a while statement that evaluates its expression at the bottom of its loop, instead of at the top. Here's the pattern a do statement must match:

```
do
    statement
while ( expression ) ;
```

Here's a sample:

```
i = 1;

do {
    printf( "%d\n", i );
    i++;
}
while ( i < 3 );

printf( "We are past the do loop." );
```

The first time through the loop, i has a value of 1. The printf() prints a 1 in the console window, and the value of i is bumped to 2. It's not until this point that the expression (i < 3) is evaluated. Since 2 is less than 3, a second pass through the loop occurs.

During this second pass, the printf() prints a 2 in the console window, and the value of i is bumped to 3. Once again, the expression (i < 3) is evaluated. Since 3 is not less than 3, we drop out of the loop to the second printf().

The important thing to remember about do loops is this: since the expression is not evaluated until the bottom of the loop, the body of the loop (the statement) is always executed at least once. Since for and while loops both check their expressions at the top of the loop, either can drop out of the loop before the body of the loop is executed.

Let's move on to a completely different type of statement, known as switch.

The switch Statement

The switch statement uses the value of an expression to determine which of a series of statements to execute. Here's an example that should make this concept a little clearer:

```
switch ( theYear ) {
    case 1066:
        printf( "Battle of Hastings" );
        break;
    case 1492:
        printf( "Columbus sailed the ocean blue" );
        break;
```

```
    case 1776:
        printf( "Declaration of Independence\n" );
        printf( "A very important document!!!" );
        break;
    default:
        printf( "Don't know what happened during this year" );
}
```

NOTE

> The switch statement and the if statement are both known as **selection statements**.

The switch is constructed of a series of cases, each case based on a specific value of theYear. If theYear has a value of 1066, execution continues with the statement following that case's colon, in this case, the following line:

```
    printf( "Battle of Hastings" );
```

Execution continues, line after line, until either the bottom of the switch (the right curly brace) or a break statement is reached. In this case, the next line is a break statement.

The break statement comes in handy when you are working with switch statements and loops. The break tells the compiler to jump immediately to the next statement after the end of the loop or switch.

Continuing with the example, if theYear has a value of 1492, the switch jumps to these lines:

```
    printf( "Columbus sailed the ocean blue" );
    break;
```

A value of 1776 jumps to the lines

```
    printf( "Declaration of Independence\n" );
    printf( "A very important document!!!" );
    break;
```

Notice that this case has two statements before the break. There is no limit to the number of statements a case can have. Having one is OK; having 653 is OK. You can even have a case with no statements at all.

The original example also contains a **default case**. If the switch can't find a case that matches the value of its expression, the switch looks for a case labeled default. If the default is present, its statements are executed. If no default is present, the switch completes without executing any of its statements.

Here's the pattern the switch tries to match:

```
switch ( expression ) {
    case constant:
        statements
    case constant:
        statements
    default:
        statements
}
```

A case with No Statements

Why would you want a case with no statements? Here's an example:

```
switch ( numberOfEggs ) {
    case 1:
    case 2:
        HardBoilThem();
        break;
    case 3:
        MakeAnOmelet();
}
```

In this example, if numberOfEggs has a value of 1 or 2, the function HardBoilThem() is called. If numberOfEggs has a value of 3, the function MakeAnOmelet() is called. If NumberOfEggs has any other value, nothing happens. Use a case with no statements when you want two different cases to execute the same statements.

But what happens if we have 4 eggs? We get no breakfast? Not cool. Here's a better plan.

```
switch ( numberOfEggs ) {
    case 1:
    case 2:
        HardBoilThem();
        break;
    case 3:
        MakeAnOmelet();
        break;
    default:
        FrenchToastForEveryone();
}
```

In this example, we've added a default case. Now, if we have 4 eggs or more, everyone will get French toast. Yay!

The Mixed Blessing of Fall-Through

Think about what happens with this example:

```
switch ( myVar ) {
    case 1:
        DoSometimes();
    case 2:
        DoFrequently();
    default:
        DoAlways();
}
```

Notice anything unusual? This code contains no break statements. If myVar is 1, all three functions will get called. This is called **fall-through**, because we execute DoSometimes(), and then fall through and execute DoFrequently(), and then fall through and execute DoAlways().

If myVar is 2, DoFrequently() and DoAlways() will get called. If myVar has any other value, DoAlways() gets called by itself.

As this example showed, fall-through allows you to layer your switch cases, adding more functionality as you fall through the cases. With careful planning, fall-through is a nice tool to have. That said, fall-through does have its downside. Imagine that you needed to modify the code. You realized that when myVar is 2, you need to call the function OnlyWhenMyVarIs2(). So you modify the code to look like this:

```
switch ( myVar ) {
    case 1:
        DoSometimes();
    case 2:
        DoFrequently();
        OnlyWhenMyVarIs2();
    default:
        DoAlways();
}
```

Do you see the problem here? In this version, OnlyWhenMyVarIs2() will get executed when myVar is 1 or 2. The lack of a break at the end of case 1 means that anything you add to case 2 will also affect case 1. Not a big deal—we can rewrite the code using breaks. The real problem is that if you have not looked at this code for a while, you might miss the fact that the break is not there and just assume each case is its own separate entity. One way to solve this problem is to heavily comment your code, making it clear for the future that you are using fall-through. Another way to solve this problem is to avoid fall-through. As always, code carefully; plan for the future.

switch Wrap-Up

At the heart of each switch is its expression. Most switch statements are based on single variables, but as we mentioned earlier, assignment statements make perfectly acceptable expressions.

Each case is based on a **constant**. Numbers (like 47 or –12,932) are valid constants. Variables, such as myVar, are not. As you'll see later, single-byte characters (like 'a' or '\n') are also valid constants. Multiple-byte character strings (like "Gummy-bear") are not.

If your switch uses a default case, make sure you use it as shown in the preceding pattern. Don't include the word case before the word default.

Breaks in Other Loops

The break statement has other uses besides the switch statement. Here's an example of a break used in a while loop:

```
i=1;

while ( i <= 9 ) {
    PlayAnInning( i );
    if ( IsItRaining() )
        break;
    i++;
}
```

This sample tries to play nine innings of baseball. As long as the function IsItRaining() returns with a value of false, the game continues uninterrupted. If IsItRaining() returns a value of true, the break statement is executed, and the program drops out of the loop, interrupting the game.

The break statement allows you to construct loops that depend on multiple factors. The termination of the loop depends on the value of the expression found at the top of the loop, as well as on any outside factors that might trigger an unexpected break.

isOdd.xcodeproj

This next program combines for and if statements to tell you whether the numbers 1 through 20 are odd or even and if they are an even multiple of 3. It also introduces a brand-new operator: the % operator. Go into the *Learn C Projects* folder, into the *06.03 - isOdd* subfolder, and open the project *isOdd.xcodeproj*.

Run *isOdd.xcodeproj*. You should see something like the console window shown in Figure 6-2, which shows a line for each number from 1 through 20. Each of the numbers will be described as either odd or even. Each of the multiples of 3 will have additional text describing them as such. Let's do a walkthrough of the code.

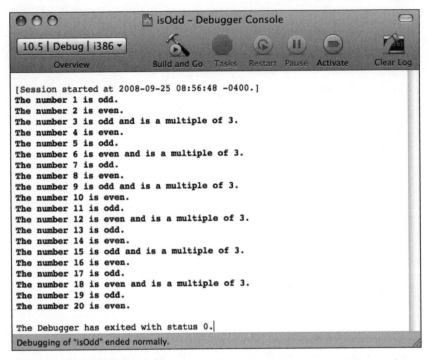

Figure 6-2. *The isOdd program steps through each number from 1 to 20, reporting whether the number is even or odd and whether the number is a multiple of 3.*

Stepping Through the isOdd Source Code

isOdd starts off with the usual `#include` and the beginning of `main()`. `main()` starts off by declaring a counter variable named `i`.

```
#include <stdio.h>

int main (int argc, const char * argv[]) {
    int     i;
```

Our goal here is to step through each of the numbers from 1 to 20. For each number, we want to check to see if the number is odd or even. We also want to check whether the number is evenly divisible by 3. Once we've analyzed a number, we'll use `printf()` to print a description of the number in the console window.

TIP

As I mentioned in Chapter 4, the scheme that defines the way a program works is called the program's algorithm. It's a good idea to try to work out the details of your program's algorithm before writing even one line of source code.

As you might expect, the next step is to set up a for loop using i as a counter. i is initialized to 1. The loop will keep running as long as the value of i is less than or equal to 20. This is the same as saying the loop will exit as soon as the value of i is found to be greater than 20. Every time the loop reaches the bottom, the third expression, i++, will be evaluated, incrementing the value of i by 1. This is a classic for loop.

```
for ( i = 1; i <= 20; i++ ) {
```

Now we're inside the for loop. Our goal is to print a single line for each number (i.e., one line each time through the for loop). If you check back to Figure 6-2, you'll notice that each line starts with the phrase

```
The number x is
```

where x is the number being described. That's the purpose of this first printf():

```
printf( "The number %d is ", i );
```

Notice that this printf() wasn't part of an if statement. We want this printf() to print its message every time through the loop. The next sequence of printf()s are a different story altogether.

The next chunk of code determines whether i is even or odd and uses printf() to print the appropriate word in the console window. Because the last printf() didn't end with a new-line character ('\n'), the word "even" or "odd" will appear immediately following

```
The number x is
```

on the *same line* in the console window.

This next chunk of code introduces a brand-new operator. % is a binary operator that returns the remainder when the left operand is divided by the right operand. For example, i % 2 divides 2 into i and returns the remainder. If i is even, this remainder will be 0. If i is odd, this remainder will be 1.

```
if ( (i % 2) == 0 )
    printf( "even" );
else
    printf( "odd" );
```

In the expression i % 3, the remainder will be 0 if i is evenly divisible by 3, and either 1 or 2 otherwise.

```
if ( (i % 3) == 0 )
    printf( " and is a multiple of 3" );
```

If i is evenly divisible by 3, we'll add the phrase

```
" and is a multiple of 3"
```

to the end of the current line. Finally, we add a period and a newline ".\n" to the end of the current line, placing us at the beginning of the next line of the console window.

```
    printf( ".\n" );
```

The loop ends with a curly brace. main() ends with our normal return and curly brace.

```
    }

    return 0;
}
```

nextPrime.xcodeproj

Our next program focuses on the mathematical concept of **prime numbers**. A prime number is any number whose only factors are 1 and itself. For example, 6 is not a prime number because its factors are 1, 2, 3, and 6. The number 5 is prime because its factors are limited to 1 and 5. The number 12 isn't prime—its factors are 1, 2, 3, 4, 6, and 12.

The program nextPrime will find the next prime number greater than a specified number. For example, if we set our starting point to 14, the program would find the next prime, 17. We have the program set up to check for the next prime after 235. Lock in your guess, and let's give it a try.

Go into the folder *Learn C Projects*, into the subfolder *06.04 - nextPrime*, and open the project *nextPrime.xcodeproj*. Run the project. You should see something like the console window shown in Figure 6-3. As you can see, the next prime number after 235 is (drum roll, please . . .) 239. Let's look at how the program works.

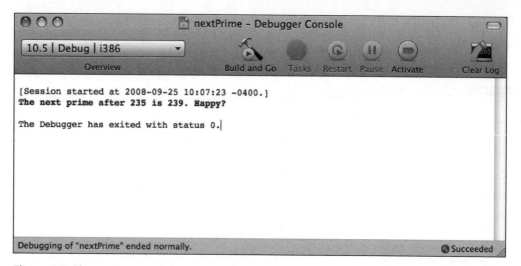

```
[Session started at 2008-09-25 10:07:23 -0400.]
The next prime after 235 is 239. Happy?

The Debugger has exited with status 0.
```

Figure 6-3. *The program nextPrime reports that the next prime after 235 is 239. I did not know that.*

Stepping Through the nextPrime Source Code

In addition to our #include of <stdio.h>, we added in a #include of <stdbool.h> to
include the definition of true and false, as well as a #include of <math.h>. <math.h> gives
us access to a series of math functions, most notably the function sqrt(). sqrt() takes
a single parameter and returns the square root of that parameter. You'll see how this works
in a minute.

```
#include <stdio.h>
#include <stdbool.h>
#include <math.h>

int main (int argc, const char * argv[]) {
```

We're going to need a boatload of variables. isPrime is defined as a bool. The rest are
defined as ints:

```
bool        isPrime;
int         startingPoint, candidate, last, i;
```

startingPoint is the number we want to start off with. We'll find the next prime after
startingPoint. candidate is the current candidate we are considering. Is candidate the
lowest prime number greater than startingPoint? By the time we are done, it will be!

```
startingPoint = 235;
```

Since 2 is the lowest prime number, if `startingPoint` is less than 2, we know that the next prime is 2. By setting `candidate` to 2, our work is done.

```
if ( startingPoint < 2 ) {
    candidate = 2;
}
```

If `startingPoint` is 2, the next prime is 3, and we'll set `candidate` accordingly.

```
else if ( startingPoint == 2 ) {
    candidate = 3;
}
```

If we got this far, we know that `startingPoint` is greater than 2. Since 2 is the only even prime number, and since we've already checked for `startingPoint` being equal to 2, we can now limit our search to odd numbers only. We'll start `candidate` at `startingPoint`, then make sure that `candidate` is odd. If not, we'll decrement `candidate`. Why decrement instead of increment? If you peek ahead a few lines, you'll see we're about to enter a do loop, and that we bump `candidate` to the next odd number at the *top* of the loop. By decrementing `candidate` now, we're preparing for the bump at the top of the loop, which will take `candidate` to the next odd number greater than `startingPoint`.

```
else {
    candidate = startingPoint;

    if (candidate % 2 == 0)
        candidate--;
```

This loop will continue stepping through consecutive odd numbers until we find a prime number. We'll start `isPrime` off as `true`, and check the current `candidate` to see if we can find a factor. If we do find a factor, we'll set `isPrime` to `false`, forcing us to repeat the loop.

```
    do {
        isPrime = true;
        candidate += 2;
```

Now we'll check to see if `candidate` is prime. This means verifying that `candidate` has no factors other than 1 and `candidate`. To do this, we'll check the numbers from 3 to the square root of `candidate` to see if any of them divide evenly into `candidate`. If not, we know we've got ourselves a prime!

```
        last = sqrt( candidate );
```

NOTE

Why don't we check from 2 up to `candidate-1`? Why start with 3? Since `candidate` will never be even, we know that 2 will never be a factor. For the same reason, we know that no even number will ever be a factor.

Why stop at the square root of `candidate`? Good question! To help understand this approach, consider the factors of 12, other than 1 and 12. They are 2, 3, 4, and 6. The square root of 12 is approximately 3.46. Notice how this fits nicely in the middle of the list of factors. Each of the factors less than the square root will have a matching factor greater than the square root. In this case, 2 matches with 6 (that is, 2 * 6 = 12) and 3 matches with 4 (that is, 3 * 4 = 12). This will always be true. If we don't find a factor by the time we hit the square root, there won't be a factor, and the candidate is prime.

Take a look at the top of the `for` loop. We start `i` at 3. Each time we hit the top of the loop (including the first time through the loop) we'll check to make sure we haven't passed the square root of `candidate`, and that `isPrime` is still `true`. If `isPrime` is `false`, we can stop searching for a factor, since we've just found one! Finally, each time we complete the loop, we bump `i` to the next odd number.

```
for ( i = 3; (i <= last) && isPrime; i += 2 ) {
```

Each time through the loop, we'll check to see if `i` divides evenly into `candidate`. If so, we know it is a factor, and we can set `isPrime` to `false`.

```
        if ( (candidate % i) == 0 )
            isPrime = false;
    }
  } while ( ! isPrime );
}
```

Once we drop out of the do loop, we use `printf()` to print both the starting point and the first prime number greater than the starting point.

```
    printf( "The next prime after %d is %d. Happy?\n",
            startingPoint, candidate );
    return 0;
}
```

If you are interested in prime numbers, play around with this program. Take a look at the exercises following this chapter for ideas.

What's Next?

Congratulations! You've made it through some tough concepts. You've learned about the C statements that allow you to control your program's flow. You've learned about C expressions and the concepts of `true` and `false`. You've also learned about the logical operators based on the values `true` and `false`. You've learned about the `if`, `if-else`, `for`, `while`, `do`, `switch`, and `break` statements. In short, you've learned a lot!

Our next chapter introduces the concept of pointers. A **pointer** to a variable is really the address of the variable in memory. If you pass the value of a variable to a function, the function can make use of the variable's value but can't *change* the variable's value. If you pass the address of the variable to the function, the function can also change the value of the variable. Chapter 7 will tell you why.

Chapter 7 will also discuss function parameters in detail. As usual, plenty of code fragments and sample applications will be presented to keep you busy. See you there.

CHAPTER 6 EXERCISES

1. What's wrong with each of the following code fragments?

   a. ```
      if   i
         i++;
      ```

   b. ```
      for ( i=0; i<20; i++ )
         i--;
      ```

   c. ```
      while ( )
         i++;
      ```

   d. ```
      do ( i++ )
         until ( i == 20 );
      ```

   e. ```
      switch (i) {
         case "hello":
         case "goodbye":
            printf("Greetings.");
            break;
         case default:
            printf("Boring.");
      }
      ```

   f. ```
      if ( i < 20 )
         if ( i == 20 )
            printf( "Lonely..." );
      ```

   g. ```
      while (done = true)
         done = ! done;
      ```

   h. ```
      for    ( i=0; i<20; i*20 )
         printf( "Modification..." );
      ```

2. Modify nextPrime to compute the prime numbers from 1 to 100.

3. Modify nextPrime to compute the first 100 prime numbers.

Pointers and Parameters

*Y*ou've come a long way. You've mastered variable basics, operators, and statements. You're about to add some powerful, new concepts to your programming toolbox.

For starters, I'll introduce the concept of pointers, also known as variable addresses. From now on, you'll use pointers in almost every C program you write. Pointers allow you to implement complex data structures, opening up a world of programming possibilities.

What Is a Pointer?

In programming, **pointers** are references to other things. When someone calls your name to get your attention, they're using your name as a pointer. Your name is one way people refer to you.

Your name and address can combine to serve as a pointer, telling the mail carrier where to deliver the new Sears catalog. Your address distinguishes your house from all the other houses in your neighborhood, and your name distinguishes you from the rest of the people living in your house.

When you declare a variable in C, memory is allocated to the variable. This memory has an address. C pointers are special variables, specifically designed to hold one of these addresses. Later in the chapter, you'll learn how to create a pointer, how to make it point to a specific variable, and how to use the pointer to change the variable's value.

Why Use Pointers?

Pointers can be extremely useful, allowing you to access your data in ways that ordinary variables just don't allow. Here's a real-world example of pointer flexibility.

When you go to the library in search of a specific title, chances are you start your search in an online catalog of some sort. Library catalogs contain thousands of entries, one for every book in the library or, in some cases, in a group of libraries. Each entry contains information about a specific book, including such information as the author's name, the book's title, and the copyright date.

Most library catalogs allow you to search using a variety of methods. For example, you might search for a book using the author's name, the book title, the subject, or some combination of all these. Figure 7-1 shows a search of the Laramie County, Wyoming library catalog. This search specifies an author named *Einstein* and a book entitled *The Meaning of Relativity*. What can I say? Einstein fascinates me.

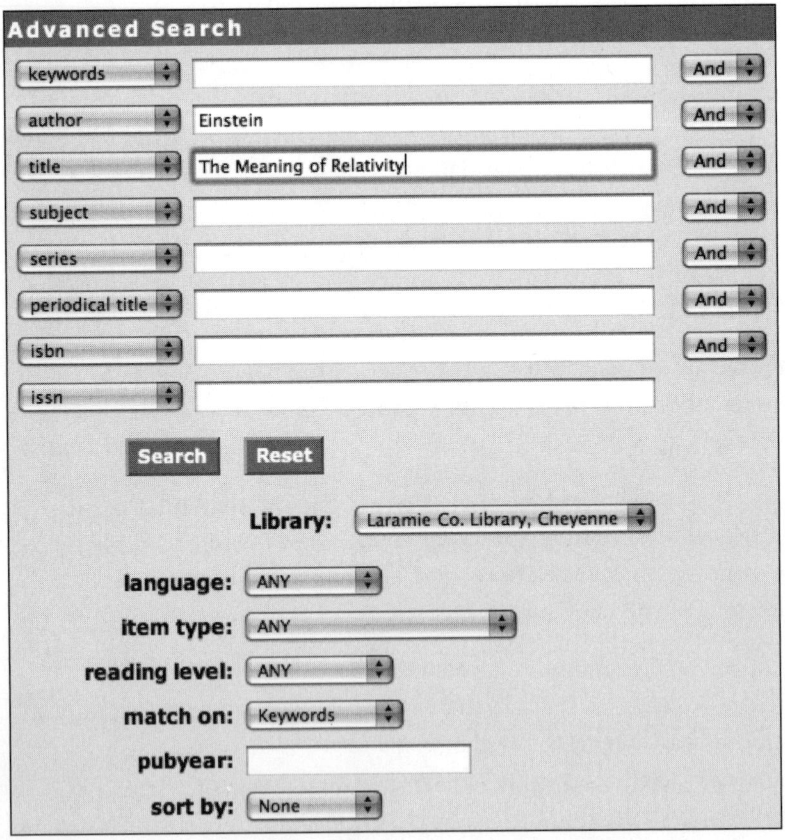

Advanced Search

keywords		And
author	Einstein	And
title	The Meaning of Relativity	And
subject		And
series		And
periodical title		And
isbn		And
issn		

Search   **Reset**

Library: Laramie Co. Library, Cheyenne

language: ANY
item type: ANY
reading level: ANY
match on: Keywords
pubyear:
sort by: None

Figure 7-1. *This is a search window from the Laramie County library in Cheyenne. In this example, we're searching using both the author field and the title field.*

Figure 7-2 shows the results of this search, a catalog entry for Albert Einstein's famous book on relativity, called *The Meaning of Relativity*. Take a minute to look over the figure. Pay special attention to the catalog number located just above the book title. The catalog number for this book is *530.1*. This number tells you exactly where to find the book among all the other books on the shelves. The books are ordered numerically, so you'll find this book in the 500 shelves, between 530 and 531.

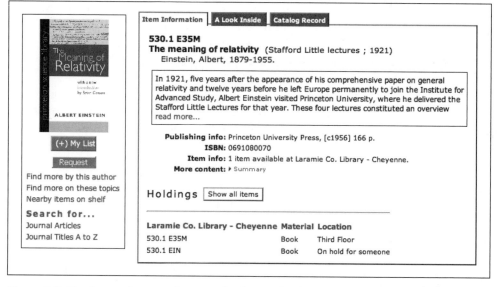

Figure 7-2. *Here's a catalog entry for our rather famous book. Note the catalog number, just above the book's title. This book can be found on the library shelf between section 530 and 531.*

In this example, the library bookshelves are like your computer's memory, with the books acting as data. The catalog number is the address of your data (a book) in memory (on the shelf).

As you might have guessed, the catalog number acts as a pointer. The library catalogs use these pointers to rearrange all the books in the library, without moving a single book. Think about it. If you search the catalog by subject, it's just as if all the books in the library are arranged by subject. Physically, the book arrangements have nothing to do with subject. The books are arranged numerically by catalog number. By adding a layer of pointers between you and the books, the librarians achieve an extra layer of flexibility.

In the same way, if you search the catalog by title, it's just as if all the books in the library are arranged alphabetically by title. Again, physically, the book arrangements have nothing to do with title. By using pointers, all the books in the library are arranged in different ways without ever leaving the shelves. The books are arranged physically (sorted by catalog number) and logically (sorted in by author, subject, title, and so on). Without the support of a layer of pointers, these logical book arrangements would be impossible.

> **NOTE**
>
> Adding a layer of pointers is also known as adding a **level of indirection**. The number of levels of indirection is the number of pointers you have to use to get to your library book (or to your data).

Checking Out of the Library

So far, we've talked about pointers in terms of library catalog numbers. The use of pointers in your C programs is not much different from this model. Each catalog number points out the location of a book on the library shelf. In the same way, each pointer in your program will point out the location of a piece of data in computer memory.

If you wrote a program to keep track of your DVD collection, you might maintain a list of pointers, each one of which might point to a block of data that describes a single DVD. Each block of data might contain such information as the name of the movie, the name of the director, the year of release, and a category (for example, drama, comedy, documentary). If you got more ambitious, you could create several pointer lists. One list might sort your DVDs alphabetically by movie title. Another might sort them chronologically by year of release. Yet another list might sort your DVDs by category. You get the picture.

There's a lot you can do with pointers. By mastering the techniques presented in these next few chapters, you'll be able to create programs that take full advantage of pointers.

The goal for this chapter is to help you master pointer basics. We'll talk about C pointers and C pointer operations. You'll learn how to create a pointer and how to make the pointer point to a variable. You'll also learn how to use a pointer to change the value of the variable the pointer points to.

Pointer Basics

Pointers are variable addresses. Instead of an address such as

```
1313 Mockingbird Lane
Raven Heights, California  90263
```

a variable's address refers to a memory location within your computer. As we discussed in Chapter 3, your computer's memory, also known as **random access memory** (**RAM**) consists of a sequence of bytes. One megabyte of RAM has exactly 2^{20} (or 1,048,576) bytes of memory, while 8 megabytes of RAM has exactly $8 * 2^{20} = 2^{23} = 8,388,608$ bytes of memory. One gigabyte of RAM has exactly 2^{30} bytes = 1,024 megabytes = 1,073,741,824 bytes of memory. And so on.

Every one of those bytes has its own unique address. Computer addresses typically start with 0 and continue up, one at a time, until they reach the highest address. The first byte has an address of 0; the next byte has an address of 1, and so on. Figure 7-3 shows the addressing scheme for a computer with a gigabyte of RAM. A gigabyte is 1,024 megabytes. Notice that the addresses run from 0 (the lowest address) all the way up to 1,073,741,823 (the highest address). The same scheme would hold true for 10 gigabytes, or even 1 terabyte (1,024 gigabytes).

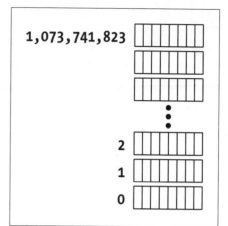

Figure 7-3. *A gigabyte's worth of bytes. The first byte of memory is number 0, and the last is number 1,073,741,823.*

Variable Addresses

When you run a program, one of the first things the computer does is allocate memory for your program's variables. When you declare an `int` in your code, like this

```
int    myVar;
```

the compiler reserves memory for the exclusive use of `myVar`.

NOTE

> As mentioned earlier in this book, the amount of memory allocated for an `int` depends on your development environment. Xcode defaults to using 4-byte `int`s.

Each of `myVar`'s bytes has a specific address. Figure 7-4 shows a 1 gigabyte chunk of memory with 4 bytes allocated to the variable `myVar`. In this picture, the 4 bytes allocated to `myVar` have the addresses 836, 837, 838, and 839.

By convention, a variable's address is said to be the address of its first byte (the first byte is the byte with the lowest numbered address). If a variable uses memory locations 836 through 839 (as `myVar` does), its address is 836 and its length is 4 bytes.

NOTE

> When more than 1 byte is allocated to a variable, the bytes will always be consecutive (next to each other in memory). You will never see an `int` whose byte addresses are 508, 509, 510, and 695. A variable's bytes are like family—they stick together!

As I showed earlier, a variable's address is a lot like the library catalog number in a library book's catalog entry. Both act as pointers, one to a book on the library shelf and the other to a variable. From now on, when we use the term "pointer" with respect to a variable, we are referring to the variable's address.

Now that you understand what a pointer is, your next goal is to learn how to use pointers in your programs. The next few sections will teach you some valuable pointer programming skills. You'll learn how to create a pointer to a variable. You'll also learn how to use that pointer to access the variable to which it points.

The C language provides you with a few key tools to help you. These tools come in the form of two special operators: & and *.

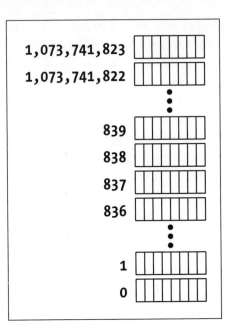

Figure 7-4. *These 4 bytes are allocated for the int named myVar. The bytes labeled 836, 837, 838, and 839 are reserved for myVar's use.*

The & Operator

The & operator (also called the **address-of operator**) pairs with a variable name to produce the variable's address. The expression

&myVar

refers to myVar's address in memory. If myVar owned memory locations 836 through 839 (as in Figure 7-4), the following expression would have a value of 836:

&myVar

The expression &myVar is a pointer to the variable myVar.

As you start programming with pointers, you'll find yourself using the & operator frequently. An expression like &myVar is a common way to represent a pointer. Another way to represent a pointer is with a **pointer variable**. A pointer variable is a variable specifically designed to hold the address of another variable.

Declaring a Pointer Variable

C supports a special notation for declaring pointer variables. The following line declares a variable named myPointer:

```
int    *myPointer;
```

Notice that the * is not part of the variable's name. Instead, it tells the compiler that the associated variable is a pointer, specifically designed to hold the address of an `int`. If there were a data type called `bluto`, you could declare a variable designed to point to a `bluto` like this:

```
bluto    *blutoPointer;
```

NOTE

This declaration is perfectly legal: `int*      myPointer;`

This line also declares a variable named `myPointer` designed to hold the address of an `int`. The fact that the white space comes after the * does not matter to the compiler. Personally, I prefer the former format, and that's what I'll use throughout this book.

For the moment, we'll limit ourselves to pointers that point to `ints`. Look at this code:

```
int    *myPointer, myVar;

myPointer = &myVar;
```

The assignment statement puts `myVar`'s address in the variable `myPointer`. If `myVar`'s address is 836, this code will leave `myPointer` with a value of 836. Note that this code has absolutely no effect on the value of `myVar`.

Oftentimes in your coding, you will have a pointer to a variable but will not have access to the variable itself. You can actually use the pointer to manipulate the value of the variable it points to. Observe:

```
int    *myPointer, myVar;

myPointer = &myVar;
*myPointer = 27;
```

As before, the first assignment statement places `myVar`'s address in the variable `myPointer`. The second assignment introduces the * operator. The * operator (called the **star** operator) converts a pointer variable to the item the pointer points to.

NOTE

The * that appears in the declaration statement isn't really an operator. It's only there to designate the variable `myPointer` as a pointer.

If myPointer contains the address of myVar, as is the case in our example, referring to *myPointer is equivalent to referring to myVar. For example, the following line:

```
*myPointer = 27;
```

is the same as this one:

```
myVar = 27;
```

Confused? An illustration should help. Figure 7-5 joins our program in progress, just after the variables myVar and myPointer were declared:

```
int    *myPointer, myVar;
```

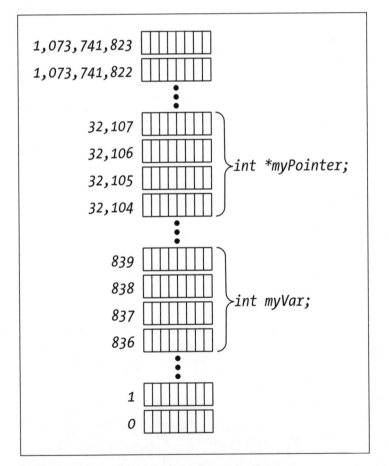

Figure 7-5. *Memory allocated for myVar and myPointer*

Notice that 4 bytes were allocated for the variable myVar and an additional 4 bytes were allocated for myPointer. Why? Because myVar is an int, and myPointer is a pointer designed to hold a 4-byte address.

Why a 4-byte address? Good question! 4 bytes is equal to 32 bits. Since memory addresses start at 0 and can never be negative, a 4-byte memory address can range from 0 up to $2^{32} - 1 = 4{,}294{,}967{,}295$. That means that a 32-bit computer can address a maximum of 4 gigabytes (4,096 megabytes) of memory.

While 4 gigabytes of memory might seem more than adequate for most folks, a number of applications that require more RAM than this already exist. After all, just a few years ago, 32 megabytes of RAM was the standard. Soon, we will look back and wonder just how we managed to live with that pesky 4-gigbyte limit!

So how do we address more than 4 gigabytes in a 32-bit computer? The short answer is, we don't. When Apple released the G5 back in 2003, they introduced their first 64-bit computer. Instead of a 4-byte address, the G5 supports an 8-byte address. An 8-byte address can hold values from 0 to $2^{64} - 1$. That is one giant number.

At the time of this writing, most of what Apple sells is limited to 32-bit addresses and a total of 4 gigabytes of memory. The Mac Pro is a 64-bit (8-byte) machine. 64 bits can address a crazy amount of memory, much more than any current computer can even come close to handling. The Mac Pro is currently limited to 32 gigabytes, but that limit will likely change in the short term. Apple's latest operating system, Snow Leopard, brings with it a technology code-named Grand Central that makes it possible for a program to address up to 16 terabytes (16,000 gigabytes) of memory. That's a *lot* of DVDs!

The point here is to be aware that the size of an address can change and the number of bytes used to represent an int can change.

NOTE

Older computers (like the Apple IIe, for example) represented an address using 2 bytes (16 bits) of memory, yielding a range of addresses from 0 to $2^{16} - 1 = 65{,}535$. Imagine having to fit your operating system, as well as all your applications in a mere 64 kilobytes of RAM (1 kilobyte = 1,024 bytes).

Years later, when the Mac first appeared, it came with 128 kilobytes of RAM and used 24-bit memory addresses, yielding a range of addresses from 0 to $2^{24} - 1 = 16{,}777{,}215$ (also known as 16 megabytes). Back then, no one could imagine a computer that actually included 16 entire megabytes of memory!

Of course, these days we are much smarter. We absolutely know for a fact that we'll never exceed the need for 64-bit addresses, right? Hmm, better not count on that. In fact, if you are a betting person, I'd wager that someday we'll see 16-byte addresses. Really!

Once memory is allocated for myVar and myPointer, we move on to the statement:

myPointer = &myVar;

The 4-byte address of the variable myVar is written to the 4 bytes allocated to myPointer. In our example, myVar's address is 836. Figure 7-6 shows the value 836 stored in myPointer's 4 bytes. Now, myPointer is said to *point to* myVar.

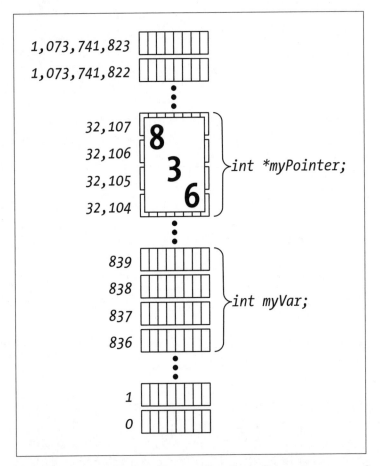

Figure 7-6. *The address of myVar is assigned to myPointer. In our example, the address of myVar is 836. The value 836 is stored in the memory allocated for the variable myPointer.*

OK, we're almost there. The next line of our example writes the value 27 to the location pointed to by myPointer:

*myPointer = 27;

Without the * operator, the computer would place the value 27 in the memory allocated to myPointer. The * operator **dereferences** myPointer. Dereferencing a pointer turns the pointer into the variable it points to. Figure 7-7 shows the end results.

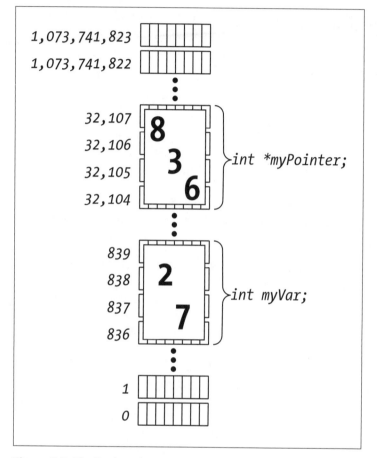

Figure 7-7. *Finally, the value 27 is assigned to *myPointer.*

If the concept of pointers seems alien to you, don't worry. You are not alone. Programming with pointers is one of the most difficult topics you'll ever take on. Just keep reading, and make sure you follow each of the examples line by line. By the end of the chapter, you'll be a pointer expert!

Function Parameters

One of the most important uses of pointers (and perhaps the easiest to understand) lies in the implementation of **function parameters**. In this section, we'll focus on parameters and, at the same time, have a chance to check out pointers in action.

What Are Function Parameters?

A function parameter is your chance to share a variable between a calling function and the called function.

Suppose you wanted to write a function called AddTwo() that took two numbers, added them together, and returned the sum of the two numbers. How would you get the two original numbers into AddTwo()? How would you get the sum of the two numbers back to the function that called AddTwo()?

As you might have guessed, the answer to both questions lies in the use of parameters. Before you can learn how to use parameters, however, you'll have to first understand the concept of scope.

Variable Scope

In C, every variable is said to have a **scope**, or range. A variable's scope defines where in the program you have access to a variable. In other words, if a variable is declared inside one function, can another function refer to that same variable?

C defines variable scope thusly: a variable declared inside a function is local to that function and may only be referenced inside that function.

This definition is important. It means you can't declare a variable inside one function, and then refer to that same value inside another function. Here's an example that will never compile:

```c
#include <stdio.h>

int main (int argc, const char * argv[]) {
    int     numDots;

    numDots = 500;
    DrawDots();

    return 0;
}

void    DrawDots( void ) {
    int    i;

    for ( i = 1; i <= numDots; i++ )
        printf( "." );
}
```

The error in this code occurs when the function DrawDots() tries to reference the variable numDots. According to the rules of scope, DrawDots() doesn't even know about the variable numDots. If you tried to compile this program the compiler would complain that DrawDots() tried to use the variable numDots without declaring it.

The problem you are faced with is getting the value of numDots to the function DrawDots() so DrawDots() knows how many dots to draw. The answer to this problem is function parameters.

NOTE

DrawDots() is another example of the value of writing functions. We've taken the code needed to perform a specific function (in this case, draw some dots) and embedded it in a function. Now, instead of having to duplicate the code inside DrawDots() every time we want to draw some dots in our program, all we'd need is a single line of code: a call to the function DrawDots().

How Function Parameters Work

Function parameters are like variables, but instead of being declared at the beginning of a function, function parameters are declared between the parentheses on the function's title line, like this:

```
void DrawDots( int numDots ) {
    /* function's body goes here */
}
```

When you call a function, you just match up the parameters, making sure you pass the function what it expects. To call the version of DrawDots() we just defined, make sure you place an int between the parentheses. The call to DrawDots() inside main() passes the value 30 into the function DrawDots():

```
int main (int argc, const char * argv[]) {
    DrawDots( 30 );

    return 0;
}
```

When DrawDots() starts executing, it sets its parameter to the passed-in value. In this case, DrawDots() has one parameter, an int named numDots. When the following call executes

```
    DrawDots( 30 );
```

the function DrawDots() sets its parameter, numDots, to a value of 30. To make things a little clearer, here's a revised version of our example:

```c
#include <stdio.h>

void    DrawDots( int numDots );

int main (int argc, const char * argv[]) {
    DrawDots( 30 );

    return 0;
}

void    DrawDots( int numDots ) {
    int    i;

    for ( i = 1; i <= numDots; i++ )
        printf( "." );
}
```

This version of drawDots will compile and run properly. It starts with the #include of <stdio.h> and follows with the function prototype for DrawDots(). Recall the concept of function prototypes that I introduced in Chapter 4. Imagine the compiler making its way down the file, processing one chunk of code at a time. Without the prototype, it would hit the call of DrawDots(30) inside main() and not have anything to verify it against. The prototype assures the compiler that we intend to provide a function named DrawDots(), that it will not return a value (that's why it is declared as void), and that it will take an int as an argument. As the compiler continues to process the file and comes across the actual call of DrawDots(), it can make an intelligent assessment of the call to decide if it was made properly.

After the DrawDots() prototype, we enter main(). main() calls DrawDots(), passing as a parameter the constant 30. DrawDots() receives the value 30 in its int parameter, num-Dots. This means that the function DrawDots() starts execution with a variable named numDots having a value of 30.

Inside DrawDots(), the for loop behaves as you might expect, drawing 30 periods in the console window. Figure 7-8 shows a picture of this program in action. You can run this example yourself. The project file, *drawDots.xcodeproj*, is located in the *Learn C Projects* folder in a subfolder named *07.01 - drawDots*.

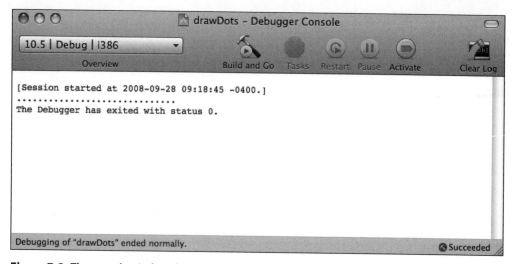

Figure 7-8. *The console window shows drawDots in action. The function DrawDots() used a for loop to draw 30 dots in a row.*

Parameters Are Temporary

When a function gets called, a temporary variable is created for each of its parameters. When the function exits (returns to the calling function), that variable goes away.

In our example, we passed a value of 30 into DrawDots() as a parameter. The value came to rest in the temporary variable named numDots. Once DrawDots() exited, numDots ceased to exist.

NOTE

Remember, a variable declared inside a function can only be referenced by that function.

It is perfectly acceptable for two functions to use the same variable names for completely different purposes. For example, using a variable name like i as a counter in a for loop is fairly standard. What happens when, in the middle of just such a for loop, you call a function that also uses a variable named i? Here's an example:

```
#include <stdio.h>

void    DrawDots( int numDots );

int main (int argc, const char * argv[]) {
    int    i;
```

```
    for ( i=1; i<=10; i++ ) {
        DrawDots( 30 );
        printf( "\n" );
    }

    return 0;
}

void    DrawDots( int numDots ) {
    int    i;

    for ( i = 1; i <= numDots; i++ )
        printf( "." );
}
```

This code prints a series of 10 rows of dots, with 30 dots in each row. After each call to DrawDots(), a carriage return (\n) is printed, moving the cursor in position to begin the next row of dots.

Notice that main() and DrawDots() each feature a variable named i. main() uses the variable i as a counter, tracking the number of rows of dots printed. DrawDots() also uses i as a counter, tracking the number of dots in the row it is printing. Won't DrawDots()'s copy of i mess up main()'s copy of i? No!

When main() starts executing, memory gets allocated for its copy of i. When main() calls DrawDots(), additional memory gets allocated for the DrawDots() copy of i. When DrawDots() exits, the memory for its copy of i is **deallocated**, freed up so it can be used again for some other variable. A variable declared within a specific function is known as a **local variable**. DrawDots() has a single local variable, the variable i.

The Difference Between Arguments and Parameters

Here's one final point: The value passed in to a function is known as an **argument**. The variable declared to receive that argument is known as a **parameter**. In this line of code:

```
DrawDots( 30 );
```

the constant 30 is an argument being passed to DrawDots(); it's not a parameter.

Many programmers use the terms "argument" and "parameter" interchangeably. For example, someone might talk about passing a parameter to a function. Strictly speaking, you pass an argument to a function to be received as a parameter. As long as you understand that point, the term "parameter passing" will do just fine.

What Does All This Have to Do with Pointers?

Now, we're getting to the crux of the whole matter. What do parameters have to do with pointers? To answer this question, you have to understand the two different methods of parameter passing.

Parameters are passed from function to function either by value or by address. Passing a parameter by value passes only the value of a variable or literal on to the called function. Take a look at this code:

```
#include <stdio.h>

void    DrawDots( int numDots );

int main (int argc, const char * argv[]) {
    int     numDots;

    numDots = 30;

    DrawDots( numDots );

    return 0;
}

void    DrawDots( int numDots ) {
    int     i;

    for ( i = 1; i <= numDots; i++ )
        printf( "." );
}
```

Here's what happens when main() calls DrawDots(): On the calling side, the expression passed as an argument to DrawDots() is resolved to a single value. In this case, the expression is simply the variable numDots. The value of the expression is the value of numDots, which is 30.

On the receiving side, when DrawDots() gets called, memory is allocated for its parameters as well as for its local variables. This means that memory is allocated for DrawDots()'s copy of numDots, as well as for its copy of i. The value passed in to DrawDots() from main() (in this case, 30) is copied into the memory allocated to DrawDots()'s copy of numDots.

It is important to understand that whatever main() passes in to DrawDots() is *copied* into DrawDots()'s local copy of the parameter. Think of DrawDots()'s copy of numDots as just another local variable that will disappear when DrawDots() exits. DrawDots() can do whatever it likes to its copy of the parameter. Since it is just a local copy, any changes will have absolutely no effect on the variable main() passes in as an argument.

Since passing parameters by value is a one-way operation, there's no way to get data back from the called function. Why would you ever want to? Several reasons. You might write a function that takes an employee number as a parameter. You might want that function to return the employee's salary in another parameter. How about a function that turns yards into meters? You could pass the number of yards as a value parameter, but how would you get back the number of meters?

Passing a parameter by address (instead of by value) solves this problem. If you pass the address of a variable, the receiving function can use the * operator to change the value of the original variable.

Here's an example:

```c
#include <stdio.h>

void    SquareIt( int  number, int    *squarePtr );

int main (int argc, const char * argv[]) {
    int    square;

    SquareIt( 5, &square );

    printf( "5 squared is %d.\n", square );

    return 0;
}

void    SquareIt( int  number, int    *squarePtr ) {
    *squarePtr = number * number;
}
```

In this example, main() calls the function SquareIt(). SquareIt() takes two parameters. As in our previous example, both parameters are declared between the parentheses on the function's title line. Notice that we used a comma to separate the parameter declarations.

The first of SquareIt()'s two parameters is an int. The second parameter is a pointer to an int. SquareIt() squares the value passed in the first parameter, using the pointer in the second parameter to return the squared value.

NOTE

In case it's been ten or more years since your last math class, squaring a number is the same as multiplying the number by itself. The square of 4 is 16, and the square of 5 is 25.

Here's `main()`'s call of `SquareIt()`:

```
SquareIt( 5, &square );
```

Here's the function prototype of `SquareIt()`:

```
void SquareIt( int  number, int    *squarePtr );
```

When `SquareIt()` gets called, memory is allocated for an `int` (number) and for a pointer to an int (squarePtr).

Once the local memory is allocated, the value 5 is copied into the local parameter `number`, and the address of `square` is copied into `squarePtr` (recall that the & operator produces the address of a variable).

Inside the function `SquareIt()`, any reference to

```
*squarePtr
```

is just like a reference to `square`. The following assignment statement

```
*squarePtr = number * number;
```

assigns the value 25 (since number has a value of 5) to the variable pointed to by `squarePtr`. This has the effect of assigning the value 25 to `square`. When `SquareIt()` returns control to `main()`, the value of `square` has been changed, as evidenced by the screen shot in Figure 7-9. If you'd like to give this code a try, you'll find it in the *Learn C Projects* folder, inside the *07.02 - squareIt* subfolder.

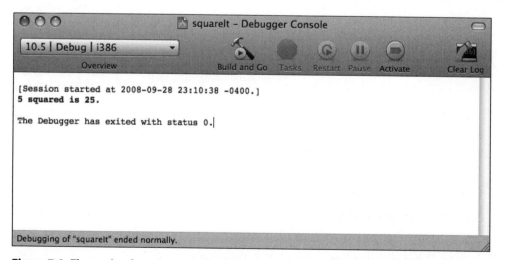

Figure 7-9. *The results of running squareIt. This program shows how to pass a parameter by address.*

You'll see lots more pointer-wielding examples throughout the rest of this book.

Global Variables and Function Returns

The combination of pointers and parameters gives us one way to share variables between different functions. This section demonstrates two more techniques for doing the same.

Global variables are variables that are accessible from inside every function in your program. By declaring a global variable, two separate functions can access the same variable without passing parameters. We'll show you how to declare a global variable, and then talk about when and when not to use global variables in your programs.

Another topic we'll discuss later in the chapter is a property common to all functions. All functions written in C have the ability to **return** a value to the function that calls them. You set this **return value** inside the function itself. You can use a function's return value in place of a parameter, use it to pass additional information to the calling function, or not use it at all. I'll show you how to add a return value to your functions.

Global Variables

Earlier in this chapter, you learned how to use parameters to share variables between two functions. Passing parameters between functions is great. You can call a function, pass it some data to work on, and when the function's done, it can pass you back the results.

Global variables provide an alternative to parameters. Global variables are just like regular variables, with one exception. Global variables are immune to C's scope rules. They can be referenced inside each of your program's functions. One function might initialize the global variable; another might change its value; and another function might print the value of the global variable in the console window.

As you design your programs, you'll have to make some basic decisions about data sharing between functions. If you'll be sharing a variable among a number of functions, you might want to consider making the variable a global. Globals are especially useful when you want to share a variable between two functions that are several calls apart.

Several calls apart? At times, you'll find yourself passing a parameter to a function, not because that function needs the parameter, but because the function calls another function that needs the parameter. Look at this code:

```c
#include <stdio.h>

void PassAlong( int myVar );
void PrintMyVar( int myVar );

int main( void ) {
    int     myVar;
```

```
    myVar = 10;

    PassAlong( myVar );

    return 0;
}

void PassAlong( int myVar ) {
    PrintMyVar( myVar );
}

void PrintMyVar( int myVar ) {
    printf( "myVar = %d", myVar );
}
```

Notice that `main()` passes `myVar` to the function `PassAlong()`. `PassAlong()` doesn't actually make use of `myVar`. Instead, it just passes `myVar` along to the function `PrintMyVar()`. `PrintMyVar()` prints `myVar` and then returns.

If `myVar` were a global, you could have avoided some parameter passing. `main()` and `PrintMyVar()` could have shared `myVar` without the use of parameters. When should you use parameters? When should you use globals?

In a nutshell, you should avoid using globals. Whenever a global variable solves a problem, there's always a way to use parameters to solve the same problem. Global variables offer a shortcut that saves you from having to pass information up and down your chain of function calls. They do save time but at the cost of proper program design. As you move on to object programming languages like Objective-C, you'll find that you just don't need globals.

So why learn about them? They are part of the C language: the concept of global variables is important to understand, and you may find yourself having to maintain or fix someone else's code. If that legacy code uses global variables, you'll need to know how they work.

Let's take a look at the proper way to add globals to your programs.

Adding Globals to Your Programs

Adding globals to your programs is easy. Just declare a variable at the beginning of your source code before the start of any of your functions. Here's the example I showed you earlier, using globals in place of parameters:

```
#include <stdio.h>

void PassAlong( void );
void PrintMyVar( void );
```

```c
int     gMyVar;

int main (int argc, const char * argv[]) {
    gMyVar = 10;

    PassAlong();

    return 0;
}

void PassAlong( void ) {
    PrintMyVar();
}

void PrintMyVar( void ) {
    printf( "gMyVar = %d", gMyVar );
}
```

This example starts with a variable declaration, right at the top of the program. Because gMyVar was declared at the top of the program, gMyVar becomes a global variable, accessible to each of the program's functions. Notice that none of the functions in this version use parameters. As a reminder, when a function is declared without parameters, use the keyword void in place of a parameter list.

NOTE

Did you notice that letter g at the beginning of the global's name? Many C programmers start each of their global variables with the letter g (for global). Doing this will distinguish your local variables from your global variables and will make your code much easier to read.

Function Returns

Before we get to our source code examples, we have one more subject to cover. In addition to passing a parameter and using a global variable, there's one more way to share data between two functions. Every function returns a value to the function that called it. You can use this return value to pass data back from a called function.

So far, all of our examples have ignored **function return values**. The return value only comes into play when you call a function in an expression, like this:

```c
#include <stdio.h>

int     AddTheseNumbers( int num1, int num2 );
```

```
int main (int argc, const char * argv[]) {
    int    sum;

    sum = AddTheseNumbers( 5, 6 );

    printf( "The sum is %d.", sum );

    return 0;
}

int    AddTheseNumbers( int num1, int num2 ) {
    return( num1 + num2 );
}
```

There are a few things worth noting in this example. First, take a look at the function declaration for AddTheseNumbers(). So far in this book, every single function other than main() has been declared using the keyword void. AddTheseNumbers(), like main(), starts with the keyword int. This keyword tells you the type returned by this function. A function declared with the void keyword doesn't return a value. A function declared with the int keyword returns a value of type int.

A function returns a value by using the return keyword, followed by an expression that represents the value you want returned. For example, take a look at this line of code from AddTheseNumbers():

```
    return( num1 + num2 );
```

This line of code adds the two variables num1 and num2 together and returns the sum. To understand what that means, take a look at this line of code from main() that calls AddTheseNumbers():

```
    sum = AddTheseNumbers( 5, 6 );
```

This line of code first calls AddTheseNumbers(), passing in values of 5 and 6 as arguments. AddTheseNumbers() adds these numbers together and returns the value 11, which is then assigned to the variable sum.

When you use a function inside an expression, the computer makes the function call and then substitutes the function's return value for the function when it evaluates the rest of the expression.

There are several ways to use `return`. To immediately exit a function, without establishing a return value, use the statement

```
return;
```

or

```
return();
```

The parentheses in a `return` statement are optional. You'd use the plain `return`, without an expression, to return from a function of type `void`. You might use this immediate `return` in case of an error, like this:

```
if ( OutOfMemory() )
     return;
```

What you'll want to remember about this form of `return` is that it does not establish the return value of the function. This works fine if your function is declared `void`:

```
void     MyVoidFunction( int myParam );
```

but won't cut it if your function is declared to return a value:

```
int     AddTheseNumbers( int num1, int num2 );
```

NOTE

> If you forget to specify a return value, some compilers will say nothing, some will print warnings, and others will report errors.

`AddTheseNumbers()` is declared to return a value of type `int`. Here is one version of the `AddTheseNumbers()` return statement:

```
return( num1 + num2 );
```

and here's another:

```
return num1 + num2;
```

Notice that the second version did not include any parentheses. Since `return` is a keyword and not a function call, either of these forms is fine.

You can find a version of this program on your hard drive. Look in the folder *Learn C Projects*, in the subfolder *07.03 - addThese*. Figure 7-10 shows the output of this program.

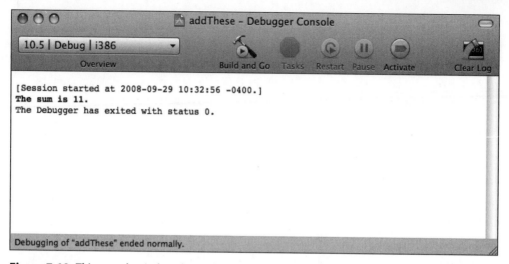

Figure 7-10. *This console window shows the results of the program addThese, which demonstrates a function that adds two numbers together and returns the sum to the calling function.*

printf() Returns a Value

It is worth noting that printf() is actually declared to return an int that reflects the number of characters generated or a negative value if an error occurs. The vast majority of programmers ignore this return value, but it is an important programming practice to be aware of the return value of every single function that you call.

Danger! Avoid Uninitialized Return Values!

Before we leave the topic of function return values, there's one pitfall worth mentioning. If you're going to use a function in an expression, make sure the function provides a return value. For example, this code will produce unpredictable results:

```c
#include <stdio.h>

int     AddTheseNumbers( int num1, int num2 );

int main (int argc, const char * argv[]) {
    int     sum;

    sum = AddTheseNumbers( 5, 6 );

    printf( "The sum is %d.", sum );

    return 0;
}

int     AddTheseNumbers( int num1, int num2 ) {
```

```
        return;    /* Yikes! We forgot to
                      set the return value */
}
```

When AddTheseNumbers() returns, what will its value be? No one knows! When I ran the preceding on my computer, Xcode reported two warnings (as it should) and ran the program, generating a sum of 0. Unpredictable results! Don't forget to set a return value if you intend to use a function in an expression. And be sure to pay attention to warnings.

To Return or Not to Return?

Should you use a return value or a passed-by-address parameter? Which is correct? This is basically a question of functional fit. Use whichever works best for you. Just remember that a function can have only one return value but an unlimited number of parameters. If you need to get more than one piece of data back to the calling function, your best bet is to use parameters.

The function AddTheseNumbers() was a natural fit for the return statement. It took in a pair of numbers (the input parameters) and needed to return the sum of those numbers. Since it needed to return only a single value, the return statement worked perfectly.

Another nice thing about using the return statement is that it frequently allows us to avoid declaring an extra variable. In addThese, we declared sum to receive the value returned by AddTheseNumbers(). Since all we did with sum was print its value, we could have accomplished the same thing with this version of main():

```
int main (int argc, const char * argv[]) {
    printf( "The sum is %d.", AddTheseNumbers( 5, 6 ) );

    return 0;
}
```

See the difference? We included the call to AddTheseNumbers() in the printf(), bypassing sum entirely. When AddTheseNumbers() returns its int, that value is passed on to printf().

More Sample Programs

Are you ready for some more code? The next few sample programs make use of pointers, function parameters, global variables, and function returns. Fire up your Mac, crank up your iPod, and break out the pizza. Let's code!

listPrimes.xcode

Our next sample program is an updated version of Chapter 6's prime number program, nextPrime, which found the next prime number following a specified number. The example we presented reported that the next prime number after 19 was 23.

This program, called listPrimes, uses a function named IsItPrime() and lists all the prime numbers between 1 and 50. Open the project *listPrimes.xcodeproj*. You'll find it in the *Learn C Projects* folder, inside the subfolder named *07.04 - listPrimes*. Run listPrimes, and compare your results with the console window shown in Figure 7-11.

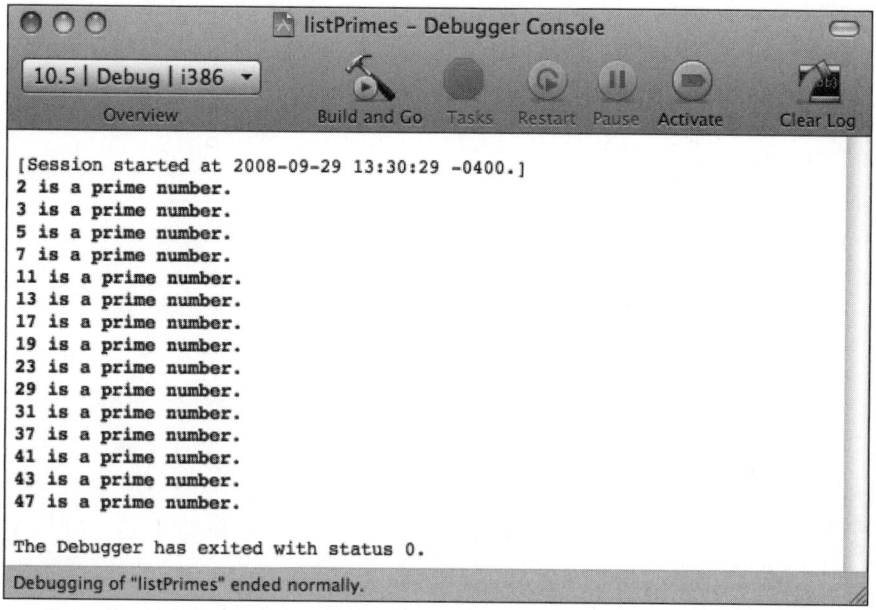

Figure 7-11. *The listPrimes program lists the prime numbers from 1 through 50.*

Let's take a look at the source code.

Stepping Through the listPrimes Source Code

listPrimes consists of two functions: main() and IsItPrime(). IsItPrime() takes a single parameter, an int named candidate, which is passed by value. IsItPrime() returns a value of true if candidate is a prime number and a value of false otherwise.

listPrimes starts off with three #includes. stdio.h gives us access to the function prototype of printf(); stdbool.h gives us access to the type bool and the definitions of true and false; and math.h gives us access to the function prototype for sqrt().

```
#include <stdio.h>
#include <stdbool.h>
#include <math.h>
```

Next comes the function prototype for `IsItPrime()`. The compiler will use this function prototype to make sure that all calls to `IsItPrime()` pass the right number of arguments (in this case, one), that the arguments are of the correct type (in this case, a single `int`), and that the return value expected is a `bool`.

```
bool    IsItPrime( int candidate );
```

`main()` defines a single variable, an `int` named `i`. We'll use `i` as a counter to step through the integers from 1 to 50. We'll pass each number to `IsItPrime()`, and if the result is `true`, we'll report the number as prime.

```
int main (int argc, const char * argv[]) {
    int    i;

    for ( i = 1; i <= 50; i++ ) {
        if ( IsItPrime( i ) )
            printf( "%d is a prime number.\n", i );
    }

    return 0;
}
```

NOTE

As usual, `main()` ends with a `return` statement. By convention, returning a value of 0 tells the outside world that everything ran just hunky-dory. If something goes wrong (if we ran out of memory perhaps), the same convention calls for us to return a negative number from `main()`. Some operating systems will make use of this return value; others won't. It doesn't cost you anything to follow the convention, so go ahead and follow it.

`IsItPrime()` first checks to see if the number passed in is less than 2. If so, `IsItPrime()` returns `false`, since 2 is the first prime number.

```
bool    IsItPrime( int candidate ) {
    int    i, last;

    if ( candidate < 2 )
        return false;
```

If `candidate` has a value of 2 or greater, we'll step through all the numbers between 2 and the square root of `candidate` looking for a factor. If this algorithm is new to you, go back to the previous chapter and check out the program nextPrime. If we find a factor, we know the number isn't prime, and we'll return `false`.

```
    else {
        last = sqrt( candidate );

        for ( i = 2; i <= last; i++ ) {
            if ( (candidate % i) == 0 )
                return false;
        }
    }
}
```

If we get through the loop without finding a factor, we know candidate is prime, and we return true.

```
    return true;
}
```

NOTE

> If candidate is equal to 2, last will be equal to 1.414, which will get truncated to 1, since last is an int. If last is 1, the for loop won't even get through one iteration and will fall through to the statement: return true;.
>
> The same thing happens if candidate is 3. Since 2 and 3 are both prime, this works just fine. On the other hand, this little example shows you how careful you have to be to check your code, to make sure it works in all cases.

Consider the function name IsItPrime(). In C, when you name a function in the form of a true or false question, returning a value of true or false is good form. The question this function answers is, "Is the candidate prime?" It is critical that IsItPrime() return true if the candidate was prime and false otherwise. When main() calls IsItPrime(), main() is asking the question, "Is the candidate prime?" In the case of the following if statement:

```
if ( IsItPrime( i ) )
    printf( ... );
```

main() is saying, "If i is prime, do the printf()." Make sure your function return values make sense!

power.xcodeproj

Our next program combines a global variable, a pointer parameter, and some value parameters. At the heart of the program is a function, called DoPower(), that takes three parameters. DoPower() takes a base and an exponent, raises the base to the exponent power, and returns the result in a parameter. Raising a base to an exponent power is the same as multiplying the base by itself, an exponent number of times.

For example, raising 2 to the fifth power (written as 2^5) is the same as saying $2 * 2 * 2 * 2 * 2$, which is equal to 32. In the expression 2^5, 2 is the base, and 5 is the exponent. The function DoPower() takes a base and an exponent as parameters and raises the base to the exponent power. DoPower() uses a third parameter to return the result to the calling function.

Running power

You'll find *power.xcodeproj* in the *Learn C Projects* folder, in the *07.05 - power* subfolder. Run power, and compare your results with the console window shown in Figure 7-12. This output was produced by three consecutive calls to the function DoPower(). The three calls calculated the result of the expressions 2^5, 3^4, and 5^3. Let's consider how the program works.

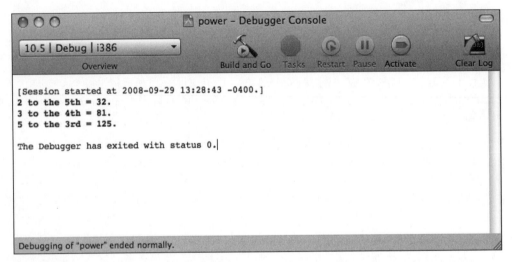

Figure 7-12. *The program power raises its first parameter to the power of the second parameter, returning the results in the third parameter.*

Stepping Through the power Source Code

The power program starts with #includes of <stdio.h> and <stdbool.h> and the function prototype for DoPower(). Notice that DoPower() is declared to be of type void, telling you that DoPower() doesn't return a value. As you read through the code, think about how you might rewrite DoPower() to return its result using the return statement instead of via a parameter.

```
#include <stdio.h>
#include <stdbool.h>

void    DoPower( int *resultPtr, int base, int exponent );
```

Next comes the declaration of our global, gPrintTraceInfo. Once again, notice that the global starts with g. We're using this global variable to **trace** our path through the program.

```
bool    gPrintTraceInfo;
```

main() starts off by setting gPrintTraceInfo to false. Next, we check to see if tracing is turned on. If so, we'll print a message telling us we've entered main(). Since we set gPrintTraceInfo to false, the trace messages will not be printed.

```
int main (int argc, const char * argv[]) {
    int     power;

    gPrintTraceInfo = false;

    if ( gPrintTraceInfo )
        printf( "---> Starting main()...\n" );
```

NOTE

C guarantees that it will initialize all global variables to 0. Since false is equivalent to 0, we could have avoided setting gPrintTraceInfo to false, but that would have been a mistake. Explicitly setting the global to a value makes the code easier to read and is the right thing to do!

Here are our three calls to DoPower(), each of which is followed by a printf() reporting our results. If DoPower() returned its results via a return statement, we could have eliminated the variable power and embedded the call to DoPower() inside the printf() in power's place.

```
    DoPower( &power, 2, 5 );
    printf( "2 to the 5th = %d.\n", power );

    DoPower( &power, 3, 4 );
    printf( "3 to the 4th = %d.\n", power );

    DoPower( &power, 5, 3 );
    printf( "5 to the 3rd = %d.\n", power );
```

If tracing is turned on, we'll print a message saying that we are leaving main():

```
    if ( gPrintTraceInfo )
        printf( "---> Leaving main()...\n" );

    return 0;
}
```

The function DoPower() takes three parameters. resultPtr is a pointer to an int. We'll use that pointer to pass back the function results. base and exponent are value parameters that represent the—guess what?—base and exponent.

```
void    DoPower( int *resultPtr, int base, int exponent )
{
    int    i;
```

Once again, check the value of gPrintTraceInfo. If it's true, print a message telling us we're at the beginning of DoPower(). Notice the tab character (represented by the characters \t) at the beginning of the printf() quoted string. You'll see what this was for when we set gPrintTraceInfo to true.

```
    if ( gPrintTraceInfo )
        printf( "\t---> Starting DoPower()...\n" );
```

The following three lines calculate base raised to the exponent power, accumulating the results in the memory pointed to by resultPtr. When main() called DoPower(), it passed &power as its first parameter. This means that resultPtr contains the address of (points to) the variable power. Changing *resultPtr is exactly the same as changing power. When DoPower() returns to main(), the value of power will have been changed. power was passed by address (also called by reference), instead of by value.

```
    *resultPtr = 1;
    for ( i = 1; i <= exponent; i++ )
        *resultPtr *= base;
```

Finally, if gPrintTraceInfo is true, print a message telling us we're leaving DoPower().

```
    if ( gPrintTraceInfo )
        printf( "\t---> Leaving DoPower()...\n" );
}
```

Change the initial value of gPrintTraceInfo to true, and run the program again. Figure 7-13 shows the console window when power is run with gPrintTraceInfo set to true. See the trace information? Find the lines printed when you enter and exit DoPower(). The leading tab characters help distinguish these lines.

Here's one final thought before we move on: there are no rigid rules when it comes to returning results to a calling function. My general approach is to use a return type if I only need to return a single piece of data. If I'm returning more than one, I turn to a parameter, passed by address. Think about this rule and about how you might rewrite power to return its results via the return statement, instead of via a parameter (this is one of the exercises at the end of this chapter).

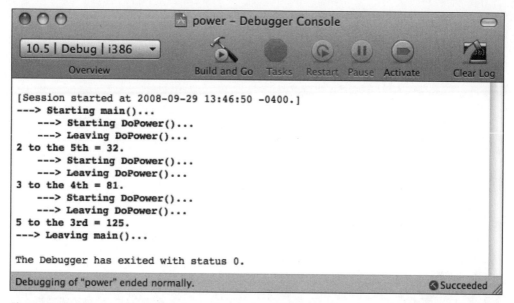

Figure 7-13. *This console window shows the output of the power program when the global variable gPrintTraceInfo was set to true. Notice all the trace messages telling you when you enter and leave each function.*

Using the Debugger

The tracing information in power was turned on and off by a single global variable. You can see how useful this information was. But there's actually a much simpler and much more powerful way to trace your way through your program's execution. Most modern development environments include a **debugger** that helps you track down bugs in your code. Let's take a look at Xcode's debugger.

The first thing we'll want to do is set a breakpoint in our source code. A breakpoint tells the debugger to stop just before a specified line of code so we can examine the value of various variables and expressions in our source code. Breakpoints are incredibly useful. In fact, once you see how breakpoints work, you'll never find a need for the global variable, printf(), and trace method I just showed you.

In the power project window, double-click the filename *main.c* in the *Groups & Files* pane to open *main.c* in a new editing window. Next, scroll *main.c* until the first few lines of the DoPower() function come into view. This next step is a bit tricky. Move your cursor into the leftmost part of the source code window, and click to the left of the first if statement in DoPower(). A thick blue arrow should appear, just like the one shown in Figure 7-14. You've just set a breakpoint. This tells the debugger to stop just before this if statement when it starts running your program.

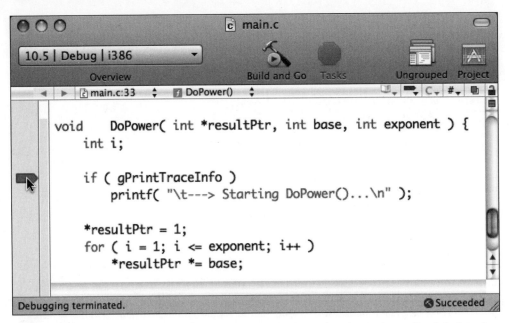

```c
void    DoPower( int *resultPtr, int base, int exponent ) {
    int i;

    if ( gPrintTraceInfo )
        printf( "\t---> Starting DoPower()...\n" );

    *resultPtr = 1;
    for ( i = 1; i <= exponent; i++ )
        *resultPtr *= base;
```

Figure 7-14. *In this source code window, the cursor has just set a breakpoint immediately before the first if in DoPower(). When we run the program, the debugger will stop at this breakpoint.*

Now select **Debug** from the **Run** menu. Xcode will use the Free Software Foundation's GNU Debugger (GDB) to run your program in debug mode. Your program will start running, and some text will appear in the console window, along with the output from our first printf(). Finally, the program will come to rest at our first breakpoint. Figure 7-15 shows our source code window stopped at our breakpoint.

Now, let's use the power of the debugger to look at the value of a few of our variables. Go to the **Run** menu and then to the **Show** submenu, and select the subitem **Expressions….** This will bring up the *Expressions* window, which will allow us to type an expression or variable name and see its current value.

In the *Expressions* window, type the variable name *gPrintTraceInfo* in the *Expression:* field at the bottom of the window, and press return. The variable name *gPrintTraceInfo* and its value will appear in the window (see Figure 7-16). As you can see, when I ran this version of my program, gPrintTraceInfo had a value of true.

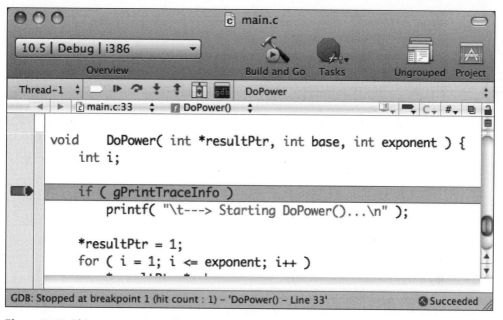

Figure 7-15. *This source code window shows that the debugger stopped at our breakpoint.*

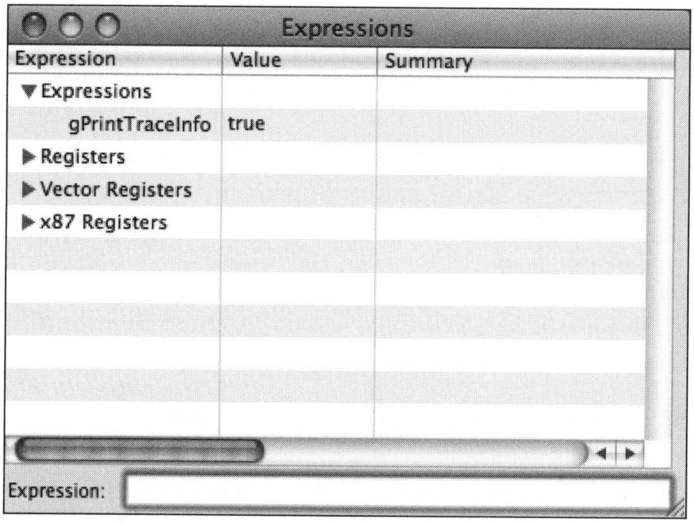

Figure 7-16. *The Expressions window showing the current value of gPrintTraceInfo*

Let's add another variable to the list. Type i, and press Return. Since we have not yet initialized i, it has an undefined value. That's fine. My updated *Expressions* window is shown in Figure 7-17.

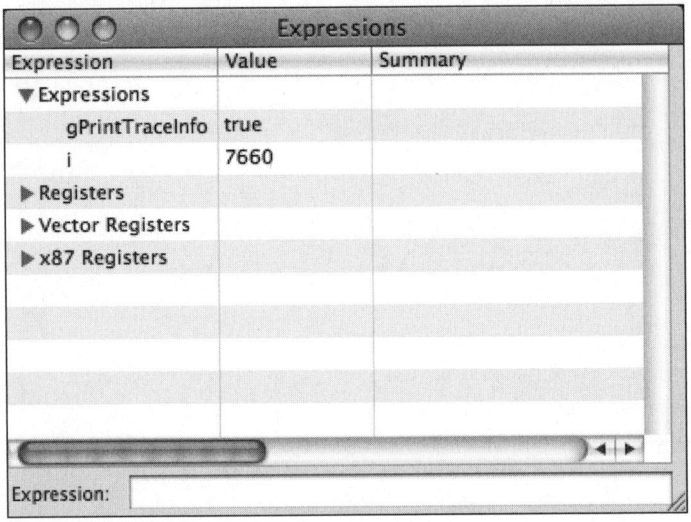

Expression	Value	Summary
▼ Expressions		
gPrintTraceInfo	true	
i	7660	
▶ Registers		
▶ Vector Registers		
▶ x87 Registers		

Expression:

Figure 7-17. *The Expressions window, now showing the current value of gPrintTraceInfo and the undefined value of i. The value of i is shown as 7660. That is the value that happened to be in i's memory location before our program set its value.*

Let's step through the program. Keep your eye on the variable i in the *Expressions* window as we move along. Select **Step Over** from the **Run** menu. The debugger will step to and execute the next line of code. If you open your console window, you'll see the text --> *Starting DoPower()...* appear. So far, so good.

Keep selecting **Step Over** from the **Run** menu. As you enter the body of the for loop, you'll see the value of i change to *1*.

Next, go to the *Expression:* field, and type the variable name *power*. When you press Return, the *Summary* column for power will say *out of scope* (see Figure 7-18). This is because power is local to main(), and we are currently running inside the function DoPower(). Keep your eye on power once we pop out of DoPower() and return to main().

Keep selecting **Step Over** from the **Run** menu. Watch the value of i change. Once your for loop exits, keep stepping until you hit the end of DoPower() and return to main(). Did you notice that i became *out of scope* and power's value changed to *32*?

There is so much more to the debugger. You can double-click a value in the *Expressions* window and change it while the program is running. Obviously, be extremely careful with this feature, or you could put out all the lights on the eastern seaboard. Well, maybe not, but you should be careful!

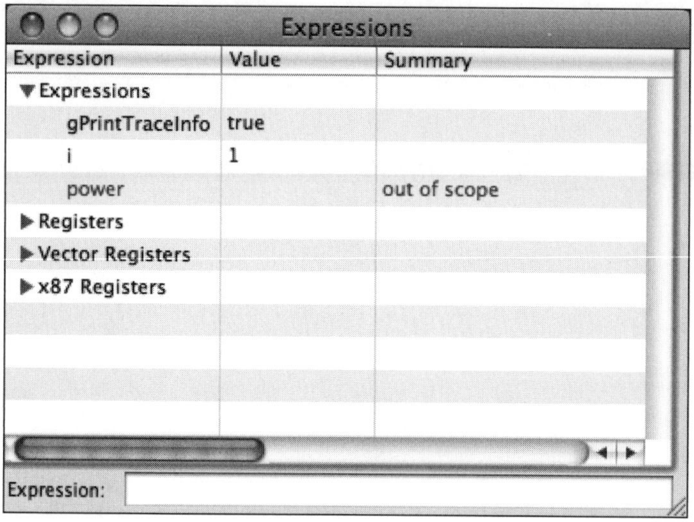

Figure 7-18. *The Expressions window, now showing that the variable is out of scope*

Select **Continue** from the **Run** menu, and you'll continue until you hit the breakpoint again. Keep doing this until the program exits normally.

If the debugger interests you, dig into the documentation and learn more. It is an incredibly powerful tool. Here's a link to a page on Apple's web site that is chock full of Xcode documentation:

```
http://developer.apple.com/documentation/DeveloperTools/Xcode-date.html
```

Check out the *Xcode Debugging Guide* on that page.

What's Next?

Wow! You really are becoming a C programmer. In this chapter alone, you covered pointers, function parameters (both by value and by address), global variables, and function return values. You also learned how to use the debugger to track the progress of your program while it was running.

You're starting to develop a sense of just how powerful and sophisticated the C language really is. You've built an excellent foundation. Now you're ready to take off.

The second half of our book starts with the introduction of the concept of data types. Throughout this book, you've been working with a single data type, the int. Our next chapter will introduce the concept of arrays, strings, pointer arithmetic, and typed function return values. Let's go.

CHAPTER 7 EXERCISES

1. Predict the result of each of the following code fragments:

a.
```c
void    AddOne( int    *myVar );

int main (int argc, const char * argv[]) {
    int     num, i;

    num = 5;

    for ( i = 0; i < 20; i++ )
        AddOne( &num );

    printf( "Final value is %d.", num );

    return 0;
}

void    AddOne( int    *myVar ) {
    (*myVar) ++;
}
```

b.
```c
int     gNumber;
int     MultiplyIt( int myVar );

int main (int argc, const char * argv[]) {
    int     i;
    gNumber = 2;

    for ( i = 1; i <= 2; i++ )
        gNumber *= MultiplyIt( gNumber );

    printf( "Final value is %d.", gNumber );

    return 0;
}

int     MultiplyIt( int myVar ) {
    return( myVar * gNumber );
}
```

```
c. int     gNumber;
   int     DoubleIt( int     myVar );

   int main (int argc, const char * argv[]) {
       int    i;
       gNumber = 1;

       for ( i = 1; i <= 10; i++ )
           gNumber = DoubleIt( gNumber );

       printf( "Final value is %d.", gNumber );

       return 0;
   }

   int    DoubleIt( int     myVar ) {
       return 2 * myVar;
   }
```

2. Modify power. Delete the first parameter of the function DoPower(), modifying the routine to return its result as a function return value instead.

3. Modify listPrimes. Instead of printing prime numbers, print only nonprime numbers. In addition, print one message for nonprimes that are multiples of 3 and a different message for nonprimes that are not multiples of 3.

Chapter 8

Variable Data Types

*n*ow we're cooking! You may now consider yourself a C Programmer, First Class. At this point, you've mastered all the basic elements of C programming. You know that C programs are made up of functions, one—and only one!—of which is named `main()`. Each of these functions uses keywords (such as `if`, `for`, and `while`), operators (such as `=`, `++`, and `*=`), and variables to manipulate the program's data.

Sometimes, you'll use a parameter to share a variable between a calling and a called function. Sometimes, these parameters are passed by value, and other times, pointers are used to pass a parameter by address. Some functions return values. Others, declared with the `void` keyword, don't return a value.

In this chapter, we'll focus on **variable types**. Each of the variables in the previous example programs has been declared as an `int`. As you'll soon see, many other data types are out there.

Data Types Beyond int

So far, the focus has been on `int`s, which are extremely useful when it comes to working with numbers. You can add two `int`s together. You can check if an `int` is even, odd, or prime. There are a lot of things you can do with `int`s, as long as you limit yourself to whole numbers.

NOTE

Just as a reminder, 527, 33, and −2 are all whole numbers, while 35.7, 92.1, and −1.2345 are not whole numbers.

What do you do if you want to work with nonwhole numbers, such as 3.14159 and –98.6? Check out this slice of code:

```
int myNum;

myNum = 3.5;
printf( "myNum = %d", myNum );
```

Since myNum is an int, the number 3.5 will be truncated before it is assigned to myNum. When this code ends, myNum will be left with a value of 3 and not 3.5 as intended. Do not despair. There are several special C data types created especially for working with nonwhole, or **floating point numbers**.

NOTE

The name **floating point** refers to the decimal point found in all floating point numbers.

The three floating point data types are float, double, and long double. The differences among these types is the number of bytes allocated to each and, therefore, the range of values each can hold. The relative sizes of these three types are completely implementation dependent. Let's look at a program you can run to tell you the size of these three types in your development environment and to show you various ways to use printf() to print floating point numbers.

floatSizer

Look inside the *Learn C Projects* folder, inside the subfolder named *08.01 - floatSizer*, and open the project named *floatSizer.xcodeproj*. Figure 8-1 shows the results when I ran float-Sizer on my Mac using Xcode. The first three lines of output tell you the size, in bytes, of the types float, double, and long double, respectively.

Never assume the size of a type. As you'll see when we go through the source code, C gives you everything you need to check the size of a specific type in your development environment. If you need to be sure of a type's size, write a program to check the size for yourself.

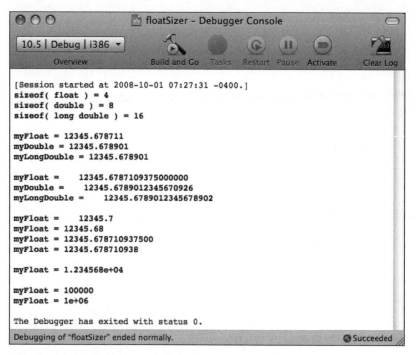

Figure 8-1. *The output from floatSizer*

Walking Through the floatSizer Source Code

floatSizer starts with the standard #include:

```
#include <stdio.h>
```

main() defines three variables, a float, a double, and a long double.

```
int main (int argc, const char * argv[]) {
    float           myFloat;
    double          myDouble;
    long double     myLongDouble;
```

Next, we assign a value to each of the three variables. Notice that we've assigned the same number to each. The F at the end of the number assigned to myFloat tells the compiler that this constant is of type float. We could also have used an f at the end of the constant to say the same thing. The L at the end of the constant assigned to myLongDouble signifies a long double. An l would have accomplished the same thing. Floating point constants with no letter at the end are assumed to be of type double.

```
    myFloat = 12345.67890123456789F;
    myDouble = 12345.67890123456789;
    myLongDouble = 12345.67890123456789L;
```

Why do we care about this? Assigning the right type to a constant ensures that the appropriate amount of memory is allocated for each constant. As you'll see as we get further into the program, a float (4 bytes) is not nearly large enough to hold this constant at the number of decimal places it requires. A double (8 bytes) is close to large enough but not quite. Declaring the constant as a float or double means that some rounding will occur before the first assignment is even performed. Only the long double (16 bytes) is large enough to hold the entire value of the constant without rounding.

Let's continue walking through the source code. main() uses C's sizeof operator to print the size of each of our three floating point types. Even though sizeof doesn't look like the other operators we've seen (+, *, /, and so on), it is indeed an operator. Stranger still, sizeof is typically followed by a pair of parentheses surrounding a single operand and looks much like a function call. The operand is either a type or a variable. sizeof returns the size, in bytes, of its operand.

```
printf( "sizeof( float ) = %d\n", (int)sizeof( float ) );
printf( "sizeof( double ) = %d\n", (int)sizeof( double ) );
printf( "sizeof( long double ) = %d\n\n", (int)sizeof( long double ) );
```

NOTE

Like return, sizeof doesn't always *require* a pair of parentheses. If the sizeof operand is a type, the parentheses are required. If the sizeof operand is a variable, the parentheses are optional. Rather than trying to remember this rule, avoid confusion, and always use parentheses with sizeof.

Did you notice the (int) to the left of each sizeof? This is known as a **typecast**. A typecast tells the compiler to convert a value of one type to a specified type. In this case, we are taking the type returned by sizeof and converting it to an int. Why do this? sizeof returns a value of type size_t (weird type name, eh?), and printf() doesn't have a format specifier that corresponds to a size_t. By converting the size_t to an int, we can use the %d format specifier to print the value returned by sizeof. Notice the extra \n at the end of the third printf() that gives us a blank line between the first three lines of output and the next line of output.

If the concept of typecasting is confusing to you, have no fear. We'll get into typecasting in Chapter 11. Until then, you can use this method whenever you want to print a value returned by sizeof. Alternatively, you might declare a variable of type int, assign the value returned by sizeof to the int, and then print the int:

```
int   myInt;
myInt = sizeof( float );
printf( "sizeof( float ) = %d\n", myInt );
```

Use whichever method works for you.

The rest of this program is dedicated to various and sundry ways you can print your floating point numbers. So far, all of our programs have printed ints using the %d format specifier. The Standard Library has a set of format specifiers for all of C's built-in data types, including several for printing floating point numbers.

The format specifer %f is used to print float and double variables and %Lf is used to print long double variables, all in their natural, decimal format.

```
printf( "myFloat = %f\n", myFloat );
printf( "myDouble = %f\n", myDouble );
printf( "myLongDouble = %Lf\n\n", myLongDouble );
```

Here's the result of these three printf()s:

```
myFloat = 12345.678711
myDouble = 12345.678901
myLongDouble = 12345.678901
```

As a reminder, all three of these numbers were assigned the value

```
12345.67890123456789
```

Notice that each of the printed numbers was cut off six digits after the decimal place. That is the default for the %f and %Lf format specifiers. The fact that myDouble and myLongDouble are a bit more accurate than myFloat makes sense, since myFloat is only 4 bytes long— less memory, less accuracy. If we were dealing with a number like 3.275, a float would be plenty big, and six digits after the decimal place would be plenty wide enough to accommodate our number. As is, the 4-byte limit of the float is causing our original number to be rounded, and the six digits past the decimal limit is causing our double and long double to be clipped. Let's keep going.

Format Specifier Modifiers

Our next three printf()s use format specifier **modifiers** to more closely specify the output produced by printf(). By using %25.16f instead of %f, we tell printf() to print the floating point number with an accuracy of 16 places past the decimal and to add spaces if necessary so the number takes up at least 25 character positions.

```
printf( "myFloat = %25.16f\n", myFloat );
printf( "myDouble = %25.16f\n", myDouble );
printf( "myLongDouble = %25.16Lf\n\n", myLongDouble );
```

Here's the result of these three `printf()`s:

```
myFloat =     12345.6787109375000000
myDouble =    12345.6789012345670926
myLongDouble =     12345.6789012345678902
```

`printf()` printed each of these numbers to 16 places past the decimal place (count the digits yourself), padding each result with zeros as needed. Since the 16 digits to the right of the decimal, plus one space for the decimal, plus the five digits to the left of the decimal is equal to 22 (16 + 1 + 5 = 22), and we asked `printf()` to use 25 character positions, `printf()` added three spaces to the left of each number.

STORING FLOATING POINT NUMBERS

We originally asked `printf()` to print a `float` with the following value:

12345.67890123456789

The best approximation of this number we were able to represent by a `float` is this:

12345.6787109375000000

Where did this approximation come from? The answer has to do with the way your computer stores floating point numbers.

The fractional part of a number (the number to the right of the decimal) is represented in binary just like an integer. Instead of the sum of powers of 2, the fractional part is represented as the sum of powers of 1/2. For example, the number .75 is equal to 1/2 + 1/4. In binary, that's 11.

The problem with this representation is that it's impossible to represent some numbers with complete accuracy. If you need a higher degree of accuracy, use `double` or `long double` instead of `float`. Unless you cannot afford the extra memory that the larger data types require, you are probably better off using a `double` or `long double` in your programs instead of a `float` for all your floating point calculations.

Note that even a 16-byte `long double` is not big enough to perfectly represent our original number. Pretty darn close, though!

The next four `printf()`s show you the result of using different modifier values to print the same `float`:

```
printf( "myFloat = %10.1f\n",myFloat );
printf( "myFloat = %.2f\n", myFloat );
printf( "myFloat = %.12f\n", myFloat );
printf( "myFloat = %.9f\n\n", myFloat );
```

Here's the output produced by each of the `printf()`s:

```
myFloat =     12345.7
myFloat = 12345.68
myFloat = 12345.678710937500
myFloat = 12345.678710938
```

The specifier `%10.1f` told `printf()` to print one digit past the decimal and to use ten character positions for the entire number. The specifier `%.2f` told `printf()` to print two digits past the decimal and to use as many character positions as necessary to print the entire number. Notice that `printf()` rounds off the result for you and doesn't simply cut off the number after the specified number of places.

The specifier `%.12f` told `printf()` to print 12 digits past the decimal, and the specifier `%.9f` told `printf()` to print 9 digits past the decimal. Again, notice the rounding that takes place.

Unless you need to exactly control the total number of characters used to print a number, you'll probably leave off the first modifier and just specify the number of digits past the decimal you want printed, using specifiers like `%.2f` and `%.9f`.

If you do use a two-part modifier like `%3.2f`, `printf()` will never cut off numbers to the left of the decimal. For example, this code

```
myFloat = 255.543;
printf( "myFloat = %3.2f", myFLoat );
```

will produce this output

```
myFloat = 255.54
```

Even though you told `printf()` to use three character positions to print the number, `printf()` was smart enough to not lose the numbers to the left of the decimal.

Scientific Notation

The next `printf()` uses the specifier %e, asking `printf()` to print the `float` using **scientific** or **exponential** notation.

```
    printf( "myFloat = %e\n\n", myFloat );
```

Here's the corresponding output:

```
myFloat = 1.234568e+04
```

1.234568e + 04 is equal to 1.234568 times 10 to the fourth power (1.234568 * 10^4 or 1.234568 * 10,000), which is equal to 12,345.68. The next two `printf()`s uses the specifier %g, letting `printf()` decide whether decimal or scientific notation will be the most efficient way to represent this number. The first %g deals with a `myFloat` value of 100,000:

```
myFloat = 100000;
printf( "myFloat = %g\n", myFloat );
```

Here's the output:

```
myFloat = 100000
```

Next, `myFLoat`'s value is changed to 1,000,000, and %g is used once again:

```
myFloat = 1000000;
printf( "myFloat = %g\n", myFloat );

    return 0;
}
```

Here's the result of this last `printf()`. As you can see, this time `printf()` decided to represent the number using exponential notation:

```
myFloat = 1e+06
```

The lesson here is to use `floats` if you want to work with floating point numbers. Use `doubles` or `long doubles` for extra accuracy, but be aware of the extra cost in memory usage. Use `ints` for maximum speed if you want to work exclusively with whole numbers or if you want to truncate a result.

The Integer Types

So far, you've learned about four different types—three floating point types (`float`, `double`, and `long double`) and one integer type (`int`). In this section, I'll introduce the remaining integer types: `char`, `short`, and `long`. As was the case with the three floating point types, the size of each of the four integer types is implementation dependent. Our next program, intSizer, proves that point. You'll find *intSizer.xcodeproj* in the *Learn C Projects* folder, in the *08.02 - intSizer* subfolder.

intSizer consists of four `printf()`s, one for each of the integer types:

```
printf( "sizeof( char ) = %d\n", (int)sizeof( char ) );
printf( "sizeof( short ) = %d\n", (int)sizeof( short ) );
printf( "sizeof( int ) = %d\n", (int)sizeof( int ) );
printf( "sizeof( long ) = %d\n", (int)sizeof( long ) );
```

SHORT AND LONG INTS

Though these forms are rarely used, a `short` is also known as a `short int` and a `long` is also known as a `long int`. As an example, these declarations are perfectly legal:

```
short int    myShort;
long int     myLong;
```

Though the preceding declarations are just fine, you are more likely to encounter declarations like these:

```
short     myShort;
long      myLong;
```

As always, choose your favorite style and be consistent.

Like their floatSizer counterparts, these `printf()`s use `sizeof` to determine the size of a char, a short, an int, and a long. When I ran intSizer on my Mac, here's what I saw:

```
sizeof( char ) = 1
sizeof( short ) = 2
sizeof( int ) = 4
sizeof( long ) = 4
```

Again, the point to remember is that there are *no* guarantees. Don't assume the size of a type. Write a program to check for yourself.

Type Value Ranges

All the integer types can be either `signed` or `unsigned`. This obviously affects the range of values handled by that type. For example, a `signed` 1-byte `char` can store a value from –128 to 127, while an `unsigned` 1-byte `char` can store a value from 0 to 255. If this clouds your mind with pain, now might be a good time to go back and review Chapter 5.

A `signed` 2-byte `short` can store values ranging from –32,768 to 32,767, while an `unsigned` 2-byte `short` can store values ranging from 0 to 65,535.

A `signed` 4-byte `long` or `int` can store values ranging from –2,147,483,648 to 2,147,483,647, while an `unsigned` 4-byte `long` or `int` can store values ranging from 0 to 4,294,967,295.

A 4-byte `float` can range in value from –3.4e + 38 to 3.4e + 38. An 8-byte `double` or `long double` can range in value from –1.7e + 308 to 1.7e + 308.

Memory Efficiency vs. Safety

Each time you declare one of your program's variables, you'll have a decision to make. What's the best type for this variable? In general, it's a good policy not to waste memory. Why use a `long` when a `short` will do just fine? Why use a `double` when a `float` will do the trick?

There is a danger in being too concerned with memory efficiency. For example, suppose a customer asked you to write a program designed to print the numbers 1 through 100, one number per line. Sounds pretty straightforward—just create a `for` loop and embed a `printf()` in the loop. In the interests of memory efficiency, you might use a `char` to act as the loop's counter. After all, if you declare your counter as an `unsigned char`, it can hold values ranging from 0 to 255. That should be plenty, right?

```
unsigned char    counter;

for ( counter=1; counter<=100; counter++ )
    printf( "%d\n", counter );
```

This program works just fine. But suppose your customer comes back with a request, asking you to extend the program to count from 1 to 1,000 instead of just to 100. You happily change the 100 to 1,000, like so, and take it for a spin:

```
unsigned char    counter;

for ( counter=1; counter<=1000; counter++ )
    printf( "%d\n", counter );
```

What do you think will happen when you run it? To find out, open the *Learn C Projects* folder, the *08.03 - typeOverflow* subfolder, and the project *typeOverflow.xcodeproj*.

Instead of just running the project this time, let's take things a bit slower. Start by compiling your code. Select **Build** from the **Build** menu. You should see a warning, just like the one shown in Figure 8-2. The warning tells us that the `for` loop comparison will always be true (`counter` will never exceed 1,000) due to the limited range of the `unsigned char` named `counter`. Good compiler!

Even though we got a warning, we can still run our project. As a rule, I always fix my code before I run it, but in this case, I want you to see what happens when we run this program as is. Select **Run** from the **Run** menu, and then bring up the console window. As you'll see if you scroll through the console window, the program generates the numbers 1 through 255, one number per line, and then goes to 0 and starts climbing again (see Figure 8-3). This repeats on and on, ad infinitum. Congratulations on your first infinite loop!

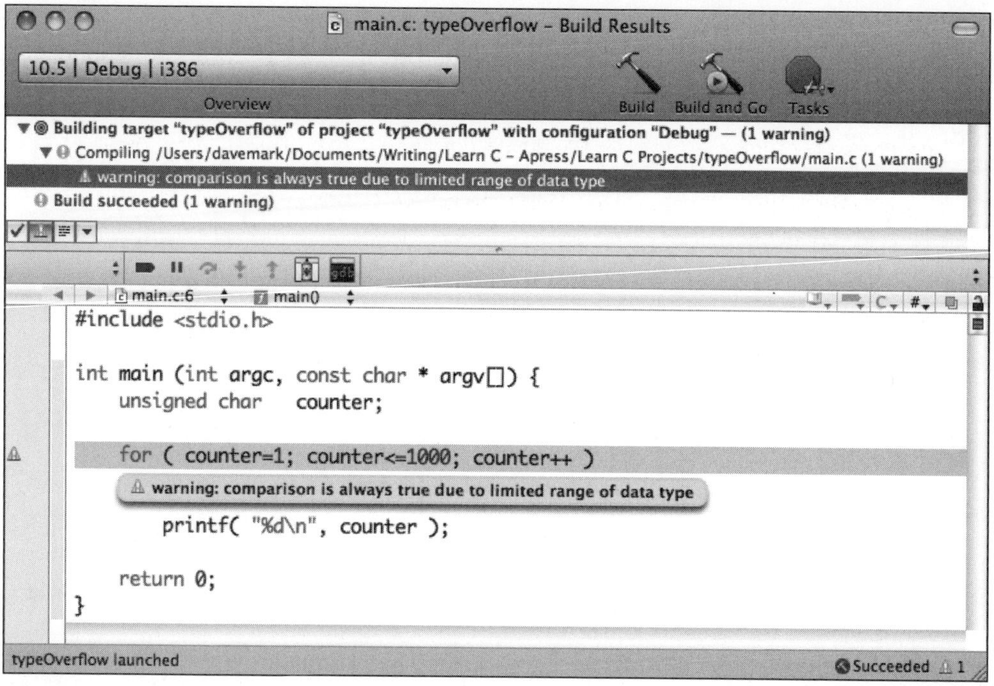

Figure 8-2. *The warning generated by the compiler when our code exceeded the range of our data type*

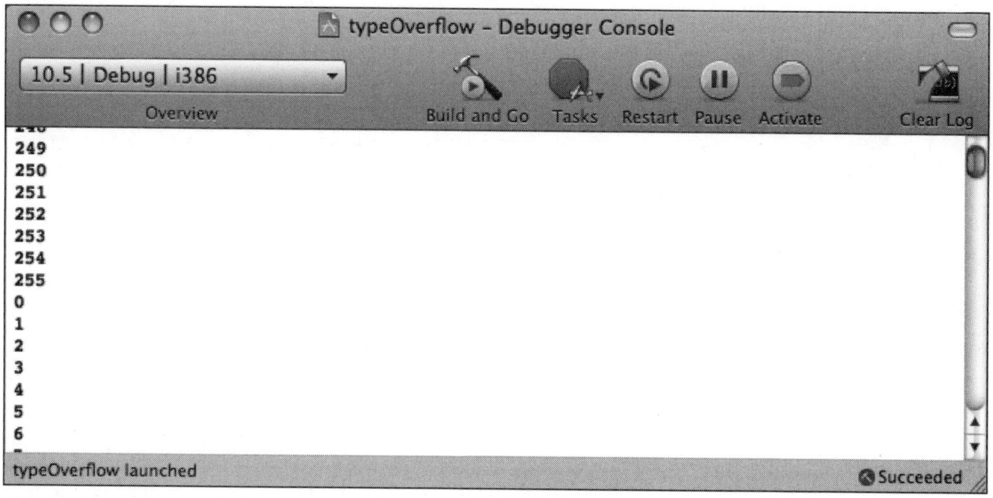

Figure 8-3. *When I ran typeOverflow, the program kept running in an infinite loop. Notice the change from 255 back to 0 in the console window.*

Click the red stop sign icon in the console window's tool bar, or select **Stop** from the **Run** menu to stop the program.

The problem with this program occurs when the for loop increments counter when it has a value of 255. Since an unsigned char can hold a maximum value of 255, incrementing it gives it a value of 0 again. Since counter can never get higher than 255, the for loop never exits.

Just for kicks, edit the code and change the unsigned char to a signed char. What do you think will happen? Try it!

The real solution here is to use the right type for your situation and to test, test, test your code. As your programming skills mature, start reading up on the process of testing your code. Testing your code is a vital part of delivering a successful product.

Working with Characters

With its minimal range, you might think that a char isn't good for much. Actually, the C deities created the char for a good reason. It is the perfect size to hold a single alphabetic character. In C, an alphabetic character is a single character placed between a pair of single quotes (' '). Here's a test to see if a char variable contains the letter 'a':

```
char    c;

c = 'a';

if ( c == 'a' )
    printf( "The variable c holds the character 'a'." );
```

As you can see, the character 'a' is used in both an assignment statement and an if statement, just as if it were a number or a variable.

The ASCII Character Set

In C, a signed char takes up a single byte and can hold a value from –128 to 127. Now, how can a char hold a numerical value, as well as a character value, such as 'a' or '+'? The answer lies with the **ASCII character set**.

NOTE

ASCII stands for the American Standard Code for Information Interchange.

The ASCII character set is a set of 128 standard characters, featuring the 26 lowercase letters, the 26 uppercase letters, the 10 numerical digits, and an assortment of other exciting characters, such as } and =. Each of these characters corresponds exactly to a value between 0 and 127. The ASCII character set ignores the values between –128 and –1.

For example, the character 'a' has an ASCII value of 97. When a C compiler sees the character 'a' in a piece of source code, it substitutes the value 97. Each of the values from 0 to 127 is interchangeable with a character from the ASCII character set.

WIDE CHARACTER DATA TYPES

Though we'll make use of the ASCII character set throughout this book, you should know that there are other character sets out there. Some foreign alphabets have more characters than can be represented by a single byte. To accommodate these multibyte characters, ISO C features **wide character** and **wide string** data types.

Though we won't get into multibyte character sets in this book, you should keep these things in mind as you write your own code. Read up on the multibyte extensions introduced as part of the ISO C standard. There's an excellent write-up in Samuel Harbison and Guy Steele's *C: A Reference Manual*; the fifth edition was released in 2002 (Prentice Hall)—a terrific C reference and well worth the purchase price.

Here's an article whose title tells it all: "The Absolute Minimum Every Software Developer Absolutely, Positively Must Know About Unicode and Character Sets (No Excuses!)" by Joel Spolsky:

`http://joelonsoftware.com/articles/Unicode.html`

Rock on, Joel!

ascii.xcodeproj

Here's a program that will make the ASCII character set easier to understand. Go into the *Learn C Projects* folder and then into the *08.04 - ascii* subfolder, and open the project *ascii.xcodeproj*.

Before we step through the project source code, let's take it for a spin. Select **Build and Run** from the **Build** menu. A console window similar to the one shown in Figure 8-4 should appear. The first line of output shows the characters corresponding to the ASCII values from 32 to 47. Why start with 32? As it turns out, the ASCII characters between 0 and 31 are nonprintable characters like the backspace (ASCII 8) or the carriage return (ASCII 13); see Table 8-1 later in this section for a rundown of these characters.

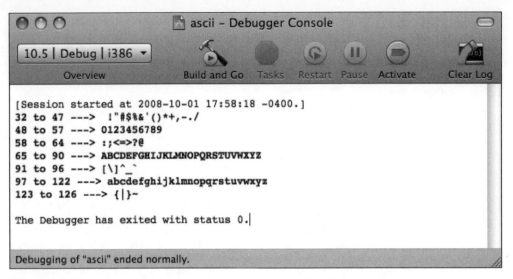

Figure 8-4. *The ascii program generates this list of the printable ASCII characters.*

Notice that ASCII character 32 is a space, also known as ' '. ASCII character 33 is '!'. ASCII character 47 is '/'. This presents some interesting coding possibilities. For example, this code is perfectly legitimate:

```
int     sumOfChars;

sumOfChars = '!' + '/';
```

What a strange piece of code! Though you will probably never do anything like this, try to predict the value of the variable sumOfChars after the assignment statement. And the answer is . . . The character '!' has a value of 33 and the character '/' has a value of 47. Therefore, sumOfChars will be left with a value of 80 following the assignment statement. C allows you to represent any number between 0 and 127 in two different ways: as an ASCII character or as a number. Let's get back to the console window in Figure 8-4.

The second line of output shows the ASCII characters from 48 through 57. As you can see, these ten characters represent the digits 0 through 9. Here's a little piece of code that converts an ASCII digit to its numerical counterpart:

```
char    digit;
int     convertedDigit;

digit = '3';

convertedDigit = digit - '0'; // That is a zero and not a lower-case o
```

This code starts with a char named digit, initialized to hold the ASCII character '3'. The character '3' has a numerical value of 51. The next line of code subtracts the ASCII character '0' from digit. Since the character '0' has a numerical value of 48, and digit started with a numerical value of 51, convertedDigit ends up with a value of 51 – 48, also known as 3. Isn't that interesting?

NOTE

Subtracting '0' from any ASCII digit yields that digit's numerical counterpart. Though this is a great trick if you know you're working with ASCII, your code will fail if the digits of the current character set are not represented in the same way as they are in ASCII. For example, if you were on a machine that used a character set where the digits were sequenced from 1 to 9, followed by 0, the trick wouldn't work.

The next line of the console window shown in Figure 8-4 shows the ASCII characters with values ranging from 58 to 64. The following line is pretty interesting. It shows the range of ASCII characters from 65 to 90. Notice anything familiar about these characters? They represent the complete, uppercase alphabet.

The next line in Figure 8-4 lists ASCII characters with values from 91 through 96. The following line lists the ASCII characters with values ranging from 97 through 122. These 26 characters represent the complete lowercase alphabet.

NOTE

Adding 32 to an uppercase ASCII character yields its lowercase equivalent. Likewise, subtracting 32 from a lowercase ASCII character yields its uppercase equivalent.

Guess what? You never want to take advantage of this information! Instead, use the Standard Library routines tolower() and toupper() to do the conversions for you.

As a general rule, try not to make assumptions about the order of characters in the current character set. Use Standard Library functions rather than working directly with character values. Though it is tempting to do these kinds of conversions yourself, by going through the Standard Library, you know your program will work across single-byte character sets.

The final line in Figure 8-4 lists the ASCII characters from 123 to 126. As it turns out, the ASCII character with a value of 127 is another nonprintable character. Table 8-1 shows a table of these unprintables. The left column shows the ASCII code. The right column shows the keyboard equivalent for that code along with any appropriate comments. The characters with comments by them are probably the only unprintables you'll ever make use of.

Table 8-1. *The ASCII Unprintables*

ASCII Code	Keyboard Equivalent
0	Used to terminate text strings (explained in the "Text Strings" section)
1	Control-A
2	Control-B
3	Control-C
4	Control-D (the end-of-file mark; see Chapter 10)
5	Control-E
6	Control-F
7	Control-G (beep; works in Terminal but not in Xcode)
8	Control-H (backspace)
9	Control-I (tab)
10	Control-J (line feed)
11	Control-K (vertical feed)
12	Control-L (form feed)
13	Control-M (carriage return, no line feed)
14	Control-N
15	Control-O
16	Control-P
17	Control-Q
18	Control-R
19	Control-S
20	Control-T
21	Control-U
22	Control-V
23	Control-W
24	Control-X
25	Control-Y
26	Control-Z
27	Control-[(escape character)
28	Control-|
29	Control-]
30	ontrol-^
31	Control-_
127	Delete

Stepping Through the acsii Source Code

Before we move on to our next topic, let's take a look at the source code that generated the ASCII character listing in Figure 8-4. ascii starts off with the usual #include and follows it by a function prototype of the function PrintChars(). PrintChars() takes two parameters that define a range of chars to print:

```
#include <stdio.h>

void    PrintChars( char low, char high );
```

main() calls PrintChars() seven times in an attempt to functionally organize the ASCII characters:

```
int main (int argc, const char * argv[]) {
    PrintChars( 32, 47 );
    PrintChars( 48, 57 );
    PrintChars( 58, 64 );
    PrintChars( 65, 90 );
    PrintChars( 91, 96 );
    PrintChars( 97, 122 );
    PrintChars( 123, 126 );

    return 0;
}
```

PrintChars() declares a local variable, c, to act as a counter as we step through a range of chars:

```
void    PrintChars( char low, char high ) {
    char    c;
```

We'll use low and high to print a label for the current line, showing the range of ASCII characters to follow. Notice that we use %d to print the integer version of these chars. %d can handle any integer types no bigger than an int.

```
    printf( "%d to %d ---> ", low, high );
```

Next, a for loop is used to step through each of the ASCII characters, from low to high, using printf() to print each of the characters next to each other on the same line. The printf() bears closer inspection. Notice the use of %c (instead of our usual %d) to tell printf() to print a single ASCII character.

```
    for ( c = low; c <= high; c++ )
        printf( "%c", c );
```

Once the line is printed, a single new line is printed, moving the cursor to the beginning of the next line in the console window. Thus ends `PrintChars()`.

```
    printf( "\n" );
}
```

The char data type is extremely useful to C programmers (such as yourself). The next two topics, arrays and text strings, will show you why. As you read through these two sections, keep the concept of ASCII characters in the back of your mind. As you reach the end of the section on text strings, you'll see an important relationship develop among all three topics.

Arrays

The next topic for discussion is **arrays**. An array turns a single variable into a list of variables. For example, this declaration

```
int     myNumber[ 3 ];
```

creates three separate `int` variables, referred to in your program as `myNumber[ 0 ]`, `myNumber[ 1 ]`, and `myNumber[ 2 ]`. Each of these variables is known as an **array element**. The number between the brackets ([and] are known as brackets or square brackets) is called an **index**. In this declaration

```
char    myChar[ 20 ];
```

the name of the array is `myChar`. This declaration will create an array of type char with a **dimension** of 20. The dimension of an array is the array's number of elements. The array elements will have **indexes** (indices, indexes—we're talking more than one index here) that run from 0 to 19.

NOTE

In C, array indexes always run from 0 to one less than the array's dimension.

This slice of code first declares an array of 100 `ints`, and then assigns each `int` a value of 0:

```
int     myNumber[ 100 ], i;

for ( i=0; i<100; i++ )
    myNumber[ i ] = 0;
```

You could have accomplished the same thing by declaring 100 individual ints and initializing each individual int. Here's what that code might look like:

```
int     myNumber0, myNumber1, ..., myNumber99;

myNumber0 = 0;
myNumber1 = 0;
      .
      .
      .
myNumber99 = 0;
```

Note that the dots in this last chunk of code are not valid C syntax. They are there to save my fingers some typing. It would take 100 lines of code just to initialize these variables! By using an array, we've accomplished the same thing in just a few lines of code. Look at this code fragment:

```
sum = 0;
for ( i=0; i<100; i++ )
    sum += myNumber[ i ];

printf( "The sum of the 100 numbers is %d.", sum );
```

This code adds together the value of all 100 elements of the array myNumber.

NOTE

In the preceding example, the for loop is used to **step through** an array, performing some operation on each of the array's elements. You'll use this technique frequently in your own C programs.

Why Use Arrays?

Programmers would be lost without arrays. Arrays allow you to keep lists of things. For example, if you need to maintain a list of 50 employee numbers, declare an array of 50 ints. You can declare an array using any C type. For example, this code

```
float     salaries[ 50 ];
```

declares an array of 50 floating point numbers. This might be useful for maintaining a list of employee salaries.

Use an array when you want to maintain a list of related data. Here's an example.

dice.xcode

Look in the *Learn C Projects* folder, inside the *08.05 - dice* subfolder, and open the project *dice. xcodeproj*. dice simulates the rolling of a pair of dice. After each roll, the program adds the two dice together, keeping track of the total. It rolls the dice 1,000 times and then reports on the results. Give it a try!

Run dice by selecting **Build and Run** from the **Build** menu. A console window should appear, similar to the one shown in Figure 8-5. Take a look at the output—it's pretty interesting. The first column lists all the possible totals of two dice. Since the lowest possible roll of a pair of six-sided dice is a one and a one, the first entry in the column is 2. The column counts all the way up to 12, the highest possible roll (achieved by a roll of a six and a six).

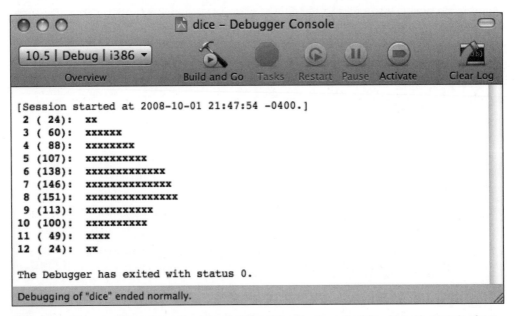

Figure 8-5. *This graph was the result of simulating 1,000 rolls of a pair of dice. Note that totals of 6, 7, and 8 are the most popular results. Your mileage may vary!*

The number in parentheses is the total number of rolls (out of 1,000) that matched that row's number. For example, the first row describes the dice rolls that total 2. In this run, the program rolled 24 twos. Finally, the program prints an x for every ten of these rolls. Since 24 twos were rolled, two xs were printed at the end of the twos' row. Since 146 sevens were rolled, 14 xs were printed at the end of the sevens' row.

NOTE

Recognize the curve depicted by the xs in Figure 8-4? The curve represents a "normal" probability distribution, also known as a **bell curve**. According to the curve, you are about 6.1 times more likely to roll a 7 as you are to roll a 12. Want to know why? Check out a book on probability and statistics.

Let's take a look at the source code that makes this possible.

Stepping Through the dice Source Code

dice starts off with three #includes. <stdlib.h> gives us access to the routines rand() and srand(); <time.h> gives us access to clock(); and <stdio.h> gives us access to printf().

```
#include <stdlib.h>
#include <time.h>
#include <stdio.h>
```

Here are the function prototypes for RollOne(), PrintRolls(), and PrintX(). You'll see how these routines work as we walk through the code.

```
int     RollOne( void );
void    PrintRolls( int rolls[] );
void    PrintX( int howMany );
```

main() declares an array of 13 ints named rolls. rolls will keep track of the 11 possible types of dice rolls. rolls[2] will keep track of the total number of twos, rolls[3] will keep track of the total number of threes, and so on, up until rolls[12] which will keep track of the total number of twelves rolled. Since there is no way to roll a 0 or a 1 with a pair of dice, rolls[0] and rolls[1] will go unused.

```
int main (int argc, const char * argv[]) {
    int       rolls[ 13 ], twoDice, i;
```

NOTE

We could have rewritten the program using an array of 11 ints, thereby saving two ints worth of memory. If we did that, rolls[0] would track the number of twos rolled, rolls[1] would track the number of threes rolled, and so on. This would have made the program a little harder to read, since rolls[i] would be referring to the number of (i+2) values rolled.

In general, it is OK to sacrifice memory to make your program easier to read, as long as program performance isn't compromised.

The function srand() is part of the Standard Library. It initializes a random number generator, using a seed provided by another Standard Library function, clock(). Once the random number generator is initialized, another function, rand(), will return an int with a random value.

```
srand( clock() );
```

Why random numbers? Sometimes, you want to add an element of unpredictability to your program. For example, in our program, we want to roll a pair of dice again and again. The program would be pretty boring if it rolled the same numbers over and over. By using a random number generator, we can generate a random number between 1 and 6, thus simulating the roll of a single die!

main()'s next step is to initialize each of the elements of the array rolls to 0. This is appropriate since no rolls of any kind have taken place yet.

```
for ( i=0; i<=12; i++ )
    rolls[ i ] = 0;
```

Let's roll some dice! This for loop rolls the dice 1,000 times. As you'll see, the function RollOne() returns a random number between 1 and 6, simulating the roll of a single die. By calling it twice and storing the sum of the two rolls in the variable twoDice, we've simulated the roll of two dice.

```
for ( i=1; i <= 1000; i++ ) {
    twoDice = RollOne() + RollOne();
```

The next line is pretty tricky, so hang on. At this point, the variable twoDice holds a value between 2 and 12, the total of two individual dice rolls. We'll use that value to specify which of the rolls' ints to increment. If twoDice is 12 (if we rolled a pair of sixes) we'll increment rolls[12]. Get it? If not, go back and read through this again. If you still feel stymied (and it's OK if you do), find a C buddy to help you through this. It is important that you get this concept. Be patient.

```
    ++ rolls[ twoDice ];
}
```

Once we're finished with our 1,000 rolls, we'll pass rolls as a parameter to PrintRolls():

```
PrintRolls( rolls );

return 0;
}
```

Notice that we used the array name, without the brackets (rolls instead of rolls[]). The name of an array is a pointer to the first element of the array. If you have access to this pointer, you have access to the entire array. You'll see how this works when we look at PrintRolls().

AN ARRAY'S NAME IS A POINTER TO ITS FIRST ELEMENT

Just remember that passing the name of an array as a parameter is exactly the same as passing a pointer to the first element of the array. To prove this, edit *main.c* and change this line of code

```
PrintRolls( rolls );
```

to

```
PrintRolls( &( rolls[0] ) );
```

These two lines are exactly equivalent! The second form passes the address of the first array element. If you think back to our last chapter, we use the & operator to pass a parameter by reference instead of by value. By passing the address of the first array element, you give `PrintRolls()` the ability to both access and modify all of the array elements. This is an important concept!

RollOne() first calls rand() to generate a random number, ranging from 0 to 32,767 (actually, the upper bound is defined by the constant RAND_MAX, which is guaranteed to be at least 32,767). Next, the % operator is used to return the remainder when the random number is divided by 6. This yields a random number ranging from 0 to 5. Finally, 1 is added to this number, converting it to a number between 1 and 6, and that number is returned.

```
int     RollOne( void ) {
    return (rand() % 6) + 1;
}
```

PrintRolls() starts off by declaring a single parameter, an array pointer named rolls. Notice that rolls was declared using square brackets, telling the compiler that rolls is a pointer to the first element of an array (in this case, to an array of ints):

```
void    PrintRolls( int rolls[] ) {
    int         i;
```

The for loop steps through the rolls array, one int at a time, starting with rolls[2] and making its way to rolls[12]. For each element, PrintRolls() first prints the roll number and then, in parentheses, the number of times (out of 1,000) that roll occurred. Next, PrintX() is called to print a single x for every ten rolls that occurred. Finally, a carriage return is printed, preparing the console window for the next roll:

```
    for ( i=2; i<=12; i++ ) {
        printf( "%2d (%3d):  ", i, rolls[ i ] );
        PrintX( rolls[ i ] / 10 );
        printf( "\n" );
    }
}
```

ROLLS[] IS THE SAME AS *ROLLS

`PrintRolls()` could have declared its parameter using this notation

```
void    PrintRolls( int *rolls )
```

instead of

```
void    PrintRolls( int rolls[] )
```

Both of these notations describe a pointer to an `int`, and both can be used to access the elements of an array. You'll learn more about the close relationship between pointers and arrays as you make your way through the rest of this book.

For now, remember this convention: If you are declaring a parameter that will point to an array, use the square bracket form. Otherwise, use the normal pointer form.

`PrintX()` is pretty straightforward. It uses a `for` loop to print the number of xs specified by the parameter howMany:

```
void    PrintX( int     howMany ) {
    int     i;

    for ( i=1; i<=howMany; i++ )
        printf( "x" );
}
```

Danger, Will Robinson!

Before we move on to our next topic, there is one danger worth discussing at this point. See if you can spot the potential hazard in this piece of code:

```
int     myInts[ 3 ];

for ( i=0; i<20; i++ )
    myInts[ i ] = 0;
```

Yikes! The array `myInts` consists of exactly 3 array elements, yet the `for` loop tries to initialize 20 elements. This is called **exceeding the bounds** of your array. Because C is such an informal language, it will let you get away with this kind of source code. To you, that means Xcode will compile this code without complaint. Your problems will start as soon as the program tries to initialize the fourth array element, which was never allocated.

What will happen? The safest thing to say is that the results will be unpredictable. The problem is that the program is trying to assign a value of 0 to a block of memory that it doesn't necessarily own. Anything could happen. The program would most likely crash, which means it stops behaving in a rational manner. I've seen some cases where the computer actually leaps off the desk, hops across the floor, and jumps face first into the trash can.

Well, OK, not really. Modern operating systems protect the boundaries of individual applications to prevent one application from crashing another. But odd things will happen if you don't keep your array references in bounds. C programmers are treated like grown-ups. C gives you incredible power. With that power comes great responsibility. Test your code. Make smart decisions about your program design. Comment your code. You get the idea.

NOTE

As you code, be aware of the limitations of your variables. For example, a `char` is limited to values from −128 to 127. Don't try to assign a value such as 536 to a `char`. Don't reference `myArray[ 27 ]` if you declared `myArray` with only ten elements. Be careful!

Text Strings

The first C program in this book made use of a text string:

```
printf( "Hello, world!" );
```

This section will teach you how to use text strings like `"Hello, world!"` in your own programs. It will teach you how these strings are stored in memory and how to create your own strings from scratch.

A Text String in Memory

Take a look at Figure 8-6. This figure represents the text string `"Hello, world!"`, as it exists in memory. The string is stored as a sequence of 14 consecutive bytes. The first 13 bytes consist of the 13 ASCII characters in `"Hello, world!"`. Note that the seventh byte contains a space (on an ASCII-centric computer, that translates to a value of 32).

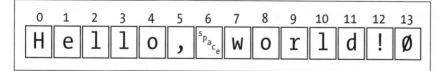

Figure 8-6. The "Hello, world!" text string. Don't forget: byte 13, which is actually the fourteenth byte, contains a 0.

The final byte has a value of 0, not to be confused with the ASCII character '0'. The zero is what makes this string a C string. Every C string ends with a byte having a value of 0. The zero identifies the end of the string.

Notice that the bytes in the string are numbered from 0 up to 13, instead of from 1 to 14. In effect, a string is an array of chars, and in C, arrays are zero-based.

When you use a quoted string like "Hello, world!" in your code, the compiler creates the string for you. This type of string is called a **string constant**. When you use a string constant in your code, the detail work is done for you automatically. In this example

```
printf( "Hello, world!" );
```

the 14 bytes needed to represent the string in memory are allocated automatically. The 0 is placed in the fourteenth byte automatically. You don't have to worry about these details when you use a string constant.

String constants are great, but they are not always appropriate. For example, suppose you want to read in somebody's name and then pass the name on to printf() to display in the console window. Since you won't be able to predict the name that will be typed in, you can't predefine the name as a string constant. Let's look at an example.

nameBad.xcodeproj

Look in the *Learn C Projects* folder, inside the *08.06 - nameBad* subfolder, and open the project *nameBad.xcodeproj*. Why is this program called nameBad? You will see; you will see. Just follow along and I promise, you will learn something awesome.

nameBad will ask you to type your first name on the keyboard. Once you've typed your first name, the program will use your name to create a custom welcome message. Then, nameBad will tell you how many characters long your name is. How useful!

To run nameBad, select **Build and Run** from the **Build** menu. A console window will appear, prompting you for your first name, like this:

```
Type your first name, please:
```

Type your first name, and then press Return. When I did, I saw the output shown in Figure 8-7. Let's take a look at the source code that generated this output.

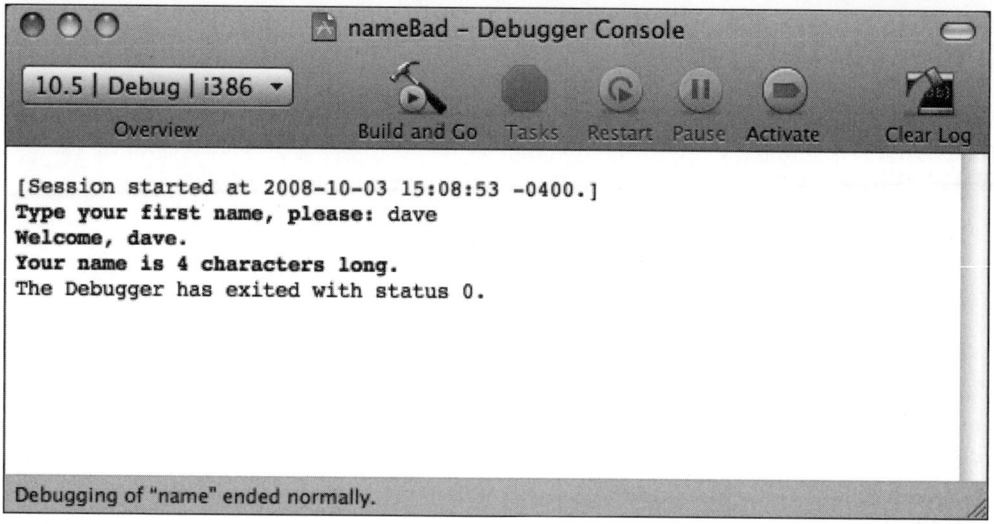

Figure 8-7. *The name program prompts you to type in your name and then tells you how long your name is.*

Stepping Through the nameBad Source Code

At the heart of nameBad is a Standard Library function called scanf(). scanf() is the source of the badness of nameBad. Keep reading, and you'll see why. scanf() uses the same format specifiers as printf() to read text in from the keyboard.

This code will read in an int:

```
int    myInt;

scanf( "%d", &myInt );
```

The %d tells scanf() to read in an int. Notice the use of the & before the variable myInt. This passes myInt's address to scanf(), allowing scanf() to change myInt's value.

nameBad starts off with a pair of #includes. <string.h> gives us access to the Standard Library function strlen(), and <stdio.h>, well, you know what we get from <stdio.h>. printf(), right? Right.

```
#include <string.h>
#include <stdio.h>
```

To read in a text string, you have to first declare a variable to place the text characters in. nameBad uses an array of characters for this purpose:

```
int main (int argc, const char * argv[]) {
    char    name[ 50 ];
```

The array name is big enough to hold a 49-byte text string. When you allocate space for a text string, remember to save 1 byte for the 0 that terminates the string.

The program starts by printing a **prompt**. A prompt is a text string that lets the user know the program is waiting for input:

```
printf( "Type your first name, please: " );
```

The Input Buffer

Before we get to the scanf() call, you should understand how the computer handles input from the keyboard. When the computer starts running your program, it automatically creates a big array of chars for the sole purpose of storing keyboard input to your program. This array is known as your program's **input buffer**. The input buffer is carriage-return based. Every time you hit a carriage return, all the characters typed since the last carriage return are appended to the current input buffer.

When your program starts, the input buffer is empty. If you type this line using your keyboard:

123 abcd

and follow it with a carriage return, the input buffer will look like Figure 8-8. The computer keeps track of the current end of the input buffer. The space character between the '3' and the 'a' has an ASCII value of 32. Notice that the carriage return was actually placed in the input buffer.

NOTE

The ASCII value of the character used to indicate a carriage return is implementation dependent. In most consoles, ASCII 10 indicates a carriage return. On some, ASCII 13 indicates a carriage return. Use the '\n' character, and you'll always be safe.

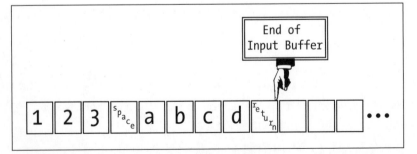

Figure 8-8. *A snapshot of the input buffer, which includes a space character and a carriage return*

Given the input buffer shown in Figure 8-8, suppose your program called `scanf()`, like this:

```
scanf( "%d", &myInt );
```

`scanf()` starts at the beginning of the input buffer and reads a character at a time until it hits one of the nonprintables (that is, a carriage return, tab, space, or a 0), until it hits the end of the buffer, or until it hits a character that conflicts with the format specifier (if %d was used and the letter 'a' was encountered, for example).

After the `scanf()`, the input buffer looks like Figure 8-9. Notice that the characters passed on to `scanf()` were removed from the input buffer and that the rest of the characters slid over to the beginning of the buffer. `scanf()` took the characters '1', '2', and '3' and converted them to the integer 123, placing 123 in the variable `myInt`.

Figure 8-9. *A second snapshot of the input buffer, after scanf() pulled out the number 123*

If you then typed the following line

```
3.5 Dave
```

followed by a carriage return, the input buffer would look like Figure 8-10. At this point the input buffer contains two carriage returns. To the input buffer, a carriage return is just like any other character. To a function like `scanf()`, the carriage return is white space.

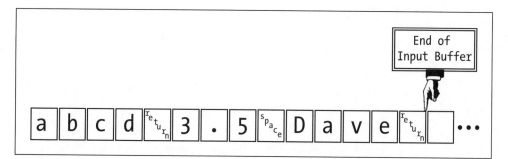

Figure 8-10. *A third snapshot of the input buffer, after a bit more was typed in*

> **NOTE**
>
> If you forgot what white space is, now would be a good time to turn back to Chapter 5, where white space was first described.

On with the Program

Before we started our discussion on the input buffer, `main()` had just called `printf()` to prompt for the user's first name:

```
printf( "Type your first name, please: " );
```

Next, we called `scanf()` to read the first name from the input buffer:

```
scanf( "%s", name );
```

Since the program just started, the input buffer is empty. `scanf()` will wait until characters appear in the input buffer, which will happen as soon as you type some characters and press Return. Type your first name, and press Return.

> **NOTE**
>
> `scanf()` will ignore white space characters in the input buffer. For example, if you type a few spaces and tabs and then press Return, `scanf()` will still sit there, waiting for some real input. Try it!

Once you type your name, `scanf()` will copy the characters, a byte at a time, into the `char` array pointed to by name. Remember, because name was declared as an array, name points to the first of the 50 bytes allocated for the array.

If you type in the name Dave, `scanf()` will place the four characters `'D'`, `'a'`, `'v'`, and `'e'` in the first four of the 50 bytes allocated for the array. Next, `scanf()` will set the fifth byte to a value of 0 to terminate the string properly (see Figure 8-11). Since the string is properly terminated by the 0 in name[4], we don't really care about the value of the bytes name[5] through name[49].

Next, we pass name on to `printf()`, asking it to print the name as part of a welcoming message. The `%s` tells `printf()` that name points to the first byte of a zero-terminated string. `printf()` will step through memory, one byte at a time, starting with the byte that name points to. `printf()` will print each byte in turn until it hits a byte with a value of 0. The zero byte marks the end of the string.

```
printf( "Welcome, %s.\n", name );
```

Figure 8-11. *Here's the array name after the string "Dave" is copied to it. Notice that name[4] has a value of 0.*

NOTE

> If name[4] didn't contain a zero, the string wouldn't be properly terminated. Passing a nonterminated string to printf() is a sure way to confuse printf(). printf() will step through memory one byte at a time, printing a byte and looking for a zero. It will keep printing bytes until it happens to encounter a byte set to 0. Remember, C strings must be terminated!

The next line of the program calls another Standard Library function, called strlen(). strlen() takes a pointer as a parameter and returns the length, in bytes, of the string pointed to by the parameter. strlen() depends on the string being zero-terminated. Just like sizeof(), strlen() returns a value of type size_t. We'll use a typecast to convert the value to an int and print it using %d. Again, we'll cover typecasting later in the book.

```
    printf( "Your name is %d characters long.", (int)strlen( name ) );

    return 0;
}
```

The Problem with nameBad

So far, the program looks great. nameBad seems to run just fine. What is so bad about scanf()?

Imagine what would happen if you typed a 50-character or longer name in response to the console window prompt. No white space, just a 50-character name. I realize that very few of you have a name that long, but just bear with me. The name array is only long enough to hold a 49-character name, reserving one byte for the string terminating 0. scanf() is not smart enough to recognize when the characters passed to it are too long for the char array receiving the data. When scanf() receives data too long for its char array, it writes the data in anyway, even if it means stepping off the end of the array. When scanf() writes that fifty-first character in an array defined to have a length of 50, where does that extra byte go?

Bottom line—the extra character goes into the memory location immediately after the array. Unfortunately, that memory location could have been reserved for another variable. That extra data you entered could be writing over some critical piece of your program's data. The results are unpredictable, and the results will be bad.

When you run the program using Xcode, overflowing data will frequently, but not always, cause your program to drop into GDB, the built-in debugger that comes along with the GCC compiler. Go ahead; give it a try. Run nameBad, and when prompted for your name, type a string of 70 characters, like so:

1234567890123456789012345678901234567890123456789012345678901234567890

When you press the carriage return, scanf() will load these 70 characters into the array, and tack on a zero at the end. Chances are pretty good that this will cause control to be passed to GDB (see Figure 8-12). If this happens to you, stop the program by clicking the stop sign icon in the console window toolbar or selecting **Stop** from the **Run** menu.

Figure 8-12. *When I typed a 70-character name, nameBad dumped me into the GBD debugger.*

Being dumped into the debugger was not the result you were looking for. In fact, you've just done your first bit of hacking, causing a program to crash by overflowing its input buffer.

The moral of this story? Don't ever, ever use scanf(). Instead, use the function fgets(). fgets() reads in a line of input from the specified file and saves it into the specified char array. fgets() has three parameters. The first is the char array. The second is an int that specifies the length of the char array. The third is the file specifier. We'll get into file specifiers in Chapter 10, and we'll use fgets() in several of this book's programs. For now, let's take a quick look at a better and safer version of our program.

The nameGood Source Code

Our new, improved version of the name program is found in *Learn C Projects*, in the folder *08.07 – nameGood*. Open the project *nameGood.xcodeproj*. Take a look at the source code. Most of it is the same.

We start with the usual #includes, define the name char array, and add an int named nameLength. We then use printf() to print the prompt:

```
#include <stdio.h>
#include <string.h> //This is to bring in the declaration of strlen()

int main (int argc, const char * argv[]) {
    char    name[ 50 ];
    int     nameLength;

    printf( "Type your first name, please: " );
```

In the next three lines, we veer away from scanf(). First, we call fgets(), telling it to read a max of 50 characters and asking it to read from the standard input. stdin is a file specifier that stands for the standard input. Again, we'll get into all that in Chapter 10.

One problem with fgets() is that it sticks the carriage return in the name array. If we leave things as they are, when we print our welcome message, the period at the end of the sentence will appear by itself on the next line. Our solution? First, we get the length of the name, which includes the carriage return. If the name was four characters long, the carriage return will add a fifth character. nameLength will be 5, and the carriage return will appear in name[4]. We then set name[4] to 0, terminating the string after the last character of the name instead of after the carriage return.

```
    fgets( name, 50, stdin );
    nameLength = strlen( name );
    name[ nameLength - 1 ] = 0;
```

```
    printf( "Welcome, %s.\n", name );
    printf( "Your name is %d characters long.", (int)strlen( name ) );

    return 0;
}
```

Take some time to go through the previous paragraph. Make sure you understand why this worked. Don't move on until you understand why this code works the way it does. The most important thing to understand is why we placed a 0 in name[4] after the user typed four-character name. Once you understand that, you're ready to move on.

Our last program for this chapter demonstrates a few more character-handling techniques, a new Standard Library function, and an invaluable programmer's tool, the #define directive.

The #define Directive

When you send your .c file to the compiler, the compiler first invokes a preprocessor, asking it to go through the source code file and perform a series of tasks to prepare the source code for the actual compilation. Here's a link to an excellent Wikipedia article that describes the C preprocessor:

http://en.wikipedia.org/wiki/C_preprocessor

One of the last things the preprocessor does is to scan the file for preprocessor directives. One preprocessor directive you've already experienced is the #include directive. Another preprocessor directive, the #define (pronounced "pound-define"), tells the compiler to substitute one piece of text for another throughout your source code. This statement

```
#define kMaxPlayers     6
```

tells the compiler to substitute the character 6 every time it finds the text kMaxPlayers in the source code. kMaxPlayers is known as a **macro**. As the preprocessor goes through your code, it enters all the #defines into a list, known as a **dictionary**, performing all the #define substitutions as it goes.

NOTE

It's important to know that the compiler never actually modifies your source code. The dictionary it creates as it goes through your code is separate from your source code, and the substitutions it performs are made as the source code is translated into machine code.

Here's an example of a #define in action:

```
#define kMaxArraySize     100

int main (int argc, const char * argv[]) {
    char    myArray[ kMaxArraySize ];
    int     i;

    for ( i=0; i<kMaxArraySize; i++ )
        myArray[ i ] = 0;

    return 0;
}
```

The #define at the beginning of this example substitutes 100 for kMaxArraySize every-where it appears in the source code file. In this example, the substitution will be done twice. Though your source code is not actually modified, here's the effect of this #define:

```
int main (int argc, const char * argv[]) {
    char    myArray[ 100 ];
    int         i;

    for ( i=0; i<100; i++ )
        myArray[ i ] = 0;

    return 0;
}
```

Note that a #define must appear in the source code file before it is used. In other words, this code won't compile:

```
int main (int argc, const char * argv[]) {
    char    myArray[ kMaxArraySize ];
    int     i;
#define kMaxArraySize     100
    for ( i=0; i<kMaxArraySize; i++ )
        myArray[ i ] = 0;
    return 0;
}
```

Having a #define in the middle of your code is just fine. The problem here is that the decla-ration of myArray references a #define that hasn't occurred yet!

If you use #defines effectively, you'll build more flexible code. In the previous example, you can change the size of the array by modifying a single line of code, the #define. If your pro-gram is designed correctly, if you change the line to

```
#define kMaxArraySize     200
```

and recompile your code, your program should still work properly. A good sign that you are using #defines properly is an absence of constants in your code. In the preceding examples, the constant 100 was replaced by kMaxArraySize.

NOTE

Many programmers use a naming convention for #defines that's similar to the one they use for global variables. Instead of starting the name with a g (as in gMyGlobal), a #define constant starts with a k (as in kMyConstant).

Unix programmers tend to name their #define constants using all uppercase letters, sprinkled with underscores (_) to act as word dividers (as in MAX_ARRAY_SIZE).

As you'll see in our next program, you can put practically anything, even source code, into a #define. Take a look:

```
#define kPrintReturn     printf( "\n" );
```

While not particularly recommended, this #define will work just fine, substituting the following statement

```
printf( "\n" );
```

for every occurrence of the text kPrintReturn in your source code. You can base one #define on a previous #define:

```
#define kSideLength     5
#define kArea           kSideLength * kSideLength
```

NOTE

Interestingly, you could have reversed the order of these two #defines, and your code would still have compiled. As long as both entries are in the dictionary, their order of occurrence in the dictionary is not important. What is important is that #define appear in the source code before any source code that refers to it.

If this seems confusing, don't sweat it. It won't be on the test.

Function-Like #define Macros

You can create a #define macro that takes one or more arguments. Here's an example:

```
#define kSquare( a )    ((a) * (a))
```

This macro takes a single argument. The argument can be any C expression. If you called the macro like this:

```
myInt = kSquare( myInt + 1 );
```

the compiler would use its first pass to turn the line into this:

```
myInt = (( myInt + 1 ) * ( myInt + 1 ));
```

Notice the usefulness of the parentheses in the macro. If the macro were defined like this

```
#define kSquare( a )    a * a
```

the compiler would have produced

```
myInt = myInt + 1 * myInt + 1;
```

which is not what we wanted. The multiplication that gets performed by this statement is 1 * myInt, because the * operator has a higher precedence than the + operator.

Be sure you pay strict attention to your use of white space in your #define macros. For example, there's a world of difference between this macro

```
#define kSquare( a )    ((a) * (a))
```

and this macro

```
#define kSquare ( a )    ((a) * (a))
```

Note the space between kSquare and (a). This second form creates a #define constant named kSquare which is defined as (a)   ((a) * (a)). A call to this macro won't even compile, because the compiler doesn't know what a is.

Here's another interesting macro side effect. Imagine calling this macro

```
#define kSquare( a )    ((a) * (a))
```

like this

```
mySquare = kSquare( myInt++ );
```

The preprocessor pass expands this macro call to this:

```
mySquare = ((myInt++) * (myInt++));
```

Do you see the problems here? First off, `myInt` will get incremented twice by this macro call (probably not what was intended). Second, the first `myInt++` will get executed before the multiplication happens, yielding a final result of `myInt*(myInt+1)`, definitely not what you wanted! The point here is to be careful when you pass an expression as a parameter to a macro.

Here's one final point. Keeping all your `#define` statements together toward the top of the file is good form. Don't place a `#define` inside a function, for example. People generally expect to find a `#define` at the top of the file, not in the middle.

Let's move on to this chapter's final example.

wordCount.xcodeproj

Look in the *Learn C Projects* folder, inside the *08.08 - wordCount* subfolder, and open the project *wordCount.xcodeproj*. wordCount will ask you to type a line of text and will count the number of words in the text you type.

To run wordCount, select **Build and Run** from the **Build** menu. wordCount will prompt you to type a line of text:

```
Type a line of text, please:
```

Type at least a few words of text, and end your line by pressing Return. When you press Return, wordCount will report its results. wordCount will ignore any white space, so feel free to sprinkle your input with tabs, spaces, and the like. My output is shown in Figure 8-13. Let's take a look at the source code that generated this output.

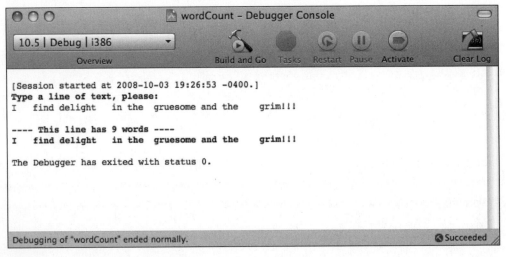

Figure 8-13. *wordCount, doing its job*

Stepping Through the wordCount Source Code

We start wordCount with the usual #includes and then add a new one. <ctype.h> includes the prototype of the function isspace(), which takes a char as input and returns a non-zero number if the char is either a tab ('\t'), hard carriage return (return without a line feed: '\r'), newline (return with a line feed: '\n'), vertical tab ('\v'), form feed ('\f'), or space (' '), and returns 0 otherwise.

```
#include <stdio.h>
#include <stdbool.h>
#include <ctype.h>
```

NOTE

Older C environments may include a variant of isspace() called iswhite().

Next, we define a pair of constants. kMaxLineLength specifies the largest line this program can handle. 200 bytes should be plenty. kZeroByte has a value of 0 and is used to mark the end of the line of input (more on this in a bit):

```
#define kMaxLineLength      200
#define kZeroByte           0
```

Here are the function prototypes for the two functions ReadLine() and CountWords(). ReadLine() reads in a line of text and CountWords() takes a line of text and returns the number of words in the line:

```
void    ReadLine( char *line );
int     CountWords( char *line );
```

main() starts by defining an array of chars that will hold the line of input we type and an int that will hold the result of our call to CountWords():

```
int main (int argc, const char * argv[]) {
    char    line[ kMaxLineLength ];
    int     numWords;
```

Once we type the prompt, we'll pass line to ReadLine(). Remember that line is a pointer to the first byte of the array of chars. When ReadLine() returns, line contains a line of text, terminated by a zero byte, making line a legitimate, zero-terminated C string. We'll pass that string on to CountWords().

```
    printf( "Type a line of text, please:\n" );

    ReadLine( line );
    numWords = CountWords( line );
```

We then print a message telling us how many words we just counted:

```
printf( "\n---- This line has %d word", numWords );

if ( numWords != 1 )
    printf( "s" );

printf( " ----\n%s\n", line );

return 0;
}
```

This last bit of code shows attention to detail, something very important in a good program. Notice that the first `printf()` ended with the characters "word". If the program found either no words or more than one word, we want to say

```
This line has 0 words.
```

or

```
This line has 2 words.
```

If the program found exactly one word, the sentence should read

```
This line has 1 word.
```

The last `if` statement makes sure the "s" gets added if needed.

In `main()`, we defined an array of `char`s to hold the line of characters we type in. When `main()` called `ReadLine()`, it passed the name of the array as a parameter to `ReadLine()`:

```
char        line[ ];

ReadLine( line );
```

As I said earlier, the name of an array also acts as a pointer to the first element of the array. In this case, `line` is equivalent to `&(line[0])`. `ReadLine()` now has a pointer to the first byte of `main()`'s `line` array.

```
void    ReadLine( char *line ) {
```

`numCharsRead` will track how many characters we've read so far. We'll use it to make sure we don't read more characters into `line` than `line` can hold.

```
int     numCharsRead = 0;
```

This `while` loop calls `getchar()` to read a character at a time from the input buffer. `getchar()` returns the next character in the input buffer, or if there's an error, it returns the constant EOF. You'll learn more about EOF in Chapter 10.

The first time through the loop, `line` points to the first byte of `main()`'s `line` array. At this point, the expression `*line` is equivalent to the expression `line[0]`. The first time through the loop, we're getting the first character from the input buffer and copying it into `line[0]`.

The `while` loop continues as long as the character we just read in is not `'\n'` (as long as we have not yet retrieved the return character from the input buffer). In addition, we increment `numCharsRead` every time we read in a character. If `numCharsRead` ever gets as big as one less than the size of the buffer, we'll break out of the loop. We use `kMaxLineLength-1` here so we leave room for the terminating zero.

```
while ( (*line = getchar()) != '\n' ) {
    line++;
    if ( ++numCharsRead >= kMaxLineLength-1 )
        break;
}
```

Each time through the loop, we'll increment `ReadLine()`'s local copy of the pointer `line`, so it points to the next byte in `main()`'s `line` array. The next time through the loop, we'll read a character into the second byte of the array, and then the third byte, and so on, until we read in a `'\n'` and drop out of the loop.

Once we drop out of the loop, we'll place a 0 in the next position of the array. This turns the line into a zero-terminated string we can print using `printf()`.

```
    *line = kZeroByte;
}
```

`CountWords()` also takes a pointer to the first byte of `main()`'s `line` array as a parameter. `CountWords()` will step through the array, looking for non–white-space characters. When one is encountered, `CountWords()` sets `inWord` to `true` and increments `numWords` and keeps stepping through the array looking for a white-space character that marks the end of the current word. Once the white space is found, `inWord` is set to `false`.

```
int    CountWords( char *line ) {
    int        numWords, inWord;

    numWords = 0;
    inWord = false;
```

POINTER ARITHMETIC

This technique is known as **pointer arithmetic.** When you increment a pointer that points into an array, the value of the pointer is actually incremented just enough to point to the next element of the array. For example, if `line` were an array of 4-byte `float`s instead of `char`s, this line of code

```
line++;
```

would increment `line` by four instead of by one. In both cases, `line` would start off pointing to `line[0]`, and after the statement `line++`, `line` would point to `line[1]`.

Take a look at this code:

```
char    charPtr;
float   floatPtr;
double  doublePtr;

charPtr++;
floatPtr++;
doublePtr++;
```

In the last three statements, `charPtr` gets incremented by 1 byte, `floatPtr` gets incremented by 4 bytes, and `doublePtr` gets incremented by 8 bytes (assuming 1-byte `char`s, 4-byte `float`s, and 8-byte `double`s).

This is an extremely important concept to understand. If it seems fuzzy to you, go back and reread this sidebar, and then write some code to make sure you truly understand how pointers work, especially as they relate to arrays.

This process continues until the zero byte marking the end of the line is encountered:

```
while ( *line != kZeroByte ) {
    if ( ! isspace( *line ) ) {
        if ( ! inWord ) {
            numWords++;
            inWord = true;
        }
    }
    else
        inWord = false;

    line++;
}
```

Once we drop out of the loop, we'll return the number of words in the line.

```
    return numWords;
}
```

MAIN()'S PARAMETERS

Now that you've seen arrays and pointers, there's something you should know. Every program in this book features a `main()` function that takes a pair of parameters:

```
int main (int argc, const char * argv[])
```

Though we won't make use of these parameters in this book, here are the basics. The first parameter, `argc`, is an `int` that tells you how many parameters are folded into the second parameter, `argv`. `argv` is an array of pointers, each of which points to a parameter.

"And," you may ask, "where do these parameters come from?" Great question! They are passed to the program by whatever entity launches the program. If you launch your program from Terminal, you can specify parameters in the Unix command line. For example, suppose we wrote a program that counted the number of words in a text file. In the Unix universe, we'd typically start the program like this:

```
$ countWords
```

The dollar sign ($) is the Unix command-line prompt, and `countWords` is the name of the program we are running. countWords might prompt us for the name of a text file and then go count its words.

Another approach would be to launch the program like so:

```
$ countWords myFile.txt
```

Now, when countWords gets launched, `argc` will have a value of 1, and `argv` will contain a single array element, a pointer to a char `array` containing the string `"myFile.txt"`. Just thought you might be wondering!

What's Next?

Congratulations! You've made it through one of the longest chapters in this book. You've mastered several new data types, including `floats` and `chars`. You've learned how to use arrays, especially in conjunction with `chars`. You've also learned about C's text-substitution mechanism, the #define preprocessor directive.

Chapter 9 will teach you how to combine C's built-in data types to create your own customized data types called `structs`. So go grab some lunch. When you return, lean back, prop up your feet, and turn the page.

CHAPTER 8 EXERCISES

1. What's wrong with each of the following code fragments?

   a.
   ```
   char    c;
   int     i;

   i=0;
   for ( c=0; c<=255; c++ )
       i += c;
   ```

   b.
   ```
   float    myFloat;

   myFloat = 5.125;
   printf( "The value of myFloat is %d.\n", f );
   ```

   c.
   ```
   char    c;

   c = "a";

   printf( "c holds the character %c.", c );
   ```

   d.
   ```
   char    c[ 5 ];

   c = "Hello, world!";
   ```

   e.
   ```
   char    c[ kMaxArraySize ]

   #define kMaxArraySize    20

   int     i;

   for ( i=0; i<kMaxArraySize; i++ )
       c[ i ] = 0;
   ```

   f.
   ```
   #define kMaxArraySize    200

   char    c[ kMaxArraySize ];

   c[ kMaxArraySize ] = 0;
   ```

   g.
   ```
   #define kMaxArraySize    200

   char    c[ kMaxArraySize ], *cPtr;
   int        i;

   cPtr = c;
   for ( i=0; i<kMaxArraySize; i++ )
       cPtr++ = 0;
   ```

h. #define kMaxArraySize   200

```
    char     c[ kMaxArraySize ];
    int         i;

    for ( i=0; i<kMaxArraySize; i++ ) {
        *c = 0;
        c++;
    }
```

i. #define kMaxArraySize   200;

2. Rewrite dice, showing the possible rolls using three dice instead of two.

3. Rewrite wordCount, printing each of the words on its own line.

Chapter 9

Designing Your Own Data Structures

C hapter 8 introduced several new data types, such as float, char, and short. We discussed the range of each type and the format specification characters necessary to print each type using printf(). Next, I introduced the concept of arrays, focusing on the relationship between char arrays and text strings. Along the way, you discovered the #define statement, C's text substitution mechanism.

This chapter will show you how to use existing C types as building blocks to design your own customized data structures.

Bundling Your Data

There will be times when your programs will want to bundle certain data together. For example, suppose you were writing a program to organize your DVD collection. Imagine the type of information you'd like to access for each DVD. At the very least, you'd want to keep track of the movie's title. You might also want to rate each DVD on a scale from one to ten. Finally, let's add in a comment field you can use to describe your feelings about the movie or perhaps note to whom you loaned this particular movie.

In the next few sections, we'll look at two separate approaches to a basic DVD-tracking program. Each approach will revolve around a different set of data structures. One will make use of arrays and the other a set of custom designed data structures.

Model A: Three Arrays

One way to model your DVD collection is with a separate array for each DVD's attributes:

```
#define kMaxDVDs            5000
#define kMaxTitleLength    256
#define kMaxCommentLength  256

char    rating[ kMaxDVDs ];
char    title[ kMaxDVDs ][ kMaxTitleLength ];
char    comment[ kMaxDVDs ][ kMaxCommentLength ];
```

This code fragment uses three #defines. kMaxDVDs defines the maximum number of DVDs this program will track. kMaxTitleLength defines the maximum length of a DVD title. kMaxCommentLength defines the maximum length of a DVD comment.

rating is an array of 5,000 chars, one char per DVD. Each of the chars in this array will hold a number from 1 to 10, the rating we've assigned to a particular DVD. This line of code assigns a value of 8 to DVD 37:

```
rating[ 37 ] = 8;    /* A pretty good DVD */
```

The arrays title and comment are each known as **multidimensional arrays**. A normal array, like rating, is declared using a single dimension. The following statement

```
float    myArray[ 5 ];
```

declares a normal or one-dimensional array containing five floats, namely:

```
myArray[ 0 ]
myArray[ 1 ]
myArray[ 2 ]
myArray[ 3 ]
myArray[ 4 ]
```

This statement

```
float      myArray[ 3 ][ 5 ];
```

declares a two-dimensional array, containing 15 floats (3 * 5 = 15), namely:

```
myArray[0][0]
myArray[0][1]
myArray[0][2]
```

```
myArray[0][3]
myArray[0][4]
myArray[1][0]
myArray[1][1]
myArray[1][2]
myArray[1][3]
myArray[1][4]
myArray[2][0]
myArray[2][1]
myArray[2][2]
myArray[2][3]
myArray[2][4]
```

Think of a two-dimensional array as an array of arrays. `myArray[0]` is an array of five `float`s. `myArray[1]` and `myArray[2]` are also arrays of five `float`s each.

Here's a three-dimensional array:

```
float        myArray[ 3 ][ 5 ][ 10 ];
```

How many `float`s does this array contain? Tick, tick, tick—got it? 3 * 5 * 10 = 150. This version of `myArray` contains 150 `float`s.

NOTE

> C allows you to create arrays of any dimension, though you'll rarely have a need for more than a single dimension.

Why would you ever want a multidimensional array? If you haven't already guessed, the answer to this question is going to lead us back to our DVD-tracking example.

Here are the declarations for our three DVD-tracking arrays:

```
#define kMaxDVDs            5000
#define kMaxTitleLength     256
#define kMaxCommentLength   256

char    rating[ kMaxDVDs ];
char    title[ kMaxDVDs ][ kMaxTitleLength ];
char    comment[ kMaxDVDs ][ kMaxCommentLength ];
```

Once again, rating contains one char per DVD. title, on the other hand, contains an array of chars whose length is kMaxTitleLength for each DVD. Each of title's arrays is large enough to hold a title up to 255 bytes long with a single byte left over to hold the terminating zero byte.

comment contains an array of chars whose length is kMaxCommentLength for each DVD. Each of comment's arrays is large enough to hold a comment up to 255 bytes long with a single byte left over to hold the terminating zero byte.

multiArray.xcodeproj

Here's a sample program that brings this concept to life. multiArray defines the two-dimensional array title (as described previously), prompts you to type a series of DVD titles, stores the titles in the two-dimensional title array, and then prints out the contents of title.

Open the *Learn C Projects* folder, go inside the folder *09.01 - multiArray*, and open the project *multiArray.xcodeproj*. Run multiArray by selecting **Build and Run** from the **Build** menu. multiArray will first tell you how many bytes of memory are allocated for the entire title array:

```
The title array takes up 1024 bytes of memory.
```

To see where this number came from, here's the declaration of title from multiArray:

```
#define kMaxDVDs            4
#define kMaxTitleLength    256

char    title[ kMaxDVDs ][ kMaxTitleLength ];
```

By performing the #define substitution yourself, you can see that title is defined as a 4-by-256 array: 4 * 256 = 1,024, matching the result reported by multiArray.

After multiArray reports the title array size, it enters a loop, prompting you for your list of favorite movies:

```
Title of DVD #1:
```

Enter a DVD title, and press Return. You'll be prompted to enter a second DVD title. Type in a total of four DVD titles, pressing Return at the end of each one.

multiArray will then step through the array, using printf() to list the DVDs you've entered. If your entire DVD collection consists entirely of classic TV boxed sets and obscure anime, feel free to use my list, shown in Figure 9-1.

Let's take a look at the source code.

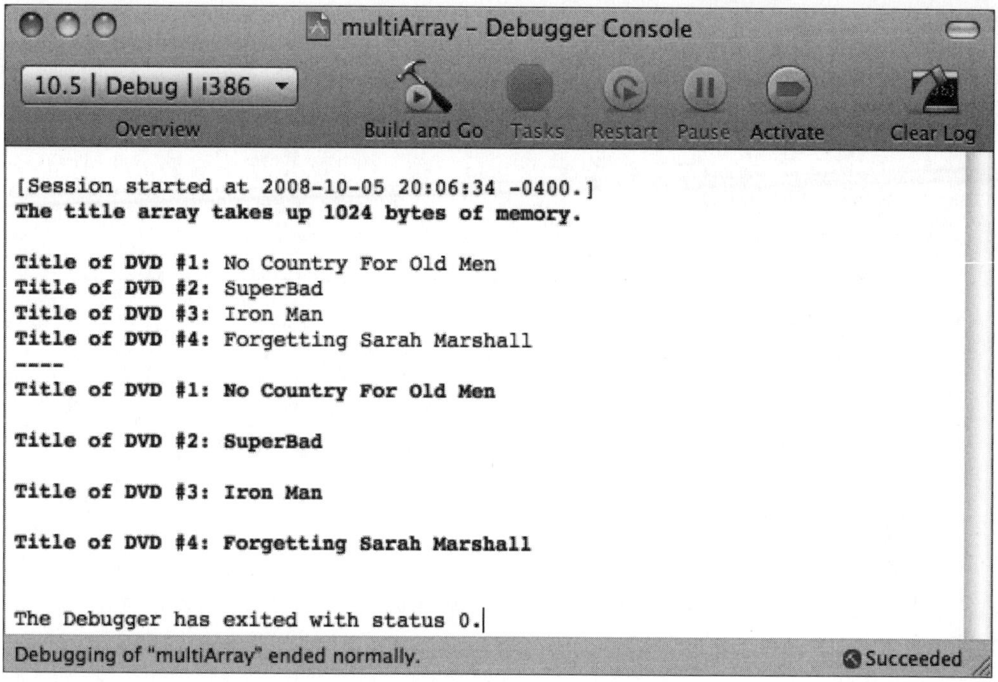

Figure 9-1. *multiArray in action. Have you seen all four of these movies?*

Stepping Through the multiArray Source Code

multiArray starts with a standard #include. <stdio.h> gives us access to both printf()
and fgets(). As a reminder, you used fgets() in Chapter 8 as an alternative to scanf() to
read a line of text from the console's input buffer (also known as stdin).

```
#include <stdio.h>
```

These two #defines will be used throughout the code:

```
#define kMaxDVDs         4
#define kMaxTitleLength  256
```

Let's look at the function prototypes for PrintDVDTitle(). PrintDVDTitle() prints out
the specified DVD title. Note the return type of void. This means that this function does not
return a value.

```
void PrintDVDTitle( int dvdNum, char title[][ kMaxTitleLength ] );
```

NOTE

> Back in the olden days, before black-hat hackers, when everyone was nice and good, programmers used a function called `gets()` to read data from the console. The problem is, just like `scanf()`, `gets()` uses a finite buffer to store a potentially infinite amount of input. Once again, `fgets()` comes to the rescue. As you saw in Chapter 8, `fgets()` asks you to specify the size of your buffer and will read at most one less `char` than will fit in the buffer, leaving you room for a trailing zero.
>
> If you look up `gets()` in the Standard Library documentation, you'll see the notation that you should not use `gets()` because of the potential for buffer overflow. Check this out for yourself: `http://www.infosys.utas.edu.au/info/documentation/C/CStdLib.html`.
>
> Here's an interesting article on buffer overflows, as used by black-hat hackers to attack individual computers and the Internet itself: `http://www.spirit.com/Network/net0999.txt`.

`main()` starts off by defining `title`, our two-dimensional array. `title` is large enough to hold four movie titles. The name of each title can be up to 255 bytes long, plus the terminating zero byte.

```
int main (int argc, const char * argv[]) {
    char    title[ kMaxDVDs ][ kMaxTitleLength ];
```

NOTE

> Once we walk through this version of multiArray, you'll find a second version that includes some error checking. The new version of `PrintDVDTitle()` checks for errors and returns an error code that lets the calling function know if an error occurs. To keep this code as simple and as easy to read as possible, I've avoided loading down my samples with an appropriate amount of error-checking code. Take a look at the second version of multiArray. Think about the differences between the two versions and what you can do to make your own code more bulletproof.

Notice anything different about the declaration of `title` in the `PrintDVDTitle()` prototype and the declaration of `title` in `main()`? We'll discuss this difference when we get to the `PrintDVDTitle()` code in a bit.

`dvdNum` is a counter used to step through each of the DVD titles in a `for` loop:

```
    short    dvdNum;
```

This `printf()` prints out the size of the `title` array. Notice that we've used the `%ld` format specifier to print the result returned by `sizeof`. `%ld` indicates that the type you are printing is the size of a long, which is true for size_t, the type returned by sizeof. If you use %ld, you won't need the (int) typecast we used in earlier programs.

```
printf( "The title array takes up %ld bytes of memory.\n\n",
            sizeof( title ) );
```

size_t is not guaranteed to be an unsigned long, though it usually is. The only guarantee is that size_t is the same size as that returned by the sizeof operator. In our case, size_t is defined as an unsigned long, so the %ld format specifier will work just fine.

Next, let's look at the loop that reads in the title names. dvdNum starts with a value of 0, is incremented by one each time through the loop, and stops as soon as dvdNum is equal to kMaxDVDs. Why "equal to kMaxDVDs"? Since dvdNum acts as an array index, it has to start with a value of 0. Since there are four elements in the array, they range in number from 0 to 3. If dvdNum is *equal* to kMaxDVDs, we need to drop out of the loop, or we'll be trying to access title[4], which does not exist. Make sense?

```
for ( dvdNum = 0; dvdNum < kMaxDVDs; dvdNum++ ) {
```

Each time through the loop, we first print out the prompt Title of DVD #, followed by the value dvdNum + 1. Though C starts its arrays with zero, in real life we start numbering things with one.

```
printf( "Title of DVD #%d: ", dvdNum + 1 );
```

Once the prompt is printed, we'll call fgets() to read in a line of text from the console. We'll store the line in the char array title[dvdNum]. We'll tell fgets() to limit input to the length of that char array, which is kMaxTitleLength. The last parameter, stdin, tells fgets() to read its input from the console, as opposed to reading from a file.

```
    fgets( title[ dvdNum ], kMaxTitleLength, stdin );
}
```

Take a look at the first parameter we passed to fgets():

title[dvdNum]

What type is this parameter? Remember, title is a two-dimensional array, and a two-dimensional array is an array of arrays. title is an array of char arrays. title[dvdNum] is an array of chars, and thus exactly suited as a parameter to fgets().

Imagine an array of chars named blap:

char   blap[100];

FINDING THE DEFINITION OF SIZE_T

Want to learn more about `size_t`? Check the documentation. Start with the C standard. Here's a link:

`http://www.open-std.org/JTC1/SC22/WG14/www/docs/n1256.pdf`

Open the standard in Acrobat, and search it for `size_t`. The first occurrence in my copy of the standard said that `size_t` was defined in `<stddef.h>`. To find the `#include` files used by a project, start by opening your project window. Click the name of the project at the top of the *Groups & Files* pane. In our case, you'd click the name *multiArray*. Next, press ⌘I, or select **Get Info** from the **File** menu to bring up the *Info* window for this project.

My project's *Info* window is shown in the following screen shot. Notice the cursor toward the bottom of the window. It points to the pop-up menu labeled *Base SDK for All Configurations*. This tells you what **software development kit (SDK)** is being used to build this project. The SDK includes the files that make up the Standard Library, other libraries, the #include files you'll need to access these libraries, and more.

To find the copy of `<stddef.h>` used by your project, go to the Finder, and open the directory /Developer/ SDKs. Next, go into the directory that matches the selection in your project *Info* window for *Base SDK for All Configurations*. In our case, that's *MacOSX10.5.sdk*. Inside that directory, go into the *usr/include* subdirectory. That is where you'll find all your include files. Cool!

To recap, you'll find the definition of `size_t` inside this file: */Developer/SDKs/MacOSX10.5.sdk/usr/include/ stddef.h*.

Feel free to open this file and search for `size_t`. I'll warn you that this is some pretty complicated code, and your head might explode a few times before you figure it all out, but knowing where this stuff lives is good. And knowing about the project *Info* window is also good. If you go back to the project *Info* window, click the *Build* tab, and scroll down to the series of heading that start with *GCC 4.0*, you'll find a ton of settings relating to compiling your project.

If you make your way all the way down to *GCC 4.0 - Warnings*, you'll see a long series of checkboxes that determine what conditions cause the compiler to issue a warning. Consider checking every single one of these checkboxes (take a screen shot of the screen first, just in case you want to go back to your original settings), and then rebuild your code. Spend some time looking through all the project window tabs. You'll find a ton of useful settings in there.

You'd have no problem passing blap as a parameter to fgets(), right? fgets() would read the characters from the input buffer and place them in blap. title[0] is just like blap. Both are pointers to an array of chars. blap[0] is the first char of the array blap. Likewise, title[0][0] is the first char of the array title[0].

OK, let's get back to the code.

Once we drop out of the loop, we print a dividing line and then loop on a call to PrintDVDTitle() to print the contents of our array of DVD titles. The first parameter to PrintDVDTitle() specifies the number of the DVD you want printed. The second parameter is the title array pointer.

```
printf( "----\n" );

for ( dvdNum = 0; dvdNum < kMaxDVDs; dvdNum++ )
    PrintDVDTitle( dvdNum, title );
```

Finally, we return 0 and thus end main():

```
    return 0;
}
```

Take a look at the definition of `PrintDVDTitle()`'s second parameter. Notice that the first of the two dimensions is missing (the first pair of brackets is empty). While we could have included the first dimension (kMaxDVDs), the fact that we were able to leave it out makes a really interesting point. When memory is allocated for an array, it is allocated as one big block. To access a specific element of the array, the compiler uses the dimensions of the array, as well as the specific element requested to calculate an offset into this block.

```
void    PrintDVDTitle( int dvdNum, char title[][ kMaxTitleLength ] ) {
    printf( "Title of DVD #%d: %s\n",
            dvdNum + 1, title[ dvdNum ] );
}
```

In the case of `title`, the compiler allocated a block of memory 1,024 bytes long. Think of this block as four char arrays, each of which is 256 bytes long (4 * 256 = 1,024). To get to the first byte of the first array, we just use the pointer that was passed in (`title` points to the first byte of the first of the four arrays). To access the first byte of the second array (in C notation, `title[1][0]`) the compiler adds 256 to the pointer `title`. In other words, the start of the second array is 256 bytes further in memory than the start of the first array. The start of the fourth array is 768 bytes (3 * 256 = 768) further in memory than the start of the first array.

While it is nice to know how to compute array offsets in memory, the point I'm going for here is that the compiler calculates the `title` array offsets using the second dimension and not the first dimension of `title` (256 is used; 4 is not used).

You might expect the compiler to use the first array bound (4) to verify that you don't reference an array element that is **out of bounds**. For example, you might expect the compiler to complain if it sees this line of code:

```
title[5][0] = '\0';
```

Guess what? C compilers don't do bounds checking of any kind. If you want to access memory beyond the bounds of your array, no one will stop you. This is part of the "charm" of C—it gives you the freedom to write programs that crash in spectacular ways. Your job is to learn how to avoid such pitfalls.

Take another look at the `printf()` inside `PrintDVDTitle()`:

```
    printf( "Title of DVD #%d: %s\n",
            dvdNum + 1, title[ dvdNum ] );
```

Note the two format specifiers. The first, %d, is used to print the DVD number. The second, %s, is used to print the DVD title itself. The \n at the end of the string is used to force a carriage return between each of the DVD titles.

Getting Rid of the Extra Carriage Return

If you look back at Figure 9-1, you might notice an extra carriage return after each line of output produced by PrintDVDTitle(). Just as was the case in our nameGood project in Chapter 8, we'll want to replace that carriage return with a terminating zero. Add this line of code just after the call to fgets():

```
title[ dvdNum ][ strlen( title[ dvdNum ] ) - 1 ] = '\0';
```

Note that you'll need to add a #include <string.h> to the top of the file to access the strlen() function. This line of code finds the length of the string that was just typed in. Remember, that string includes a carriage return at the very end of it. We subtract one from the length, and then write a zero right where the carriage return sits, making the string 1 byte shorter. This line of code is so complex, it would be better served if it were broken into pieces and wrapped in its own function.

Here's a function that does the same thing:

```
void    ReplaceReturnAtEndOfString( char *theString ) {
    int     length = strlen( theString );

    theString[ length - 1 ] = '\0';
}
```

In the next section, we'll add some error handling code to our program, as well as a call to ReplaceReturnAtEndOfString().

Adding Error Handling

As I mentioned earlier in this chapter, the sample code in this book does not do any error checking. Many of the Standard Library functions return error codes if something goes wrong during their execution. Again, to keep things simple, I've ignored those error codes. As your programming skills mature, you'll want to add error handling to every one of your programs. You'll want to check any error codes returned by functions you call. Error checking is incredibly important.

To give you a sense of how an error-checking scheme might work, I've included a new version of multiArray with a basic error-handling scheme. I've also added in the ReplaceReturnAtEndOfString() function I described in the previous section.

You'll find the new version of multiArray in the *Learn C Projects* folder, in the *09.02 – multiArrayWithErrCode* subfolder. Open the project *multiArrayWithErrCode.xcodeproj*.

When you run the project, it will look just like the previous version of multiArray, with one exception. As you can see from Figure 9-2, the extra carriage return after each line of output has been removed. Let's take a look at the source code.

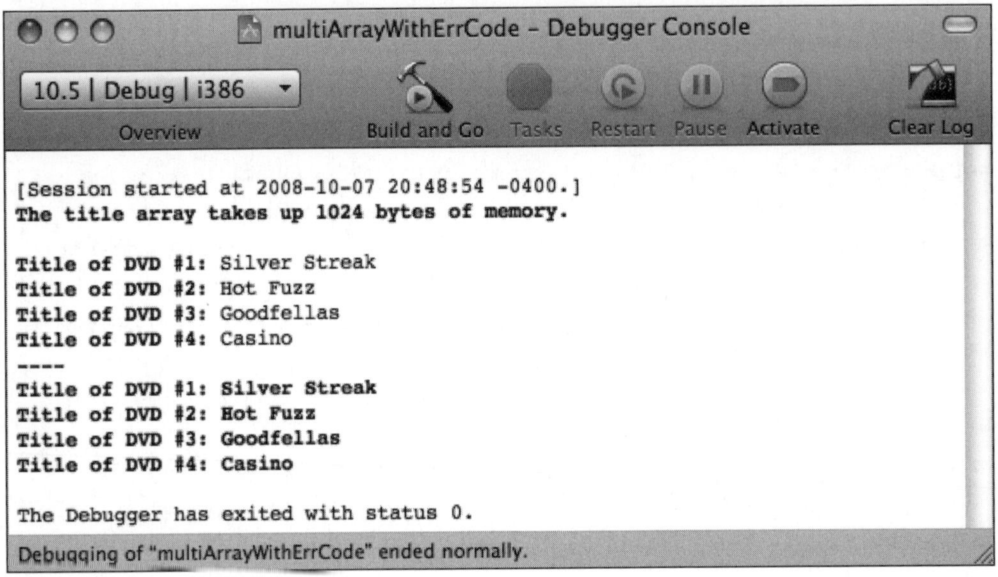

Figure 9-2. *This version of multiArray includes error handling as well as a call to the function ReplaceReturnAtEndOfString(). Notice that the extra carriage returns have been removed from the output strings.*

Walking Through the multiArrayWithErrCode Source Code

Our new version start with two #includes. The second one gives us access to `strlen()`, which is called in the function `ReplaceReturnAtEndOfString()`.

```
#include <stdio.h>
#include <string.h>
```

You've seen our first two #defines already. kError_none is used to signify success, kError_printf indicates a problem with a `printf()` call, and kError_fgets indicates a problem with an `fgets()` call.

```
#define  kMaxDVDs            4
#define  kMaxTitleLength     256
#define  kError_printf       -1
#define  kError_fgets        -2
#define  kError_none         0
```

Here are the prototypes for `PrintDVDTitle()` and `ReplaceReturnAtEndOfString()`. Notice that `PrintDVDTitle()` returns an `int`. As you'll see, it returns either kError_printf or kError_none. ReplaceReturnAtEndOfString() does not return an error code, as it does not call any functions that return an error code.

```
int     PrintDVDTitle( int dvdNum, char title[][ kMaxTitleLength ] );
void    ReplaceReturnAtEndOfString( char *theString );
```

main() starts as it did before but adds a variable named result to capture the value returned by fgets() and error to catch the value returned by printf():

```
int main (int argc, const char * argv[]) {
    char    title[ kMaxDVDs ][ kMaxTitleLength ];
    short   dvdNum;
    char    *result;
    int     error;
```

According to the C standard, printf() returns a negative value if it encounters an error. In that case, main() exits by returning the value kError_printf to the calling program:

```
    error = printf( "The title array takes up %ld bytes of memory.\n\n",
                    sizeof( title ) );

    if ( error < 0 )
        return kError_printf;
```

We use the same approach inside the for loop, exiting the program if we encounter an error with printf():

```
    for ( dvdNum = 0; dvdNum < kMaxDVDs; dvdNum++ ) {
        error = printf( "Title of DVD #%d: ", dvdNum + 1 );
        if ( error < 0 )
            return kError_printf;
```

fgets() returns NULL if it encounters an error. In that case, we exit the program with an error code of kError_fgets. If there was no error, we replace the carriage return at the end of the string with a zero byte terminator and then go back to the top of the for loop. When the for loop completes, we print the dividing line and check for an error again.

```
        result = fgets( title[ dvdNum ], kMaxTitleLength, stdin );
        if ( result == NULL ) {
            error = printf( "*** ERROR reported by fgets ***" );
            return kError_fgets;
        }
        ReplaceReturnAtEndOfString( title[ dvdNum ] );
    }

    error = printf( "----\n" );
    if ( error < 0 )
            return kError_printf;
```

In the second for loop, we check for the error returned by `PrintDVDTitle()` and exit the program if an error occurred. Once the loop exits, we return normally.

```
    for ( dvdNum = 0; dvdNum < kMaxDVDs; dvdNum++ ) {
        error = PrintDVDTitle( dvdNum, title );
        if ( error != kError_none )
            return error;
    }

    return 0;
}
```

`PrintDVDTitle()` returns an error if `printf()` returns one; otherwise, it returns kError_none:

```
int    PrintDVDTitle( int dvdNum, char title[][ kMaxTitleLength ] ) {
    int error;

    error=printf( "Title of DVD #%d: %s\n", dvdNum + 1, title[ dvdNum ] );
    if ( error < 0 )
        return kError_printf;
    else
        return kError_none;
}
```

`ReplaceReturnAtEndOfString()` does what you expect. There's no error for it to return, as `strlen()` does not return an error code:

```
void    ReplaceReturnAtEndOfString( char *theString ) {
    int    length = strlen( theString );

    theString[ length - 1 ] = '\0';
}
```

Bottom line—you should add error handling to your programs. For the remainder of this book, I'm going to stick with the simple approach to keep the code clean and readable. But please don't take that as a sign that error handling is not important. To be clear, error handling is vital and makes finding bugs in your code much simpler.

Finishing Up With Model A

Back in the beginning of the chapter, we described a program that would track your DVD collection. The goal was to look at two different approaches to solving the same problem.

The first approach, model A, uses three arrays to hold a rating, title, and comment for each DVD in the collection:

```
#define kMaxDVDs            5000
#define kMaxTitleLength     256
#define kMaxCommentLength   256

char    rating[ kMaxDVDs ];
char    title[ kMaxDVDs ][ kMaxTitleLength ];
char    comment[ kMaxDVDs ][ kMaxCommentLength ];
```

Before we move on to model B, let's take a closer look at the memory used by the model A arrays:

- The array `rating` uses 1 byte per DVD (enough for a 1-byte rating from 1 to 10).

- The array `title` uses 256 bytes per DVD (enough for a text string holding the movie title, up to 255 bytes in length, plus the terminating byte).

- The array `comment` also uses 256 bytes per DVD (enough for a text string holding a comment about the DVD, up to 255 bytes in length, plus the terminating byte).

Add those three together and you find that model A allocates 513 bytes per DVD. Since model A allocates space for 5,000 DVDs when it declares its three key arrays, it uses 2,565,000 bytes (5,000 * 513 = 2,565,000).

Since the program really only needs 513 bytes per DVD, wouldn't it be nice if you could allocate the memory for a DVD when you need it? With this type of approach, if your collection only consisted of 50 DVDs, you'd only have to use 25,650 bytes of memory (50 * 513 = 25,650), instead of 2,565,000.

NOTE

Memory usage is just one factor to take into account when deciding which data structures to use in your program. Another is ease of use. If you have plenty of memory available, model A takes less time to implement and is much easier to work with—in that case, memory be damned; go for the simpler solution. The cool thing about being the programmer is that you get to decide what's best in any given situation.

As you'll see by the end of this chapter, C provides a mechanism for allocating memory as you need it. Model B takes a first step toward memory efficiency by creating a single data structure that contains all the information relevant to a single DVD. Later in this chapter, you'll learn how to allocate just enough memory for a single structure.

Model B: The Data Structure Approach

As stated earlier, our DVD program must keep track of a rating (from 1 to 10), the DVD's title, and a comment about the DVD:

```
#define kMaxDVDs            5000
#define kMaxTitleLength     256
#define kMaxCommentLength   256

char    rating[ kMaxDVDs ];
char    title[ kMaxDVDs ][ kMaxTitleLength ];
char    comment[ kMaxDVDs ][ kMaxCommentLength ];
```

C provides the perfect mechanism for wrapping all three of these variables in one tidy bundle. A `struct` allows you to associate any number of variables together under a single name. Here's an example of a `struct` declaration:

```
#define kMaxTitleLength       256
#define kMaxCommentLength     256

struct DVDInfo {
    char    rating;
    char    title[ kMaxTitleLength ];
    char    comment[ kMaxCommentLength ];
}
```

This `struct` **type declaration** creates a new type called DVDInfo. Just as you'd use a type like short or float to declare a variable, you can use this new type to declare an individual struct. Here's an example:

```
struct DVDInfo    myInfo;
```

This line of code uses the previous type declaration as a template to create an individual struct. The compiler uses the type declaration to tell it how much memory to allocate for the struct and allocates a block of memory large enough to hold all of the individual variables that make up the struct.

The variables that form the struct are known as **fields**. A struct of type DVDInfo has three fields: a char named rating, an array of chars named title, and an array of chars named comment. To access the fields of a struct, use the . operator (C programmers typically pronounce this as the "dot" operator). Here's an example:

```
struct DVDInfo    myInfo;

myInfo.rating = 7;
```

Notice the . between the struct name (myInfo) and the field name (rating). The . following a struct name tells the compiler that a field name is to follow.

structSize.xcodeproj

Here's a program that demonstrates the declaration of a struct type, as well as the definition of an individual struct. Open the *Learn C Projects* folder, go inside the folder *09.03 - structSize*, and open the project *structSize.xcodeproj*. Run structSize.

Compare your output with the console window shown in Figure 9-3. They should be the same. The first three lines of output show the rating, title, and comment fields. To the right of each field name, you'll find printed the number of bytes of memory allocated to that field. The last line of output shows the memory allocated to the entire struct.

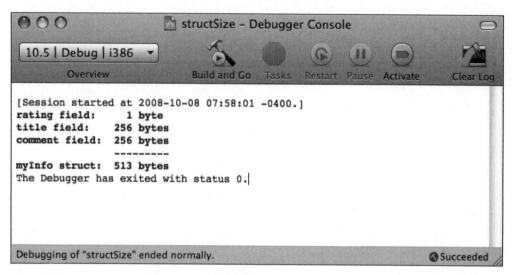

Figure 9-3. *structSize shows the size of a DVDInfo struct.*

Stepping Through the structSize Source Code

If you haven't done so already, quit structSize, and take a minute to look over the source code in *main.c*. Once you feel comfortable with it, read on.

main.c starts off with our standard #include along with a brand-new one:

```
#include <stdio.h>
#include "structSize.h"
```

The angle brackets (<>) that surround all the #include files we've seen so far tell the compiler to look in the #include file directories that it knows about. When you surround the include file name by double quotes ("") instead of angle brackets, like those around "structSize.h" in this example, you are telling the compiler to look for this #include file in the same folder as the including source code file.

Regardless of where it locates the #include file, the compiler treats the contents of the #include file as if it were actually inside the including file. In this case, the compiler treats <stdio.h> and "structSize.h" as if they were directly inside *main.c*. Strictly speaking, the preprocessor loads the #include file inside its copy of the including file before control is handed off to the compiler.

NOTE

As you've already seen, C #include files typically end in the two characters *.h*. Though you can give your #include files any name you like, the *.h* convention is one you should definitely stick with. #include files are also known as header files, which is where the "h" comes from.

Let's take a look at *structSize.h*. One way to do this is to select **Open...** from the **File** menu, navigate into the same directory as the *structSize.xcodeproj* project, and select the file.

A simpler way to do this is to use Xcode's #include file pop-up menu, shown in Figure 9-4. In the project window, look toward the right side of the window, just above the vertical scrollbar, for a pop-up menu whose label is in the shape of a *#*. Click the pop-up, and select *structSize.h* from the menu. A new window will open containing *structSize.h*. Note that this pop-up includes all included files, as well as the including file. In this case, the menu includes *stdio.h* and *main.c*.

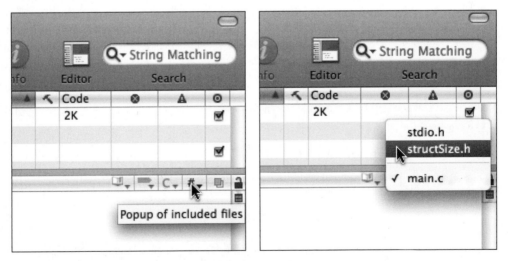

Figure 9-4. *Selecting an include file from Xcode's include file pop-up.*

Still another method is to type the character sequence ⌘⌥↑, which will toggle between the including file and the #include files.

NOTE

#include files typically contain things like #defines, global variables, and function prototypes. By embedding these things in an #include file, you remove clutter from your source code file, and more importantly, you make this common source code available to other source code files via a single #include.

structSize.h starts off with two #defines you've seen before.

```
#define kMaxTitleLength    256
#define kMaxCommentLength  256
```

Next comes the declaration of the struct type, DVDInfo:

```
/**********************/
/* Struct Declarations */
/**********************/
struct DVDInfo {
    char    rating;
    char    title[ kMaxTitleLength ];
    char    comment[ kMaxCommentLength ];
};
```

By including the header file at the top of the file (where we might place our globals), we've made the DVDInfo struct type available to all of the functions inside *main.c*. If we placed the DVDInfo type declaration inside of main() instead, our program would still have worked (as long as we placed it before the definition of myInfo), but we would not have access to the DVDInfo type outside of main().

That's all that was in the header file *structSize.h*. Back in *main.c*, main() starts by defining a DVDInfo struct named myInfo. myInfo has three fields: myInfo.rating, myInfo.title, and myInfo.comment.

```
int main (int argc, const char * argv[]) {
    struct DVDInfo    myInfo;
```

The next three statements print the size of the three myInfo fields. Notice that we are again using the %ld format specifier to print the value returned by sizeof.

```
    printf( "rating field:     %ld byte\n",
            sizeof( myInfo.rating ) );

    printf( "title field:    %ld bytes\n",
            sizeof( myInfo.title ) );

    printf( "comment field:     %ld bytes\n",
            sizeof( myInfo.comment ) );
```

This next `printf()` prints a separator line, purely for aesthetics. Notice the way everything lines up in Figure 9-3?

```
printf( "                    --------\n" );
```

Finally, we print the total number of bytes allocated to the `struct`. Do the numbers add up? They should!

```
printf( "myInfo struct: %ld bytes",
        sizeof( myInfo ) );

    return 0;
}
```

As it turns out, on some computers, the numbers will *not* add up. Here's why: Some computers follow rules to keep various data types lined up a certain way. For example, on old 680x0 machines, the compiler forces all data larger than a `char` to start on an even-byte boundary (at an even memory address). A `long` will always start at an even address. A `short` will always start at an even address. A `struct`, no matter its size, will always start at an even address. Conversely, a `char` or array of `chars` can start at either an odd or even address. In addition, on a 680x0 machine, a `struct` must always have an even number of bytes.

NOTE

> In our example, the three `struct` fields are all either `chars` or arrays of `chars`, so they are all allowed to start at either an odd or even address. The three fields total 103 bytes. Since a `struct` on a 680x0 must always have an even number of bytes, the compiler adds an extra byte (known as **padding** or a **pad byte**) at the end of the `struct`.

You might never see an example of this, but it is worth remembering that data alignment rules are not specific to the C language and can vary from CPU type to CPU type. When in doubt, write some code, and try it out.

Passing a struct As a Parameter

Think back to the DVD-tracking program we've been discussing throughout this chapter. We started off with three separate arrays, each of which tracked a separate element. One array stored the rating field, another stored the movie's title, and the third stored a pithy comment.

We then introduced the concept of a structure that would group all the elements of one DVD together, in a single `struct`. One advantage of a `struct` is that you can pass all the information about a DVD using a single pointer. Imagine a routine called `PrintDVD()`, designed to print the three elements that describe a single DVD. Using the original array-based model, we'd have to pass three parameters to PrintDVD():

```c
void    PrintDVD( char rating, char *title, char *comment ) {
    printf( "rating: %d\n", rating );
    printf( "title: %s\n", title );
    printf( "comment: %s\n", comment );
}
```

Using the struct-based model, however, we could pass the information using a single pointer. As a reminder, here's the DVDInfo struct declaration again:

```c
#define kMaxTitleLength        256
#define kMaxCommentLength      256


/***********************/
/* Struct Declarations */
/***********************/
struct DVDInfo {
    char    rating;
    char    title[ kMaxTitleLength ];
    char    comment[ kMaxCommentLength ];
};
```

This version of main() defines a DVDInfo struct and passes its address to a new version of PrintDVD() (we'll get to it next):

```c
int main (int argc, const char * argv[]) {
    struct DVDInfo     myInfo;

    PrintDVD( &myInfo );

    return 0;
}
```

Just as has been the case in earlier programs, passing the address of a variable to a function gives that function the ability to modify the original variable. Passing the address of myInfo to PrintDVD() gives PrintDVD() the ability to modify the three myInfo fields. Though our new version of PrintDVD() doesn't modify myInfo, it's important to know that the opportunity exists. Here's the new, struct-based version of PrintDVD():

```c
void    PrintDVD( struct DVDInfo *myDVDPtr ) {
    printf( "rating: %d\n", (*myDVDPtr).rating );
    printf( "title: %s\n", myDVDPtr->title );
    printf( "comment: %s\n", myDVDPtr->comment );
}
```

Notice that `PrintDVD()` receives its parameter as a pointer to (i.e., the address of) a DVDInfo struct. The first `printf()` uses the `*` operator to turn the `struct` pointer back to the struct it points to and then uses the `.` operator to access the `rating` field:

```
(*myDVDPtr).rating
```

C features a special operator, `->`, that lets you accomplish the exact same thing. The `->` operator is binary. That is, it requires both a left and right operand. The left operand is a pointer to a `struct`, and the right operand is the `struct` field. The following notation

```
myDVDPtr->rating
```

is exactly the same as

```
(*myDVDPtr).rating
```

Use whichever form you prefer. In general, most C programmers use the `->` operator to get from a `struct`'s pointer to one of the `struct`'s fields.

Passing a Copy of the struct

Here's a version of `main()` that passes the `struct` itself, instead of its address:

```
int main (int argc, const char * argv[]) {
    struct DVDInfo    myInfo;

    PrintDVD( myInfo );
}
```

As always, when the compiler encounters a function parameter, it passes a copy of the parameter to the receiving routine. The previous version of `PrintDVD()` received a copy of the address of a DVDInfo struct.

In this new version of `PrintDVD()`, the compiler passes a copy of the entire DVDInfo struct, not just a copy of its address. This copy of the DVDInfo struct includes copies of the rating field, and the title and comment arrays.

```
void    PrintDVD( struct DVDInfo myDVD ) {
    printf( "rating: %d\n", myDVD.rating );
    printf( "title: %s\n", myDVD.title );
    printf( "comment: %s\n", myDVD.comment );
}
```

<u>NOTE</u>

When a function exits, all of its local variables (except for `static` variables, which we'll cover in Chapter 11) are no longer available. This means that any changes you make to a local parameter are lost when the function returns. If this version of `PrintDVD()` made changes to its local copy of the `DVDInfo` struct, those changes would be lost when `PrintDVD()` returned.

Sometimes, you'll want to pass a copy of a `struct`. One advantage this technique offers is that there's no way that the receiving function can modify the original `struct`. Another advantage is that it offers a simple mechanism for making a copy of a `struct`. A disadvantage of this technique is that copying a `struct` takes time and uses memory. Though time won't usually be a problem, memory usage might be, especially if your `struct` gets pretty large. Just be aware that whatever you pass as a parameter is going to get copied by the compiler. Pass a `struct` as a parameter, and the compiler will copy the `struct`. Pass a pointer to a `struct`, and the compiler will copy the pointer.

paramAddress.xcodeproj

There's a sample program in the *Learn C Projects* folder, inside a subfolder named *09.04 - paramAddress*, that should help show the difference between passing the address of a `struct` and passing a copy of the `struct`. Open and run *paramAddress.xcodeproj*.

`main()` defines a `DVDInfo` struct named `myDVD` and prints the address of `myDVD`'s `rating` field:

```
printf( "Address of myDVD.rating in main():              %p\n",
        &(myDVD.rating) );
```

Notice that we print an address using the %p format specifier. The "p" stands for pointer. This is the proper way to print an address in C. Here's the output of this `printf()` on my computer:

```
Address of myDVD.rating in main():              0xbffff559
```

Next, `main()` passes the address of `myDVD` as well as `myDVD` itself as parameters to a routine named `PrintParamInfo()`:

```
PrintParamInfo( &myDVD, myDVD );
```

Here's the prototype for `PrintParamInfo()`:

```
void    PrintParamInfo( struct DVDInfo *myDVDPtr,
                struct DVDInfo myDVDCopy );
```

The first parameter is a pointer to main()'s myDVD struct. The second parameter is a copy of the same struct. PrintParamInfo() prints the address of the rating field of each version of myDVD:

```
printf( "Address of myDVDPtr->rating in PrintParamInfo(): %p\n",
        &(myDVDPtr->rating) );
printf( "Address of myDVDCopy.rating in PrintParamInfo(): %p\n",
        &(myDVDCopy.rating) );
```

Here are the results, including the line of output generated by main():

```
Address of myDVD.rating in main():                  0xbffff559
Address of myDVDPtr->rating in PrintParamInfo(): 0xbffff559
Address of myDVDCopy.rating in PrintParamInfo(): 0xbffff4d4
```

Notice that the rating field accessed via a pointer has the same address as the original rating field in main()'s myDVD struct. If PrintParamInfo() uses the first parameter to modify the rating field, it will, in effect, be changing main()'s rating field.

If PrintParamInfo() uses the second parameter to modify the rating field, main()'s rating field will remain untouched.

NOTE

By the way, most programmers use **hexadecimal** notation (**hex** for short) when they print addresses. Hex notation represents numbers as base 16 instead of the normal base 10 you are used to. Instead of the 10 digits 0 through 9, hex features the 16 digits 0, 1, 2, 3, 4, 5, 6, 7, 8, 9, a, b, c, d, e, and f. Each digit of a number represents a successive power of 16 instead of successive powers of 10.

For example, the number 532 in base ten is equal to $5 * 10^2 + 3 * 10^1 + 2 * 10^0 = 5 * 100 + 3 * 10 + 2 * 1$. The number 532 in hex is equal to $5 * 16^2 + 3 * 16^1 + 2 * 16^0 = 5 * 256 + 3 * 16 + 2 * 1 = 1,330$ in base 10. The number ff in hex is equal to $15 * 16 + 15 * 1 = 255$ in base 10. Remember, the hex digit f has a decimal (base 10) value of 15.

To represent a hex constant in C, preceded it by the characters 0x. The constant 0xff has a decimal value of 255. The constant 0xFF also has a decimal value of 255. C doesn't distinguish between uppercase and lowercase when representing hex digits.

struct Arrays

Just as you can declare an array of chars or ints, you can also declare an array of structs:

```
#define kMaxDVDs    5000

struct DVDInfo    myDVDs[ kMaxDVDs ];
```

This declaration creates an array of 5,000 structs of type DVDInfo. The array is named myDVDs. Each of the 5,000 structs will have the three fields rating, title, and comment. You access the fields of the structs as you might expect. Here's an example (note the use of the all-important . operator):

```
myDVDs[ 10 ].rating = 9;
```

We now have an equivalent to our first DVD tracking data structure. Where the first model used three arrays, we now have a solution that uses a single array. As you'll see when you start writing your own programs, packaging your data in a struct makes life a bit simpler. Instead of passing three parameters each time you need to pass a DVD to a function, you can simply pass a struct.

From a memory standpoint, both DVD-tracking solutions cost the same. With three separate arrays, the cost is as follows:

```
                    5,000 bytes /*rating array*/
5,000 * 256 = 1,280,000 bytes /*title array*/
5,000 * 256 = 1,280,000 bytes /*comment array*/
              ---------------
Total         2,565,000 bytes
```

With an array of structs, this is the cost:

```
5,000 * 513 = 2,565,000 bytes     /*Cost of array of 5,000 DVDInfo structs*/
```

So what can we do to cut this memory cost down? Thought you'd never ask!

Allocating Your Own Memory

One of the limitations of an array-based DVD-tracking model is that arrays are not resizable. When you define an array, you have to specify exactly how many elements make up your array.

For example, this code defines an array of 5,000 DVDInfo structs:

```
#define kMaxDVDs    5000

struct DVDInfo    myDVDs[ kMaxDVDs ];
```

As we calculated earlier, this array will take up 2,565,000 bytes of memory, whether we use the array to track 1 DVD or 5,000. If you know in advance exactly how many elements your array requires, arrays are just fine. In the case of our DVD-tracking program, using an array just isn't practical. For example, if my DVD collection consists entirely of a test DVD that came with my DVD burner and a rare bootleg of *Gilligan's Island* outtakes, a 5,000 struct array is overkill. Even worse, what happens if I've got more than 5,000 DVDs? No matter what number I pick for kMaxDVDs, there's always the chance that it won't prove large enough.

The problem here is that arrays are just not flexible enough to do what we want. Instead of trying to predict the amount of memory we'll need in advance, we need a method that will give us a chunk of memory the exact size of a DVDInfo struct, as we need it. In more technical terms, we need to allocate and manage our own memory.

When your program starts running, your operating system (Mac OS X, Unix, and Vista are all examples of operating systems) carves out a chunk of memory for the exclusive use of your application.

Some of this memory is used to hold the object code that makes up your application. Still more of it is used to hold things like your application's global variables. As your application runs, some of this memory will be allocated to main()'s local variables. When main() calls a function, memory is allocated for that function's local variables. When that function returns, the memory allocated for its local variables is freed up, made available to be allocated all over again.

In the next few sections, you'll learn about some functions you can call to allocate a block of memory and to free the memory (to return it to the pool of available memory). Ultimately, we'll combine these functions with a data structure called a linked list to provide a more memory efficient, more flexible alternative to the array.

Using malloc()

The Standard Library function malloc() allows you to allocate a block of memory of a specified size. To access malloc(), you'll need to include the file <stdlib.h>:

```
#include <stdlib.h>
```

malloc() takes a single parameter, the size of the requested block, in bytes. malloc() returns a pointer to the newly allocated block of memory. Here's the function prototype:

```
void *malloc( size_t size );
```

If malloc() can't allocate a block of memory the size you requested, it returns a pointer with the value NULL. NULL is a constant, usually defined to have a value of zero, used to specify an invalid pointer. In other words, a pointer with a value of NULL does not point to a legal memory address. You'll learn more about NULL and (void *) as we use them in our examples.

Here's a code fragment that allocates a single DVDInfo struct:

```
struct DVDInfo     *myDVDPtr;

myDVDPtr = malloc( sizeof( struct DVDInfo ) );
```

> **NOTE**
>
> The parameter is declared to be of type `size_t`, the same type returned by `sizeof`. Think of `size_t` as equivalent to an `unsigned long` (it's `unsigned` in that it only takes on positive values, and it's the size of a `long`). Note also that `malloc()` returns the type `(void *)`, a pointer to a `void`. A `void` pointer is essentially a generic pointer. Since there's no such thing as a variable of type `void`, the type `(void *)` is used to declare a pointer to a block of memory whose type has not been determined.
>
> In general, you'll convert the `(void *)` returned by `malloc()` to the pointer type you really want. Read on to see an example of this.

The first line of code declares a new variable, `myDVDPtr`, which is a pointer to a `DVDInfo` struct. At this time, `myDVDPtr` doesn't point to a `DVDInfo` struct. You've just told the compiler that `myDVDPtr` is designed to point to a `DVDInfo` struct.

The second line of code calls `malloc()` to create a block of memory the size of a `DVDInfo` struct. `sizeof` returns its result as a `size_t`, the type we need to pass as a parameter to `malloc()`. How convenient!

Converting the Type Returned by malloc()

On the right side of the `=` operator, we've got a `(void *)`, and on the left side, we've got a `(struct DVDInfo *)`. The compiler automatically resolves this type difference for us. We could have used a typecast here to make this more explicit:

```
myDVDPtr = (struct DVDInfo *)malloc( sizeof(struct DVDInfo) );
```

Though this explicit typecast isn't strictly necessary, it makes our intentions quite clear and allows the compiler to step in with a warning if we've got our types confused. Don't worry if this is confusing. We'll get into typecasting in Chapter 11.

Checking the malloc() Return Value

If `malloc()` was able to allocate a block of memory the size of a `DVDInfo` struct, `myDVDPtr` contains the address of the first byte of this new block. If `malloc()` was unable to allocate our new block (perhaps there wasn't enough unallocated memory left), `myDVDPtr` will be set to `NULL`. Notice that I placed `NULL` on the left side of the `==` operator. This is a good habit to get into. It protects you if you accidentally type `=` instead of `==`, since the compiler will complain if you try to change the value of `NULL`.

```
if ( NULL == myDVDPtr )
    printf( "Couldn't allocate the new block!\n" );
else
    printf( "Allocated the new block!\n" );
```

If `malloc()` succeeded, `myDVDPtr` points to a `struct` of type `DVDInfo`. For the duration of the program, we can use `myDVDPtr` to access the fields of this newly allocated `struct`:

```
myDVDPtr->rating = 7;
```

You need to understand the difference between a block of memory allocated using `malloc()` and a block of memory that corresponds to a local variable. When a function declares a local variable, the memory associated with that variable is temporary. As soon as the function exits, the block of memory associated with that memory is returned to the pool of available memory.

A block of memory that you allocate using `malloc()` sticks around until you specifically return it to the pool of available memory or until your program exits.

free()

The Standard Library provides a function, called `free()`, that returns a previously allocated block of memory back to the pool of available memory. Here's the function prototype:

```
void    free( void *ptr );
```

`free()` takes a single argument, a pointer to the first byte of a previously allocated block of memory. The following line returns the block allocated earlier to the free memory pool:

```
free( myDVDPtr );
```

Use `malloc()` to allocate a block of memory. Use `free()` to free up a block of memory allocated via `malloc()`. You are responsible for freeing up any memory that you allocate. You create it; you free it. That said, when a program exits, the operating system automatically frees up all memory allocated by that program.

CAUTION

> Never put a fork in an electrical outlet. Never pass an address to `free()` that didn't come from `malloc()`. Both will make you extremely unhappy!

Keeping Track of That Address!

The address returned by `malloc()` is critical. If you lose it, you've lost access to the block of memory you just allocated. Even worse, you can never `free()` the block, and it will just sit there, wasting valuable memory, for the duration of your program.

One great way to lose a block's address is to call `malloc()` inside a function, saving the address returned by `malloc()` in a local variable. When the function exits, your local variable goes away, taking the address of your new block with it!

There are many ways to keep track of a newly allocated block of memory. As you design your program, you'll figure out which approach makes the most sense for your particular situation. One technique you'll find very useful is to place the pointer inside a special data structure known as a linked list.

Working with Linked Lists

The linked list is one of the most widely used data structures in C. A **linked list** is a series of `struct`s, each of which contains, as a field, a pointer. Each `struct` in the series uses its pointer to point to the next `struct` in the series. Figure 9-5 shows a linked list containing three elements.

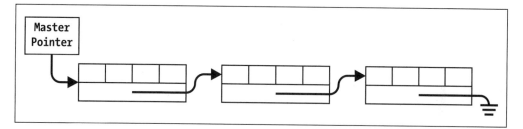

Figure 9-5. *This linked list contains three elements. The master pointer points to the first element in the list. The first element contains a pointer that points to the second element in the list, and so on. The last element contains a NULL pointer.*

A linked list starts with a **master pointer**. The master pointer is a pointer variable, typically a global, that points to the first `struct` in the list, also known as the **head**. This first `struct` contains a field, also a pointer, which points to the second `struct` in the linked list. The second `struct` contains a pointer field that points to the third element. The linked list in Figure 9-5 ends with the third element. The pointer field in the last element of a linked list is typically set to NULL. The last element in the list is known as the **tail**.

NOTE

The notation used at the end of the linked list in Figure 9-5 is borrowed from our friends in electrical engineering. The funky three-line symbol at the end of the last pointer represents a NULL pointer.

Why Use Linked Lists?

Linked lists allow you to be extremely memory efficient. Using a linked list, you can imple-ment our DVD-tracking data structure, allocating exactly the number of structs that you need. Each time a DVD is added to your collection, you'll allocate a new struct and add it to the linked list.

A linked list starts out as a single master pointer. When you want to add an element to the list, call malloc() to allocate a block of memory for the new element. Next, make the master pointer point to the new block. Finally, set the new block's next element pointer to NULL.

Creating a Linked List

The first step in creating a linked list is the design of the main link, the linked list struct. Here's a sample:

```
#define kMaxTitleLength        256
#define kMaxCommentLength      256

struct DVDInfo {
    char              rating;
    char              title[ kMaxTitleLength ];
    char              comment[ kMaxCommentLength ];
    struct DVDInfo    *next;
}
```

The change here is the addition of a fourth field, a pointer to a DVDInfo struct. The next field is the key to connecting two different DVDInfo structs together. If myFirstPtr is a pointer to one DVDInfo struct and mySecondPtr is a pointer to a second struct, this line

```
myFirstPtr->next = mySecondPtr;
```

connects the two structs. Once they are connected, you can use a pointer to the first struct to access the second struct's fields! For example, the following line sets the rating field of the second struct to 7:

```
myFirstPtr->next->rating = 7;
```

Using the next field to get from one struct to the next is also known as **traversing** a linked list.

Our next (and final) program for this chapter will incorporate the new version of the DVDInfo struct to demonstrate a more memory-efficient DVD-tracking program. This program is pretty long, so you may want to take a few moments to let the dog out and answer your mail.

NOTE

There are many variants of the linked list. If you connect the last element of a linked list to the first element, you create a never-ending circular list. You can add a `prev` field to the `struct` and use it to point to the previous element in the list (as opposed to the next one). This technique allows you to traverse the linked list in two directions and creates a doubly linked list.

As you gain more programming experience, you'll want to check out some books on data structures. Three books well worth exploring are *Algorithms in C, Parts 1–5* by Robert Sedgewick (Addison-Wesley 2001), *Data Structures and C Programs* by Christopher J. Van Wyk (Addison-Wesley 1990), and my personal favorite, *Fundamental Algorithms*, volume one of Donald Knuth's *The Art of Computer Programming* series (Addison-Wesley 1997).

dvdTracker.xcodeproj

dvdTracker implements model B of our DVD-tracking system. It uses a text-based menu, allowing you to quit, add a new DVD to the collection, or list all of the currently tracked DVDs.

Open the *Learn C Projects* folder, go inside the folder *09.05 - dvdTracker*, and open the project *dvdTracker.xcodeproj*. Run dvdTracker. The console window will appear, showing the following prompt:

```
Enter command (q=quit, n=new, l=list):
```

At this point, you have three choices. You can type *q* and press Return to quit the program. You can type *n* and press Return to add a new DVD to your collection. Finally, you can type *l* and press Return to list all the DVDs in your collection.

Start by typing *l* and pressing Return. You should see this message:

```
No DVDs have been entered yet...
```

Next, the original command prompt should reappear:

```
Enter command (q=quit, n=new, l=list):
```

This time, type *n*, and press Return. You will be prompted to enter a DVD title and comment:

```
Enter DVD Title:  The Ring
Enter DVD Comment:  Scariest movie ever!
```

Next, you'll be prompted for a rating for the new DVD. The program expects a number between 1 and 10. Try typing something unexpected, such as the letter "x", followed by a carriage return:

```
Enter DVD Rating (1-10):  x
Enter DVD Rating (1-10):  9
```

The program checks your input, discovers it isn't in the proper range, and repeats the prompt. This time, type a number between 1 and 10, and press Return. The program returns you to the main command prompt:

```
Enter command (q=quit, n=new, l=list):
```

Type *l*, and press Return. The single DVD you just entered will be listed, and the command prompt will again be displayed:

```
Title:  The Ring
Comment:   Scariest move ever!
Rating:  9

----------
Enter command (q=quit, n=new, l=list):
```

Type *n*, and press Return to enter another DVD. Repeat the process one more time, adding a third DVD to the collection. Now, type *l*, and press Return to list all three DVDs. Here's my list:

```
Enter command (q=quit, n=new, l=list):  l

----------
Title:  The Ring
Comment:   Scariest move ever!
Rating:  9

----------
Title:  Tenacious D in The Pick of Destiny
Comment:   Jack Black rocks, Kyle Gass can play
Rating:  7

----------
Title:  Hot Fuzz
Comment:   Simon Pegg sleeper - must see!
Rating:  8

----------
Enter command (q=quit, n=new, l=list):
```

Finally, type *q*, and press Return to quit the program. Let's hit the source code.

Stepping Through the dvdTracker Source Code

main.c starts by including four different files. `<stdio.h>` gives us access to routines like `printf()`, `getchar()`, and `fgets()`. `<stdlib.h>` gives us access to `malloc()` and `free()`. `<string.h>` gives us access to `strlen()`. The fourth include file is our own "dvdTracker.h".

```
#include <stdio.h>
#include <stdlib.h>
#include <string.h>
```

"dvdTracker.h" starts off with three `#defines` that you should know pretty well by now:

```
/***********/
/* Defines */
/***********/
#define kMaxTitleLength      256
#define kMaxCommentLength    256
```

TIP

As you make your way through the dvdTracker source code, you'll notice I've added some decorative comments used to mark the beginning of a section of code. For example, in *dvdTracker.h*, I've added comments to mark off areas for defines, `struct` declarations, and function prototypes.

In *main.c*, I've done something similar to set off the beginning of each function. You should do this in your own code. It'll make your code easier to read.

Next comes the new and improved `DVDInfo` `struct` declaration:

```
/***********************/
/* Struct Declarations */
/***********************/
struct DVDInfo {
    char            rating;
    char            title[ kMaxTitleLength ];
    char            comment[ kMaxCommentLength ];
    struct DVDInfo  *next;
} *gHeadPtr, *gTailPtr;
```

Notice the two variables hanging off the end of this `struct` declaration. This is a shorthand declaration of two globals, each of which is a pointer to a `DVDInfo` `struct`. We'll use these two globals to keep track of our linked list.

`gHeadPtr` will always point to the first `struct` in the linked list. `gTailPtr` will always point to the last `struct` in the linked list. We'll use `gHeadPtr` when we want to step through the linked list, starting at the beginning. We'll use gTailPtr when we want to add an element to the end of the list. As long as we keep these pointers around, we'll have access to the linked list of memory blocks we'll be allocating.

We could have split this declaration into two parts, like this:

```
struct DVDInfo {
    char                rating;
    char                title[ kMaxTitleLength ];
    char                comment[ kMaxCommentLength ];
    struct DVDInfo      *next;
};

struct DVDInfo *gHeadPtr, *gTailPtr;
```

Either form is fine, though the shorthand version in *dvdTracker.h* does a better job of showing that gHeadPtr and gTailPtr belong with the DVDInfo struct declaration.

dvdTracker.h ends with a series of function prototypes:

```
/***********************/
/* Function Prototypes */
/***********************/
char                GetCommand( void );
struct DVDInfo      *ReadStruct( void );
void                AddToList( struct DVDInfo *curPtr );
void                ListDVDs( void );
void                ReplaceReturnAtEndOfString( char *theString );
void                Flush( void );
```

Let's get back to *main.c*. main() defines a char named command, which will be used to hold the single-letter command typed by the user:

```
/*************************************************> main <*/
int main (int argc, const char * argv[]) {
    char                command;
```

Next, the variables gHeadPtr and gTailPtr are set to a value of NULL. As defined earlier, NULL indicates that these pointers do not point to valid memory addresses. Once we add an item to the list, these pointers will no longer be NULL.

```
    gHeadPtr = NULL;
    gTailPtr = NULL;
```

Next, main() enters a while loop, calling the function GetCommand(). GetCommand() prompts you for a one-character command: 'q', 'n', or 'l'. Once GetCommand() returns 'q', we drop out of the while loop and exit the program.

```
    while ( (command = GetCommand() ) != 'q' ) {
```

If GetCommand() returns 'n', the user wants to enter information on a new DVD. First, we call ReadStruct(), which allocates space for a DVDInfo struct and prompts the user for the information to place in the new struct's fields. Once the struct is filled out, ReadStruct() returns a pointer to the newly allocated struct.

The pointer returned by ReadStruct() is passed on to AddToList(), which adds the new struct to the linked list.

```
        switch( command ) {
            case 'n':
                AddToList( ReadStruct() );
                break;
```

If GetCommand() returns 'l', the user wants to list all the DVDs in a collection. That's what the function ListDVDs() does.

```
            case 'l':
                ListDVDs();
                break;
        }
    }
```

Before the program exits, it says "Goodbye...".

```
    printf( "Goodbye..." );

    return 0;
}
```

Next up on the panel is GetCommand(). GetCommand() declares a char named command, used to hold the user's command:

```
/*********************************************> GetCommand <*/
char    GetCommand( void ) {
    char    command;
```

Because we want to execute the body of this next loop at least once, we used a do loop instead of a while loop. We'll first prompt the user to enter a command and then use scanf() to read a character from the input buffer. The function Flush() will read characters, one at a time, from the input buffer until it reads in a carriage return. If we didn't call Flush(), any extra characters we typed after the command (including '\n') would be picked up the next time through this loop, and extra prompt lines would appear, one per extra character. To see this effect, comment out the call to Flush(), and type more than one character when prompted for a command. We'll drop out of the loop once we get either 'q', 'n', or 'l'.

```
    do {
        printf( "Enter command (q=quit, n=new, l=list): " );
```

```
            scanf( "%c", &command );
            Flush();
        }
    while ( (command != 'q') && (command != 'n')
                    && (command != 'l') );
```

Here's a cool trick Keith Rollin (C guru extraordinaire) showed me. Instead of ending the do loop with this statement:

```
while ( (command != 'q') && (command != 'n') && (command != 'l') );
```

try this code instead:

```
while ( ! strchr( "qnl", command ) );
```

strchr() takes two parameters: a zero-terminated string and an int containing a character. It searches the string for the character and returns a pointer to the character inside the string, if it was found. If the character wasn't in the string, strchr() returns NULL. Pretty cool, eh?

Once we drop out of the loop, we'll print a separator line and return the single-letter command:

```
        printf( "\n----------\n" );
        return( command );
}
```

Next up is ReadStruct(). Notice the unusual declaration of the function name:

```
/*******************************************> ReadStruct <*/
struct DVDInfo     *ReadStruct( void ) {
```

This line says that ReadStruct() returns a pointer to a DVDInfo struct:

```
struct DVDInfo     *ReadStruct( void )
```

ReadStruct() uses malloc() to allocate a block of memory the size of a DVDInfo struct. The variable infoPtr will act as a pointer to the new block. We'll use the variable num to read in the rating, which we'll eventually store in infoPtr->rating.

```
        struct DVDInfo     *infoPtr;
        int                num;
```

ReadStruct() calls malloc() to allocate a DVDInfo struct, assigning the address of the block returned to infoPtr:

```
        infoPtr = malloc( sizeof( struct DVDInfo ) );
```

If malloc() cannot allocate a block of the requested size, it will return a value of NULL. If this happens, we'll print an appropriate message and call the Standard Library function exit(). As its name implies, exit() causes the program to immediately exit. The parameter you pass to exit() will be passed back to the operating system (or to whatever program launched your program).

```
if ( NULL == infoPtr ) {
    printf( "Out of memory!!!  Goodbye!\n" );
    exit( 0 );
}
```

If we're still here, malloc() must have succeeded. Next, we'll print a prompt for the DVD title and call fgets() to read a line from the input buffer. fgets() will place the line in the title field of the newly allocated struct. As a reminder, when you write your own programs, capture the values returned by printf() and fgets(), and handle any errors accordingly.

```
printf( "Enter DVD Title:  " );
fgets( infoPtr->title, kMaxTitleLength, stdin );
ReplaceReturnAtEndOfString( infoPtr->title );
```

Earlier in the chapter (in the multiArray sample program), we discovered that fgets() leaves '\n' in place when it reads in a line of input. As we did in multiArray, we pass the char array to ReplaceReturnAtEndOfString() to replace the '\n' with a terminating zero ('\0').

We then repeat the process to prompt for and read in the DVD title.

```
printf( "Enter DVD Comment:  " );
result = fgets( infoPtr->comment, kMaxCommentLength, stdin );
ReplaceReturnAtEndOfString( infoPtr->comment );
```

This loop prompts the user to enter a number between 1 and 10. We then use scanf() to read an int from the input buffer. Note that we used a temporary int to read in the number instead of reading it directly into infoPtr->rating. We did this because the %d format specifier expects an int and rating is declared as a char. Once we read the number, we call a function defined a bit further down in the file, called Flush(), to get rid of any other characters (including '\n').

```
do {
    num = 0;
    printf( "Enter DVD Rating (1-10):  " );
    scanf( "%d", &num );
    Flush();
}
while ( ( num < 1 ) || ( num > 10 ) );
```

ERROR CHECKING FOR SCANF()

This do loop is not as careful as it could be. If scanf() encounters an error of some kind, num will end up with an undefined value. If that undefined value happens to be between 1 and 10, the loop will exit and an unwanted value will be entered in the rating field. Though that might not be that big a deal in our case, we probably would want to drop out of the loop or, at the very least, print some kind of error message if this happens.

Here's another version of the same code:

```
do {
    num = 0;
    printf( "Enter DVD Rating (1-10):   " );
    if ( scanf( "%d", &num ) != 1 ) {
        printf( "Error returned by scanf()!\n" );
        exit( -1 );
    };
    Flush();
}
while ( ( num < 1 ) || ( num > 10 ) );
```

scanf() returns the number of items it read. Since we've asked it to read a single int, this version prints an error message and exits if we don't read exactly one item. This is a pretty simplistic error strategy, but it does make a point. Pay attention to error conditions and to function return values.

Once a number is read in that's between 1 and 10, the number is assigned to the rating field of the newly allocated struct:

```
infoPtr->rating = num;
```

Finally, a separating line is printed and the pointer to the new struct is returned:

```
printf( "\n----------\n" );

return( infoPtr );
}
```

AddToList() takes a pointer to a DVDInfo struct as a parameter. It uses the pointer to add the struct to the linked list:

```
/*********************************************> AddToList <*/
void    AddToList( struct DVDInfo *curPtr ) {
```

If gHeadPtr is NULL, the list must be empty. If so, make gHeadPtr point to the new struct:

```
if ( gHeadPtr == NULL )
    gHeadPtr = curPtr;
```

If gHeadPtr is not NULL, the linked list contains at least one element. In that case, make the next field of the very last element on the list point to the new struct:

```
else
    gTailPtr->next = curPtr;
```

In either case, set gTailPtr to point to the new last element in the list. Finally, make sure the next field of the last element in the list is NULL. You'll see why we did this in the next function, ListDVDs().

```
    gTailPtr = curPtr;
    curPtr->next = NULL;
}
```

ListDVDs() lists all the DVDs in the linked list, and the variable curPtr is used to point to the link element currently being looked at:

```
/*********************************************> ListDVDs <*/
void    ListDVDs( void ) {
    struct DVDInfo    *curPtr;
```

If no DVDs have been entered yet, we'll print an appropriate message:

```
if ( gHeadPtr == NULL ) {
    printf( "No DVDs have been entered yet...\n" );
    printf( "\n----------\n" );
}
```

Otherwise, we'll use a for loop to step through the linked list. The for loop starts by setting curPtr to point to the first element in the linked list and continues as long as curPtr is not NULL. Each time through the loop, curPtr is set to point to the next element in the list. Since we make sure that the last element's next pointer is always set to NULL, when curPtr is equal to NULL, we know we have been through every element in the list, and we are done.

```
else {
    for ( curPtr=gHeadPtr; curPtr!=NULL; curPtr = curPtr->next ) {
```

The first two `printf()`s use the "%s" format specifier to print the strings in the fields `title` and comment:

```
printf( "Title: %s\n", curPtr->title );
printf( "Comment:  %s\n", curPtr->comment );
```

Next, the `rating` field and a separating line are printed, and we head back to the top of the loop:

```
        printf( "Rating: %d\n", curPtr->rating );

        printf( "\n----------\n" );
    }
  }
}
```

`ReplaceReturnAtEndOfString()` is exactly the same function as the one in multiArray, which brings up an excellent programming point. Design your code to be reusable, and reuse your code. When I wrote the version of `ReplaceReturnAtEndOfString()` I used in multiArray, I tried to keep my code as generic as possible, avoiding any references to anything specific to multiArray. In my mind, I was writing a companion function for `fgets()`. When I got to dvdTracker, what a nice surprise! I was able to use the same function without changing a line of code.

`Flush()` uses `getchar()` to read characters from the input buffer until it reads in a carriage return. `Flush()` is a good utility routine to have around.

```
/*****************************************> Flush <*/
void    Flush( void ) {
    while ( getchar() != '\n' )
        ;
}
```

NOTE

Flush() was based on the Standard Library function `fflush()`. `fflush()` flushes the input buffer associated with a specific file. Since we haven't gotten into files yet, we wrote our own version, which as you can see, wasn't very hard.

What's Next?

This chapter covered a wide range of topics, from #include files to linked lists. The intent of the chapter, however, was to attack a real-world programming problem—in this case, a program to catalog DVDs. This chapter showed several design approaches, discussing the pros and cons of each. Finally, the chapter presented a prototype for a DVD-tracking program. The program allows you to enter information about a series of DVDs and, on request, will present a list of all the DVDs tracked.

One problem with this program is that once you exit, all of the data you entered is lost. The next time you run the program, you have to start all over again.

Chapter 10 offers a solution to this problem. The chapter introduces the concept of files and file management, showing you how to save your data from memory out to your hard disk drive and how to read your data back in again. The next chapter updates dvdTracker, storing the DVD information collected in a file on your disk drive.

CHAPTER 9 EXERCISES

1. What's wrong with each of the following code fragments?

   a. ```
      struct Employee {
          char   name[20];
          int   employeeNumber
      };
      ```

   b. ```
      while ( getchar() == '\n' ) ;
      ```

   c. ```
      #include "stdio.h"
      ```

   d. ```
      struct Link {
          name[ 50 ];
          Link    *next;
      };
      ```

   e. ```
      struct Link {
          struct Link   next;
          struct Link prev;
      }
      ```

   f. ```
      StepAndPrint( char *line ) {
          while ( *line != 0 )
              line++;

          printf( "%s", line );
      }
      ```

2. Update dvdTracker so it maintains its linked list in order from the lowest rating to the highest rating. If two DVDs have the same rating, the order is unimportant.

3. Update dvdTracker to add a prev field to the DVDInfo struct so it maintains a doubly linked list. As before, the next field will point to the next link in the list. Now, however, the prev field should point to the previous link in the list. Add an option to the menu that prints the list backward, from the last struct in the list to the first.

Chapter 10

Working with Files

C hapter 9 introduced dvdTracker, a program designed to keep track of your DVD collection. dvdTracker allowed you to enter a new DVD, as well as list all existing DVDs. dvdTracker's biggest shortcoming was that it didn't save the DVD information when it exited. If you ran dvdTracker, entered information on ten DVDs and then quit, your information would be gone. The next time you ran dvdTracker, you'd have to start from scratch.

The solution to this problem is to somehow save all of the DVD information before you quit the program. This chapter will show you how; it introduces the concept of **files**, the long-term storage for your program's data. We'll start off with the basics, learning how to open and read a file and displaying its contents in the console window. Next, you'll learn how to write data out to a file. Finally, you'll learn about a variety of file opening modes that give you more options when dealing with files.

NOTE

As you move on to other programming languages (such as Objective-C, Java, or C++), sophisticated development toolkits (such as Cocoa), and even other operating systems, you'll find there are many ways to work with files. Most of them are based on the concepts you'll learn in this chapter.

Stay with the program! Learn the basics, and you'll find moving on to other development platforms much, much easier in the long run.

What Is a File?

A file is a series of bytes residing in some storage media. Files can be stored on your hard drive, on a recordable DVD or CD, or even on your iPod. The iTunes application is made up of a collection of files, including the actual executable, the preference files, and all the song files. Your favorite word processor lives in a file, and so does each and every document you create with your word processor.

The project archive that came with this book contains many different files. Apple's developer tools are made up of hundreds of files. Each of the *Learn C* projects consists of at least two files: a project file and at least one source code file. When you compile and link a project, you produce a new kind of file, an application file.

All of these are examples of the same thing: a collection of bytes known as a file.

All of the files on your computer share a common set of traits. For example, each file has a size. The file *main.c* from the dvdTracker project takes up 4 kilobytes of disk space. The movie I made for my friend's fortieth birthday takes up 196 megabytes. Each of these files resides on my Mac's internal hard drive.

Working with Files: File Basics

In the C world, each file consists of a **stream** of consecutive bytes. When you want to access the data in a file, you first **open** the file using a Standard Library function named fopen(), pronounced "eff-open." Once your file is open, you can **read** data from the file or **write** new data back into the file using Standard Library functions like fgets(), fscanf() and fprintf(). Once you are done working with your file, you'll close it using the Standard Library function fclose().

Before we get into the specifics of opening a file, let's take a side trip and examine the rules for naming files in C.

Understanding File Names

The . (dot), / (slash), and ~ (tilde) characters have a special meaning when naming Unix and Mac OS X files. The . refers to the current directory; the / is a directory separator, and the ~ specifies your home directory.

The sequence of characters including directories, slash, dot, tilde characters, and the actual file name lead the compiler to your file. Together, this sequence is known as a **path**. A slash at the beginning of a path tells the compiler to start at the top, or **root level**, of your hard drive. Without a slash, the search starts in the current directory. Typically, the **current directory** is the directory containing your application.

For example, if you wanted to refer to the file *myFile.text* in the current directory, you'd use the string "./myFile.text". The string "/myFile.text" refers to the file named *myFile.text* at the root level of your hard drive.

CAUTION

The string "myFile.text" also refers to the file *myFile.text* in the current directory. I prefer to use "./myFile.text", as I think the intent of referring to the file *myFile.text* in the current directory is much clearer.

Two dots in a row refer to the **parent directory** of the **current directory**. An example will help clarify this point. Suppose you had a program named */Users/davemark/test/myProgram*. If myProgram referred to ".myFile.text", it would actually be referring to the file */Users/davemark/test/myFile.text*. If, instead, it referred to "../myFile.text", it would be referring to */Users/davemark/myFile.text*. If this is confusing, take another read through this.

The string "~/myFile.text" refers to the file named *myFile.text* in your home directory. On my Mac, this would be */Users/davemark/myFile.text*.

As you make your way through the programs in this chapter, play with the file names until you understand these concepts.

Opening and Closing a File

Here's the function prototype for fopen(), found in the file <stdio.h>:

```
FILE *fopen( const char *name, const char *mode );
```

The const keyword marks a variable or parameter as read-only. In other words, fopen() is not allowed to modify the array of characters pointed at by name or mode. Here's another example:

```
const int kMyInt = 27;
```

This declaration creates an int named kMyInt and assigns it a value of 27 (we'll talk about definitions that also initialize in Chapter 11). More importantly, the value of kMyInt is now permanently set. kMyInt is now read-only. As long as kMyInt remains in scope, you can't change its value. I start all my const variables with the letter k.

The first parameter to fopen(), name, tells fopen() which file you want to open.

The second parameter, mode, tells fopen() how you'll be accessing the file. The three basic file modes are "r", "w", and "a", which stand for **read**, **write**, and **append**, respectively.

CAUTION

The mode parameter is char *, *not* char. In other words, mode is a zero-terminated string, so use "r", not 'r'.

"r" tells fopen() that you want to read data from the file and that you won't be writing to the file at all. The file must already exist in order to use this mode. In other words, you can't use the mode "r" to create a file.

The mode "w" tells fopen() that you want to write to the specified file. If the file doesn't exist yet, a new file with the specified name is created. If the file does exist, fopen() deletes it and creates a new empty file for you to write into.

CAUTION

This point bears repeating: calling fopen() with a mode of "w" will delete a file (along with the file's contents!) if the file already exists, essentially starting you over from the beginning of the file. Be careful!

The mode "a" is similar to "w". It tells fopen() that you want to write to the specified file and to create the file if it doesn't exist. If the file does exist, however, the data you write to the file is appended to the end of the file.

If fopen() successfully opens the specified file, it allocates a struct of type FILE and returns a pointer to the FILE struct. The FILE struct contains information about the open file, including the current mode (e.g., "r", "w", or "a") as well as the current **file position**. The file position is a pointer into the file that acts like a bookmark in a book. When you open a file for reading, for example, the file position points to the first byte in the file. When you read the first byte, the file position moves to the next byte.

It's not really important to know the details of the FILE struct. All you need to do is keep track of the FILE pointer returned by fopen(). By passing the pointer to a Standard Library function that reads or writes, you'll be sure the read or write takes place in the right file and at the right file position. You'll see how all this works as we go through this chapter's sample code.

Here's a sample fopen() call:

```
FILE     *fp;

if ( (fp = fopen( "My Data File", "r")) == NULL ) {
    printf( "File doesn't exist!!!\n" );
    exit(1);
}
```

This code first calls fopen(), attempting to open the file named "My Data File" for reading. If fopen() cannot open the file for some reason—perhaps you've asked it to open a file that doesn't exist or you've already opened the maximum number of files—it returns NULL. In that case, we'll print an error message and exit.

NOTE

There is a limit to the number of simultaneous open files. This limit is implemented as a #define, FOPEN_MAX, defined in the file <stdio.h>. At the time of this writing, FOPEN_MAX was defined to be 20.

If fopen() does open the file, it will allocate the memory for a FILE struct, and fp will point to that struct. We can then pass fp to routines that read from the file. Once we're done with the file, we'll pass fp to the function fclose():

```
int fclose( FILE *stream );
```

fclose() takes a pointer to a FILE as a parameter and attempts to close the specified file. If the file is closed successfully, fclose() frees up the memory allocated to the FILE struct and returns a value of 0. It is very important that you match every fopen() with a corresponding fclose(); otherwise, you'll end up with unneeded FILE structs floating around in memory.

In addition, once you've passed a FILE pointer to fclose(), that FILE pointer no longer points to a FILE struct. If you want to access the file again, you'll have to make another fopen() call.

If fclose() fails, it returns the value EOF. EOF is a #define macro defined in <stdio.h> and stands for "end of file." Though my example code ignores the value returned by fclose(), do as I say, not as I do. Check the value returned by every function that returns one. You can never have too much error checking in your code. Check the value returned by fclose().

Reading a File

Once you open a file for reading, the next step is to read data from the file. Several Standard Library functions help you do just that. For starters, the function fgetc() reads a single character from a file's input buffer. Here's the function prototype:

```
int fgetc( FILE *fp );
```

The single parameter is the FILE pointer returned by fopen(). fgetc() reads a single character from the file and advances the file position pointer. If the file position pointer is already at the end of the file, fgetc() returns EOF.

USING A CHAR TO CATCH AN INT

Though `fgetc()` returns an `int`, a line like this

```
char    c;
c = fgetc( fp );
```

works just fine. When the C compiler encounters two different types on each side of an assignment operator, it does its best to convert the value on the right side to the type of the left side before doing the assignment. As long as the type of the right side is no larger than the type of the left side (as is the case here: an `int` is at least as large as a `char`), this won't be a problem.

We'll get into the specifics of typecasting in Chapter 11.

The function `fgets()`, which we made use of in Chapter 9, reads a series of characters into an array of `char`s. Here's the function prototype:

```
char *fgets( char *s, int n, FILE *fp );
```

You should already be comfortable using `fgets()`. In our previous uses, we passed `stdin` as the third parameter to `fgets()`. As it turns out, `stdin` is a `FILE` pointer automatically provided to your program when it starts. In this chapter, we'll open a file with `fopen()` and use `fgets()` to read from the file.

Here's an example:

```
#define kMaxBufferSize        200

FILE        *fp;
char        buffer[ kMaxBufferSize ];

if ( (fp = fopen( "My Data File", "r")) == NULL ) {
    printf( "File doesn't exist!!!\n" );
    exit(1);
}

if ( fgets( buffer, kMaxBufferSize, fp ) == NULL ) {
    if ( feof( fp ) )
        printf( "End-of-file!!!\n" );
    else
        printf( "Unknown error!!!\n" );
}
else
    printf( "File contents: %s\n", buffer );
```

Notice that the example calls a function named feof() if fgets() returns NULL. fgets() returns NULL no matter what error it encounters. feof() returns true if the last read on the specified file caused the end of the file to be reached, and false otherwise.

The function fscanf() is similar to scanf(), but it reads from a file instead of the keyboard. Here's the prototype:

```
int    fscanf( FILE *fp, const char* format, ... );
```

The first parameter is the FILE pointer returned by fopen(). The second parameter is a format specification embedded inside a character string. The format specification tells fscanf() what kind of data you want read from the file. The ... operator in a parameter list tells the compiler that zero or more parameters may follow the second parameter. Like scanf() and printf(), fscanf() uses the format specification to determine the number of parameters it expects to see. Be sure to pass the correct number of parameters or your program will get confused.

If possible, stick with fgets() instead of fscanf(), for the same reason I steered you to fgets() instead of scanf() earlier in the book. fgets() calls for a maximum number of characters to read, which will prevent a malicious user from overflowing the buffer you pass in as a first parameter. fscanf() does not offer that protection.

These are a few of the file access functions provided by the Standard Library. Wanna look up something? Here's that link to that online Standard Library reference I keep mentioning:

```
http://www.infosys.utas.edu.au/info/documentation/C/CStdLib.html
```

Click the link to <stdio.h> at the top of the page. You might also want to take a look at C, A Reference Manual by Samuel Harbison and Guy Steele, especially Chapter 15, "Input/Output Facilities" (Prentice Hall 2002).

In the meantime, here's an example that uses the functions fopen() and fgetc() to open a file and display its contents.

printFile.xcodeproj

printFile opens a file named *My Data File*, reads in all the data from the file one character at a time, and prints each character in the console window.

Open the *Learn C Projects* folder, go inside the folder *10.01 - printFile*, and open and run the project *printFile.xcodeproj*. Compare your output with the console window shown in Figure 10-1. They should be the same.

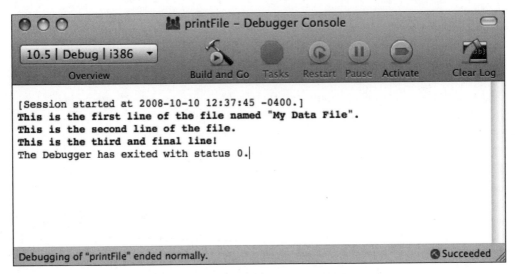

Figure 10-1. *The printFile output, showing the contents of the file My Data File*

Let's take a look at the data file read in by printFile. Select **Open...** from Xcode's **File** menu. Xcode will prompt you for a text file to open. Be sure you are in the *10.01 - printFile* directory, and select the file named *My Data File*. An editing window will open allowing you to edit the contents of *My Data File*. Feel free to make some changes to the file and run the program again. Make sure you don't change the name *or* the location of the file.

Let's take a look at the source code.

Stepping Through the printFile Source Code

Open the source code file *main.c* by double-clicking its name in the project window. Take a minute to look over the source code. Once you feel comfortable with it, read on.

main.c starts off with the usual #include:

```
#include <stdio.h>
```

main() defines two variables. fp is our FILE pointer, and c is an int that will hold the chars we read from the file:

```
int main (int argc, const char * argv[]) {
    FILE        *fp;
    int         c;
```

This call of the function `fopen()` opens the file named *My Data File* for reading, returning the file pointer to the variable `fp`:

```
fp = fopen( "../../My Data File", "r" );
```

Notice the `../../` characters at the beginning of the file name we passed to `fopen()`. As described earlier, each `../` means that the file is in the parent directory, one level up from the application. This means that our data file is two levels up from our application. But wait. The file *My Data File* is in the same directory as the project file. What gives?

The confusion stems from the location in which Xcode stores the binary it builds from our source code. Go to the Finder, and open the *10.01 - printFile* directory. Inside that folder, you'll find your project file, a few other files, and a folder named *build*. If you don't see the build folder, you haven't built your application yet. Go back and run the project, and then come back to the Finder.

Open the *build* folder. You should see a subfolder named *Debug*. Inside the *Debug* folder, you'll find the *printFile* executable. This is your program. As you can see, to get from the *print-File* executable to the file *My Data File*, you'll need to move up two levels. And that's why we pass the argument "`../../My Data File`" to `fopen()`.

If `fp` is NULL, `fpopen()` was unable to open the file and an appropriate error message is printed:

```
if ( NULL == fp ) {
    printf( "Error opening ../../MyData File", "r" );
} else {
```

If the file was opened successfully, we enter a `while` loop that continuously calls `fgetc()`, passing it the file pointer `fp`. `fgetc()` returns the next character in `fp`'s input buffer. The returned character is assigned to `c`. If `c` is not equal to EOF, `putchar()` is called, taking `c` as a parameter.

```
while ( (c = fgetc( fp )) != EOF )
    putchar( c );
```

`putchar()` prints the specified character to the console window. We could have accomplished the same thing by using `printf()`:

```
printf( "%c", c );
```

NOTE

As you program, you'll often find two different solutions to the same problem. Should you use `putchar()` or `printf()`? If performance is critical, pick the option that is more specific to your particular need. In this case, `printf()` is designed to handle many different data types. `putchar()` is designed to handle one data type, an `int`. Chances are, the source code for `putchar()` is simpler and more efficient than the source code for `printf()` *when it comes to printing an* `int`. If performance is critical, you might want to use `putchar()` instead of `printf()`. If performance isn't critical, go with your own preference.

Once we are done, we'll close the file by calling `fclose()`. Remember to always balance each call of `fopen()` with a corresponding call to `fclose()`.

```
        fclose( fp );
    }
    return 0;
}
```

stdin, stdout, and stderr

C provides you with three `FILE` pointers that are open as soon as your program starts running and available throughout your program. `stdin` represents the keyboard; `stdout` represents the console window; and `stderr` represents the file where the user wants all error messages sent. `stdin`, `stdout`, and `stderr` are normally associated with command line–oriented operating systems like Unix. As you can see, `stdin`, `stdout`, and `stderr` work just fine within Xcode. Once you move on and start working with Cocoa (for the Mac) and Cocoa Touch (for iPhone), you'll stop using `stdin`, `stdout`, and `stderr` to communicate with the user. Instead, you'll use windows, text fields, buttons, and the like. That said, many of the concepts in this chapter *will* carry forward into Cocoa and Cocoa Touch. Mastering `stdin`, `stdout`, and `stderr` along with `fpopen()` and the rest of C's file management functions is vital to your programming education and is well worth your time.

In printFile, we used the function `fgetc()` to read a character from a previously opened file. This line

```
c = fgetc( stdin );
```

will read the next character from the keyboard's input buffer. `fgetc( stdin )` is equivalent to calling `getchar()`.

As you'll see in the next few sections, whenever C provides a mechanism for reading or writing to a file, C will also provide a similar mechanism for reading from `stdin` or writing to `stdout`.

Working with Files: Writing Files

So far, you've learned how to open a file using fopen() and how to read from a file using fgetc(). You've seen, once again, that you can often use two different functions to solve the same problem. Now let's look at some functions that allow you to write data out to a file.

Writing to a File

The Standard Library offers several functions that write data out to a previously opened file. This section will introduce three of them: fputc(), fputs(), and fprintf().

fputc() takes an int holding a character value and writes the character out to the specified file. fputc() is declared as follows:

```
int    fputc( int c, FILE *fp );
```

If fputc() successfully writes the character out to the file, it returns the value passed to it in the parameter c. If the write fails for some reason, fputc() returns the value EOF.

NOTE

Note that fputc(c, stdout) is the same as calling putchar(c).

fputs() is similar to fputc(), but writes out a zero-terminated string instead of a single character. fputs() is declared as follows:

```
int    fputs( const char *s, FILE *fp );
```

fputs() writes out all the characters in the string but does not write out the terminating zero. If the write fails, fputs() returns EOF; otherwise, it returns a nonnegative number.

fprintf() works just like printf(). Instead of sending its output to the console window, fprintf() writes its output to the specified file. fprintf() is declared as follows:

```
int    fprintf( FILE *fp, const char *format, ... );
```

The first parameter specifies the file to be written to. The second is the format specification text string. Any further parameters depend on the contents of the format specification string.

dvdFiler.xcodeproj

In Chapter 9, we ran dvdTracker, a program designed to help you track your DVD collection. The big shortcoming of dvdTracker is its inability to save your carefully entered DVD data. As you quit the program, the DVD information you entered gets discarded, forcing you to start over the next time you run dvdTracker.

Our next program, dvdFiler, solves this problem by adding two special functions to dvdTracker. ReadFile() opens a file named *dvdData*, reads in the DVD data from the file, and uses the data to build a linked list of dvdInfo structs. WriteFile() writes the linked list back out to the file.

Open the *Learn C Projects* folder, go inside the folder *10.02 - dvdFiler*, and open the project *dvdFiler.xcodeproj*. Check out the *dvdFiler.xcodeproj* project window shown in Figure 10-2. Notice that there are two source code files in the project, *files.c* and *main.c*. Your project can contain as many source code files as you like. Just make sure that only one of the files has a function named main(), since that's where your program will start.

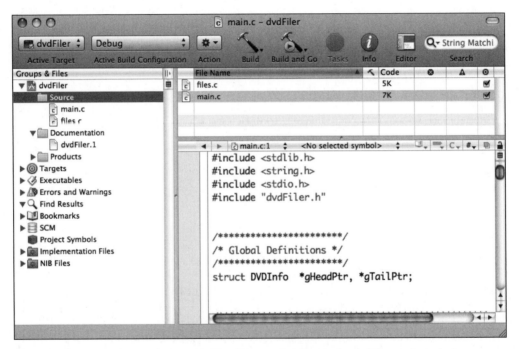

Figure 10-2. *Notice the two source code files, files.c and main.c, in the dvdFiler project window.*

The file *main.c* is almost identical to the file *main.c* from Chapter 9's *dvdTracker* program. The file *files.c* contains the functions that allow *dvdFiler* to read and write the file *dvdData*.

Creating a New Source Code File

Before we move on to the program itself, let's take a look at the process of creating a new source code file. When Xcode creates a new *Standard Tool* project, it adds a single source code file, *main.c*. To add a new file, start by clicking the *Source* folder in the project window's *Groups & Files* pane; see Figure 10-2. This tells Xcode where you want the new file placed.

Next, select **New File…** from the **File** menu. The *New File* dialog will appear, as shown in Figure 10-3. Select *C and C++* on the left side of the window and *C File* from the list that appears, and then click the *Next* button. In the next screen that appears, you'll be asked to name the file. If you want Xcode to create a matching *.h* file, check the checkbox just under the file name. When you're good to go, click the *Finish* button.

NOTE

If you just added new files to the *dvdFiler.xcodeproj* file, be sure to select any files you added, and press the Delete key to remove the files from the project.

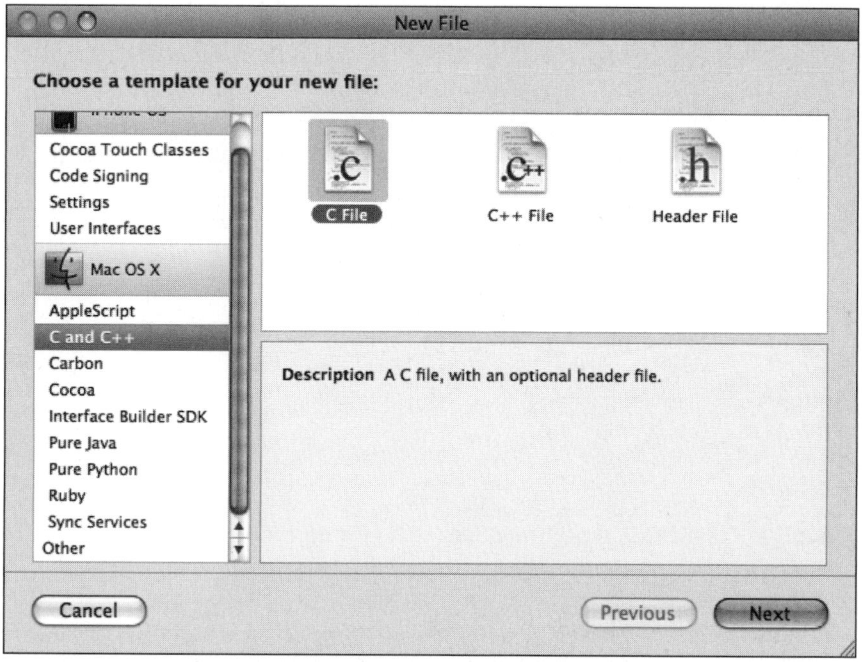

Figure 10-3. *In the New File dialog, to add a new source code file, select C and C++ on the left side of the window, and select C File from the list that appears. Then click Next.*

We now return to the program previously in progress.

Exploring dvdData

Before you run dvdFiler, use Xcode to take a quick look at the file *dvdData*. There are a number of ways to do this. You can select **Open…** from the **File** menu and select *dvdData* to open it. You can also drag *dvdData* from the Finder into the *Groups & Files* pane to add it to the project. I added my copy to the *Source* group. With the file added to the project, it becomes a snap to edit and examine any time you like.

At first glance, the contents of the file may not make much sense, but the text does follow a well-defined pattern:

```
The Ring
Scariest move ever!
9
Tenacious D in The Pick of Destiny
Jack Black rocks, Kyle Gass can play
7
Hot Fuzz
Simon Pegg sleeper - must see!
8
```

The file is organized in clusters of three lines each. Each cluster contains a one-line DVD title, a one-line DVD comment, and a one-line numerical DVD rating.

NOTE

The layout of your data files is as important a part of the software design process as the layout of your program's functions. The *dvdData* file follows a well-defined pattern. As you lay out a file for your next program, think about the future. Can you live with one-line DVD titles? Do you want the ability to add a new DVD field, perhaps the date of the DVD's release?

The time to think about these types of questions is at the beginning of your program's life, during the design phase.

Running dvdFiler

Before you run dvdFiler, be sure to save any *dvdData* text-editing windows you might have open.

Why? Suppose you make some changes to the file in Xcode but don't save your changes. Next, you run dvdFiler and make some changes, with dvdFiler saving the changes. What happens if you go back to Xcode and save your changes? Most likely, Xcode will overwrite the changes you made using dvdFiler, and the dvdFiler changes will be lost. Not good!

Once *dvdData* is saved, run dvdFiler. The console window will appear, prompting you for a *q*, *n*, or *l*:

```
Enter command (q=quit, n=new, l=list):
```

Type *l*, and press Return to list the DVDs currently in the program's linked list. If you need a refresher on linked lists, now would be a perfect time to turn back to Chapter 9.

```
Enter command (q=quit, n=new, l=list):  l
```

```
----------
Title:   The Ring
Comment:   Scariest move ever!
Rating:   9


----------
Title:   Tenacious D in The Pick of Destiny
Comment:   Jack Black rocks, Kyle Gass can play
Rating:   7


----------
Title:   Hot Fuzz
Comment:   Simon Pegg sleeper - must see!
Rating:   8


----------
Enter command (q=quit, n=new, l=list):
```

While Chapter 9's dvdTracker started with an empty linked list, dvdFiler starts with a linked list built from the contents of the *dvdData* file. The DVDs you just listed should match the DVDs you saw when you edited the *dvdData* file.

Let's add a fourth DVD to the list. Type *n*, and press Return:

```
Enter command (q=quit, n=new, l=list): n


----------
Enter DVD Title:   The Shawshank Redemption
Enter DVD Comment:   #1 movie of all time on imdb.com
Enter DVD Rating (1-10): 10


----------
Enter command (q=quit, n=new, l=list):
```

Next, type *l* to make sure your new DVD made it into the list:

```
Enter command (q=quit, n=new, l=list):   l


----------
Title:   The Ring
Comment:   Scariest move ever!
Rating:   9


----------
Title:   Tenacious D in The Pick of Destiny
Comment:   Jack Black rocks, Kyle Gass can play
Rating:   7
```

```
----------
Title:  Hot Fuzz
Comment:  Simon Pegg sleeper - must see!
Rating:  8


----------
Title:  The Shawshank Redemption
Comment:  #1 movie of all time on imdb.com
Rating:  10


----------
Enter command (q=quit, n=new, l=list):
```

Finally, type *q*, and press Return. This causes the program to write the current linked list back out to the file *dvdData*. To prove this write worked, run dvdFiler one more time. When prompted for a command, type *l* to list your current DVDs. You should find your new DVD nestled at the bottom of the list. Let's see how this works.

Stepping Through the dvdFiler Source Code

The file *dvdFiler.h* contains source code that will be included by both *main.c* and *files.c*. The #defines and struct declaration should be familiar to you.

```
/**********/
/* Defines */
/**********/
#define kMaxTitleLength        256
#define kMaxCommentLength      256

#define kDVDFileName           "../../dvdData"


/**********************/
/* Struct Declarations */
/**********************/
struct DVDInfo {
    char            rating;
    char            title[ kMaxTitleLength ];
    char            comment[ kMaxCommentLength ];
    struct DVDInfo  *next;
};
```

Just as we did in dvdTracker, we've declared two globals to keep track of the beginning and end of our linked list. The extern keyword at the beginning of the declaration tells the C compiler to link this declaration to the definition of these two globals, which can be found in *main.c*. If you removed the extern keyword from this line, the compiler would first compile *files.c*, defining space for both pointers. When the compiler went to compile *main.c*, it would complain that these globals were already declared.

The `extern` mechanism allows you to declare a global without actually allocating memory for it. Since the `extern` declaration doesn't allocate memory for your globals, you'll need a matching definition (usually found in the same file as `main()`) that *does* allocate memory for the globals. You'll see that definition in *main.c*:

```
/***********************/
/* Global Declarations */
/***********************/
  extern struct DVDInfo    *gHeadPtr, *gTailPtr;
```

Next comes the list of function prototypes. By listing all the functions in this include file, we make all functions available to be called from all other functions. As your programs get larger and more sophisticated, you might want to create a separate include file for each of your source code files. Some programmers create one include file for globals, another for defines, and another for function prototypes.

```
/******************************/
/* Function Prototypes - main.c */
/******************************/
char              GetCommand( void );
struct DVDInfo    *ReadStruct( void );
void              AddToList( struct DVDInfo *curPtr );
void              ListDVDs( void );
void              ReplaceReturnAtEndOfString( char *theString );
void              Flush( void );


/******************************/
/* Function Prototypes - files.c */
/******************************/
void    WriteFile( void );
void    ReadFile( void );
char    ReadStructFromFile( FILE *fp, struct DVDInfo *infoPtr );
```

The file *main.c* is almost exactly the same as the file *main.c* from Chapter 9's dvdTracker program. There are four differences. First, we include the file *dvdFiler.h* instead of *dvdTracker.h*:

```
#include <stdlib.h>
#include <string.h>
#include <stdio.h>
#include "dvdFiler.h"
```

Next, we include the definitions of our two globals directly in this source code file, to go along with the `extern` declarations in *dvdFiler.h*. This definition is where the memory actually gets allocated for these two global pointers:

```
/***********************/
/* Global Definitions */
/***********************/
struct DVDInfo    *gHeadPtr, *gTailPtr;
```

`main()` contains the last two differences. Before we enter the command processing loop, we call `ReadFile()` to read in the *dvdData* file and turn the contents into a linked list:

```
/************************> main <*/
int main (int argc, const char * argv[]) {
    char        command;

    gHeadPtr = NULL;
    gTailPtr = NULL;

    ReadFile();

    while ( (command = GetCommand() ) != 'q' ) {
        switch( command ) {
            case 'n':
                AddToList( ReadStruct() );
                break;
            case 'l':
                ListDVDs();
                break;
        }
    }
```

Once we drop out of the loop, we call `WriteFile()` to write the linked list out to the file *dvdData*:

```
    WriteFile();

    printf( "Goodbye..." );

    return 0;
}
```

For completeness, here's the remainder of *main.c*. Each of these functions is identical to its dvdTracker counterpart:

```
/***********************> GetCommand <*/
char    GetCommand( void ) {
    char        command;
```

```c
    do {
        printf( "Enter command (q=quit, n=new, l=list):  " );
        scanf( "%c", &command );
        Flush();
    }
    while ( (command != 'q') && (command != 'n')
                && (command != 'l') );

    printf( "\n----------\n" );
    return( command );
}


/************************> ReadStruct <*/
struct DVDInfo     *ReadStruct( void ) {
    struct DVDInfo   *infoPtr;
    int              num;
    char             *result;

    infoPtr = (struct DVDInfo *)malloc( sizeof( struct DVDInfo ) );

    if ( NULL == infoPtr ) {
        printf( "Out of memory!!!  Goodbye!\n" );
        exit( 0 );
    }

    printf( "Enter DVD Title:  " );
    fgets( infoPtr->title, kMaxTitleLength, stdin );
    ReplaceReturnAtEndOfString( infoPtr->title );

    printf( "Enter DVD Comment:  " );
    fgets( infoPtr->comment, kMaxCommentLength, stdin );
    ReplaceReturnAtEndOfString( infoPtr->comment );

    do {
        num = 0;
        printf( "Enter DVD Rating (1-10):  " );
        scanf( "%d", &num );
        Flush();
    }
    while ( ( num < 1 ) || ( num > 10 ) );

    infoPtr->rating = num;

    printf( "\n----------\n" );

    return( infoPtr );
}
```

```
/*********************************************> AddToList <*/
void    AddToList( struct DVDInfo *curPtr ) {
    if ( NULL == gHeadPtr )
        gHeadPtr = curPtr;
    else
        gTailPtr->next = curPtr;

    gTailPtr = curPtr;
    curPtr->next = NULL;
}


/*********************************************> ListDVDs <*/
void    ListDVDs( void ) {
    struct DVDInfo    *curPtr;

    if ( NULL == gHeadPtr ) {
        printf( "No DVDs have been entered yet...\n" );
        printf( "\n----------\n" );
    } else {
        for ( curPtr=gHeadPtr; curPtr!=NULL; curPtr = curPtr->next ) {
            printf( "Title:  %s\n", curPtr->title );
            printf( "Comment:   %s\n", curPtr->comment );
            printf( "Rating: %d\n", curPtr->rating );

            printf( "\n----------\n" );
        }
    }
}


/*********************> ReplaceReturnAtEndOfString <*/
void    ReplaceReturnAtEndOfString( char *theString ) {
    int    length = strlen( theString );

    theString[ length - 1 ] = '\0';
}


/*********************************************> Flush <*/
void    Flush( void ) {
    while ( getchar() != '\n' )
        ;
}
```

files.c starts out with these #includes:

```
#include <stdlib.h>
```

```
#include <stdio.h>
#include <stdbool.h>
#include "dvdFiler.h"
```

WriteFile() first checks to see if there are any DVDs to write out. If gFirstPtr is NULL (the value it was set to in main()), no DVDs have been entered yet, and we can just return:

```
/*************************> WriteFile <*/
void    WriteFile( void ) {
    FILE                *fp;
    struct DVDInfo      *infoPtr;
    int                 num;

    if ( NULL == gHeadPtr )
        return;
```

Next, we'll open the file *dvdData* for writing. If fopen() returns NULL, we know it couldn't open the file, and we'll print out an error message and return:

```
    if ( ( fp = fopen( kDVDFileName, "w" ) ) == NULL ) {
        printf( "***ERROR: Could not write DVD file!" );
        return;
    }
```

This for loop steps through the linked list, setting infoPtr to point to the first struct in the list, moving it to point to the next struct, and so on, until infoPtr is equal to NULL. Since the last struct in our list sets its next pointer to NULL, infoPtr will be equal to NULL when it points to the last struct in the list.

```
    for ( infoPtr=gHeadPtr; infoPtr!=NULL; infoPtr=infoPtr->next ) {
```

Each time through the list, we call fprintf() to print the title string followed by a carriage return and then the comment string followed by a carriage return. Remember, each of these strings was zero-terminated, a requirement if you plan on using the %s format specifier.

```
        fprintf( fp, "%s\n", infoPtr->title );
        fprintf( fp, "%s\n", infoPtr->comment );
```

Finally, we convert the rating field to an int by assigning it to the int num and print it (as well as a following carriage return) to the file using fprintf(). We converted the char to an int, because the %d format specifier was designed to work with an int, and not a char.

```
        num = infoPtr->rating;
        fprintf( fp, "%d\n", num );
    }
```

Once we finish writing the linked list into the file, we'll close the file by calling fclose():

```
    fclose( fp );
}
```

ReadFile() starts by opening the file *dvdData* for reading. If we can't open the file, we'll print an error message and return, leaving the list empty:

```
/***************************> ReadFile <*/
void    ReadFile( void ) {
    FILE              *fp;
    struct DVDInfo    *infoPtr;

    if ( ( fp = fopen( kDVDFileName, "r" ) ) == NULL ) {
        printf( "***ERROR: Could not read DVD file!" );
        return;
    }
```

With the file open, we'll enter a loop that continues as long as ReadStructFromFile() returns true. By using the do-while loop, we'll execute the body of the loop before we call ReadStructFromFile() for the first time. This is what we want. The body of the loop attempts to allocate a block of memory the size of a DVDInfo struct. If the malloc() fails, we'll bail out of the program.

```
    do {
        infoPtr = malloc( sizeof( struct DVDInfo ) );

        if ( NULL == infoPtr ) {
            printf( "Out of memory!!!  Goodbye!\n" );
            exit( 0 );
        }
    }
    while ( ReadStructFromFile( fp, infoPtr ) );
```

ReadStructFromFile() will return false when it hits the end of the file, when it can't read another set of DVDInfo fields. In that case, we'll close the file and free up the last block we just allocated, since we have nothing to store in it:

```
    fclose( fp );
    free( infoPtr );
}
```

ReadStructFromFile() uses a funky form of fscanf() to read in the first two DVDInfo fields. Notice the use of the format descriptor "%[^\n]\n". This tells fscanf() to read characters from the specified file until it hits a '\n' and then to read the '\n' character and stop. The characters [^\n] represent the set of all characters except '\n'. Note that the %[format specifier places a terminating zero byte at the end of the characters it reads in.

```
/*******************> ReadStructFromFile <*/
char    ReadStructFromFile( FILE *fp, struct DVDInfo *infoPtr ) {
    int         num;

    if ( fscanf( fp, "%[^\n]\n", infoPtr->title ) != EOF ) {
```

> **NOTE**
>
> The square brackets inside a format specifier give you much greater control over scanf(). For example, the format specifier "%[abcd]" would tell scanf() to keep reading as long as it was reading 'a', 'b', 'c', or 'd'. The first non-[abcd] character would be left in the input buffer for the next part of the format specifier or for the next read operation to pick up.
>
> If the first character in the set is the character ∧, the set represents the characters that do not belong to that set. In other words, the format specifier "%[∧abdvd]", tells scanf() to continue reading as long as it doesn't encounter any of the characters 'a', 'b', 'c', or 'd'.

If fscanf() hits the end of the file, we'll return false, letting the calling function know there are no more fields to read. If fscanf() succeeds, we'll move on to the comment field using the same technique. If this second fscanf() fails, we've got a problem, since we read a title but couldn't read a comment:

```
    if ( fscanf( fp, "%[^\n]\n", infoPtr->comment ) == EOF ) {
        printf( "Missing DVD comment!\n" );
        return false;
    }
```

You may have noticed that ReadStructFromFile() returns a char instead of a bool. Since true and false are integer values, char, short, or int will work. Personally, I think you should stick with the convention of declaring a function as bool if it strictly returns true or false Since much of the code you encounter will use the "int returning true or false" approach, I thought you should see this for yourself.

Assuming we got both the title and comment, we'll use a more normal format specifier to pick up an int and the third carriage return:

```
    else if ( fscanf( fp, "%d\n", &num ) == EOF ) {
        printf( "Missing DVD rating!\n" );
        return false;
    }
```

Assuming we picked up the int, we'll use the assignment operator to convert the int to a char and add the now-complete struct to the list by passing it to AddToList():

```
        else {
            infoPtr->rating = num;
            AddToList( infoPtr );
            return true;
        }
    }
    else
        return false;
}
```

Working with Files: Fancier File Manipulation

Now that you've mastered the basics of file reading and writing, a few more topics are worth exploring before we leave this chapter. We'll start off with a look at some additional file opening modes.

The Update Modes

So far, you've encountered the three basic file opening modes: "r", "w", and "a". Each of these modes has a corresponding **update** mode, specified by adding a plus sign (+) to the mode. The three update modes, "r+", "w+", and "a+", allow you to open a file for both reading and writing.

NOTE

> Though the three update modes do allow you to switch between read and write operations without reopening the file, you must first call either fsetpos(), fseek(), rewind(), or fflush() before you make the switch.
>
> In other words, if your file is opened using one of the update modes, you can't call fscanf() and then call fprintf() (or call fprintf() followed by fscanf()) unless you call fsetpos(), fseek(), rewind(), or fflush() in between.

A great chart in Harbison and Steele's *C: A Reference Manual* summarizes these modes quite nicely. My version of the chart is found in Table 10-1. Before you read on, take a minute to look over the chart to be sure you understand the different file modes.

Table 10-1. *Rules Associated with Each of the Basic File Opening Modes*

Mode Rules	"r"	"w"	"a"	"r+"	"w+"	"a+"
Named file must already exist	Yes	No	No	Yes	No	No
Existing file's contents are lost	No	Yes	No	No	Yes	No
Read OK	Yes	No	No	Yes	Yes	Yes
Write OK	No	Yes	Yes	Yes	Yes	Yes
Write begins at end of file	No	No	Yes	No	No	Yes

NOTE

C also allows a file mode to specify whether a file is limited to ASCII characters (text mode) or is allowed to hold any type of data at all (binary mode). To open a file in text mode, just append a "t" at the end of the mode string (like "rt" or "w+t"). To open a file in binary mode, append a "b" at the end of the mode string (like "rb" or "w+b").

If you use a file mode that doesn't include a "t" or a "b", check your development environment documentation to find out which of the two types is the default.

Random File Access

So far, each of the examples presented in this chapter have treated files as a **sequential stream of bytes**. When dvdFiler read from a file, it started from the beginning of the file and read the contents, one byte at a time or in larger chunks, but from the beginning straight through until the end. This sequential approach works fine if you intend to read or write the entire file all at once. As you might have guessed, there is another model.

Instead of starting at the beginning and streaming through a file, you can use a technique called **random file access**. The Standard Library provides a set of functions that let you reposition the file position indicator to any location within the file, so that the next read or write you do occurs exactly where you want it to.

Imagine a file filled with 100 longs, each of which was 4 bytes long. The file would be 400 bytes long. Now, suppose you wanted to retrieve the tenth long in the file. Using the sequential model, you would have to do ten reads to get the tenth long into memory. Unless you read the entire file into memory, you'll constantly be reading a series of longs to get to the long you want.

Using the random access model, you would first calculate where in the file the tenth long starts. Then, you'd jump to that position in the file and read just that long. To move the file position indicator just before the tenth long, you'd skip over the first nine longs (9 * 4 = 36 bytes).

Using Random Access Functions

There are a number of useful functions you'll need to know about in order to randomly access your files. `fseek()` moves the file position indicator to an offset you specify, relative to either the beginning of the file, the current file position, or the end of the file:

```
int    fseek( FILE *fp, long offset, int whence );
```

You'll pass your `FILE` pointer as the first parameter, a `long` offset as the second parameter, and `SEEK_SET`, `SEEK_CUR`, or `SEEK_END` as the third parameter. `SEEK_SET` represents the beginning of the file. `SEEK_CUR` represents the current position, and `SEEK_END` represents the end of the file (in which case you'll probably use a negative `offset`).

`ftell()` takes a `FILE` pointer as a parameter and returns a `long` containing the value of the file position indicator:

```
long    ftell( FILE *fp );
```

`rewind()` takes a `FILE` pointer as a parameter and resets the file position indicator to the beginning of the file:

```
void    rewind( FILE *fp );
```

NOTE

The functions `fsetpos()` and `fgetpos()` were introduced as part of ISO C and allow you to work with file offsets that are larger than will fit in a `long`. You can look these two functions up in the usual places.

dinoEdit.xcodeproj

The last sample program in this chapter, dinoEdit, is a simple example of random file access. It allows you to edit a series of dinosaur names stored in a file named *MyDinos*. Each dinosaur name in *MyDinos* is 20 characters long. If the actual dinosaur name is shorter than 20 characters, the appropriate number of spaces is added to the name to bring the length up to 20. Adding the spaces makes the size of each item in the file a fixed length. You'll see why this is important as we go through the source code. For now, let's take *dinoEdit* for a spin.

Open the *Learn C Projects* folder, go inside the folder *10.03 - dinoEdit*, and open and run *dinoEdit.xcodeproj*. dinoEdit will count the number of dinosaur names in the file *My Dinos* and will use that number to prompt you for a dinosaur number to edit:

```
Enter number from 1 to 5 (0 to exit):
```

Since the file *My Dinos* has five dinosaurs, enter a number from 1 to 5:

```
Enter number from 1 to 5 (0 to exit): 3
```

If you type the number *3*, for example, dinoEdit will fetch the third dinosaur name from the file and ask you to enter a new name for the third dinosaur. When you type a new name, dinoEdit will overwrite the existing name with the new name:

```
Dino #3: Gallimimus
Enter new name: Euoplocephalus
```

Either way, `dinoEdit` will prompt you to enter another dinosaur number. Reenter the same number, so you can verify that the change was made in the file:

```
Enter number from 1 to 5 (0 to exit): 3
Dino #3: Euoplocephalus
Enter new name: Gallimimus
Enter number from 1 to 5 (0 to exit): 0
Goodbye...
```

It's not the most efficient dinosaur editor I've used, but it'll do. Let's take a look at the source code.

Stepping Through the dinoEdit Source Code

The file *dinoEdit.h* starts off with a few `#defines`. `kDinoRecordSize` defines the length of each dinosaur record. Note that the dinosaur file doesn't contain any carriage returns, just 100 bytes (5 * 20 = 100) of pure dinosaur pleasure!

`kMaxLineLength` defines the length of an array of `chars` we'll use to read in any new dinosaur names. `kDinoFileName` is the name of the dinosaur file.

```
/***********/
/* Defines */
/***********/
#define kDinoRecordSize      20
#define kMaxLineLength       100
#define kDinoFileName        "../../My Dinos"
```

Next come the function prototypes for the functions in *main.c*:

```
/*******************************/
/* Function Prototypes - main.c */
/*******************************/
int    GetNumber( void );
int    GetNumberOfDinos( void );
void   ReadDinoName( int number, char *dinoName );
bool   GetNewDinoName( char *dinoName );
```

```
void    WriteDinoName( int number, char *dinoName );
void    Flush( void );
void    DoError( char *message );
```

main.c starts with four #includes. <stdlib.h> gives us access to the function exit().
<stdio.h> gives us access to a number of functions, including printf() and all the file
manipulation functions, types, and constants. <string.h> gives us access to the function
strlen(). You've already seen what "dinoEdit.h" brings to the table.

```
#include <stdlib.h>
#include <stdio.h>
#include <string.h>
#include <stdbool.h>

#include "dinoEdit.h"
```

NOTE

If you ever want to find out which of the functions you call are dependent on which of your include files,
just comment out the #include statement in question and recompile. The compiler will spew out an
error message (or a whole bunch of messages) telling you it couldn't find a prototype for a function you
called.

main() basically consists of a loop that first prompts for a dinosaur number at the top of the
loop and processes the selection in the body of the loop:

```
/********************************> main <*/
int    main( void ) {
    int     number;
    char    dinoName[ kDinoRecordSize+1 ];
```

GetNumber() prompts for a dinosaur number between 0 and the number of dinosaur
records in the file. If the user types *0*, we'll drop out of the loop and exit the program.

```
    while ( (number = GetNumber() ) != 0 ) {
```

If we made it here, GetNumber() must have returned a legitimate record number.
ReadDinoName() takes the dinosaur number and returns the corresponding dinosaur
name from the file. The returned dinosaur name is then printed.

```
        ReadDinoName( number, dinoName );

        printf( "Dino #%d: %s\n", number, dinoName );
```

GetNewDinoName() prompts the user for a new dinosaur name to replace the existing name. GetNewDinoName() returns true if a name is entered and false if the user just presses return. If the user entered a name, we'll pass it on to WriteDinoName(), which will write the name in the file, overwriting the old name.

```
        if ( GetNewDinoName( dinoName ) )
            WriteDinoName( number, dinoName );
    }

    printf( "Goodbye..." );

    return 0;
}
```

GetNumber() starts off with a call to GetNumberOfDinos(). As its name implies, GetNumberOfDinos() goes into the dinosaur file and returns the number of records in the file:

```
/*************************> GetNumber <*/
int     GetNumber( void ) {
    int         number, numDinos;

    numDinos = GetNumberOfDinos();
```

GetNumber() then continuously prompts for a dinosaur number until the user enters a number between 0 and numDinos:

```
    do {
        printf( "Enter number from 1 to %d (0 to exit): ", numDinos );
        scanf( "%d", &number );
        Flush();
    }
    while ( (number < 0) || (number > numDinos));

    return( number );
}
```

GetNumberOfDinos() starts our file management adventure. First, we'll open *My Dinos* for reading only:

```
/********************> GetNumberOfDinos <*/
int     GetNumberOfDinos( void ) {
    FILE    *fp;
    long    fileLength;

    if ( (fp = fopen( kDinoFileName, "r" )) == NULL )
        DoError( "Couldn't open file...Goodbye!" );
```

TIP

Notice that we've passed an error message to a function called `DoError()` instead of printing it with `printf()`. There are several reasons for doing this. First, since `DoError()` executes two lines of code (calls of `printf()` and `exit()`), each `DoError()` call saves a bit of code.

More importantly, this approach encapsulates all our error handling in a single function. If we want to send all error messages to a log file, all we have to do is edit `DoError()` instead of hunting down all the error messages and attaching a few extra lines of code.

Next, we'll call `fseek()` to move the file position indicator to the end of the file. Can you see what's coming?

```
if ( fseek( fp, 0L, SEEK_END ) != 0 )
    DoError( "Couldn't seek to end of file...Goodbye!" );
```

Now, we'll call `ftell()` to retrieve the current file position indicator, which also happens to be the file length. Cool!

```
if ( (fileLength = ftell( fp )) == -1L )
    DoError( "ftell() failed...Goodbye!" );
```

Now that we have the file length, we can close the file:

```
fclose( fp );
```

Finally, we'll calculate the number of dinosaur records by dividing the file length by the number of bytes in a single record. For simplicity's sake, we'll convert the number of records to an `int` before we return it. That means that we can't deal with a file that contains more than 32,767 dinosaur records. How many dinosaurs can you name?

```
    return( (int)(fileLength / kDinoRecordSize) );
}
```

`ReadDinoName()` first opens the file for reading only:

```
/***********************> ReadDinoName <*/
void    ReadDinoName( int number, char *dinoName ) {
    FILE    *fp;
    long    bytesToSkip;

    if ( (fp = fopen( kDinoFileName, "r" )) == NULL )
        DoError( "Couldn't open file...Goodbye!" );
```

Since we'll be reading dinosaur number number, we have to move the file position indicator to the end of dinosaur number number-1. That means we'll need to skip over number-1 dinosaur records.

```
bytesToSkip = (long)((number-1) * kDinoRecordSize);
```

We'll use fseek() to skip the appropriate number of bytes from the beginning of the file (that's what the constant SEEK_SET is for):

```
if ( fseek( fp, bytesToSkip, SEEK_SET ) != 0 )
    DoError( "Couldn't seek in file...Goodbye!" );
```

Finally, we'll call fread() to read the dinosaur record into the array of chars pointed to by dinoName. The first fread() parameter is the pointer to the block of memory where the data will be read. The second parameter is the number of bytes in a single record. fread() expects both the second and third parameters to be of type size_t, so we'll use a typecast to make the compiler happy. (Gee, by the time we talk about typecasting in Chapter 11, you'll already be an expert!) The third parameter is the number of records to read in. We want to read in one record of kDinoRecordSize bytes. The last parameter is the FILE pointer we got from fopen().

fread() returns the number of records read. Since we asked fread() to read one record, we expect fread() to return a value of 1. If that doesn't happen, something is dreadfully wrong (perhaps the file got corrupted, or that Pepsi you spilled in your hard drive is finally starting to take effect):

```
if ( fread( dinoName, (size_t)kDinoRecordSize,
        (size_t)1, fp ) != 1 )
    DoError( "Bad fread()...Goodbye!" );
```

Once again, we close the file when we're done working with it:

```
    fclose( fp );
}
```

GetNewDinoName() starts by prompting for a new dinosaur name. Then, it calls fgets() to read in a line of text. We'll use our strlen() trick to replace the '\n' with a '\0':

```
/*********************> GetNewDinoName <*/
bool    GetNewDinoName( char *dinoName ) {
    char    line[ kMaxLineLength ];
    int     i, nameLen;

    printf( "Enter new name: " );
```

```
if ( fgets( line, kMaxLineLength, stdin ) == NULL )
    DoError( "Bad fgets()...Goodbye!" );

line[ strlen( line ) - 1 ] = '\0';
```

Our next step is to fill the `dinoName` array with spaces. We'll then call `strlen()` to find out how many characters the user typed. We'll copy those characters back into the `dinoName` array, leaving `dinoName` with a dinosaur name followed by a bunch of spaces.

```
for ( i=0; i<kDinoRecordSize; i++ )
    dinoName[i] = ' ';
```

`strlen()` takes a pointer to a zero-terminated string and returns the length of the string, not including the zero terminator.

```
nameLen = strlen( line );
```

If the user typed a dinosaur name larger than 20 characters long, we'll only copy the first 20 characters:

```
if ( nameLen > kDinoRecordSize )
    nameLen = kDinoRecordSize;
```

Here's where we copy the characters from `line` into `dinoName`:

```
for ( i=0; i<nameLen; i++ )
    dinoName[i] = line[i];
```

Finally, we'll return `true` to let the calling function know that the name is ready:

```
    return true;
}
```

`WriteDinoName()` opens the file for reading and writing. Since we used a mode of `"r+"` instead of `"w+"`, we won't lose the contents of *MyDinos* (in other words, *MyDinos* won't be deleted and re-created):

```
/***********************> WriteDinoName <*/
void    WriteDinoName( int number, char *dinoName ) {
    FILE    *fp;
    long    bytesToSkip;

    if ( (fp = fopen( kDinoFileName, "r+" )) == NULL )
        DoError( "Couldn't open file...Goodbye!" );
```

Next, we calculate the number of bytes we need to skip to place the file position indicator at the beginning of the record we want to overwrite and then call `fseek()` to move the file position indicator:

```
bytesToSkip = (long)((number-1) * kDinoRecordSize);

if ( fseek( fp, bytesToSkip, SEEK_SET ) != 0 )
    DoError( "Couldn't seek in file...Goodbye!" );
```

We then call `fwrite()` to write the dinosaur record back out. `fwrite()` works exactly the same way as `fread()`, including returning the number of records written:

```
if ( fwrite( dinoName, (size_t)kDinoRecordSize,
        (size_t)1, fp ) != 1 )
    DoError( "Bad fwrite()...Goodbye!" );

fclose( fp );
}
```

You've seen this function before:

```
/*****************************> Flush <*/
void    Flush( void ) {
    while ( getchar() != '\n' )
        ;
}
```

`DoError()` prints the error message, adding a carriage return, and then exits:

```
/*****************************> DoError <*/
void    DoError( char *message ) {
    printf( "%s\n", message );
    exit( 0 );
}
```

What's Next?

This chapter has covered a lot of material. You've learned about file names and paths and learned how to open and close a file. We then moved on to reading and writing files and explored the update file opening modes. Finally, you learned all about random file access.

Chapter 11 tackles a wide assortment of programming topics. We'll look at typecasting, the technique used to translate from one type to another. We'll cover recursion, the ability of a function to call itself. We'll also examine function pointers, variables that can be used to pass a function as a parameter.

CHAPTER 10 EXERCISES

1. What's wrong with each of the following code fragments?

    a.
```
FILE    *fp;

fp = fopen( "w", "My Data File" );
if ( fp != NULL )
    printf( "The file is open." );
```

    b.
```
char    myData = 7;
FILE    *fp;

fp = fopen( "r", "My Data File" );
fscanf( "Here's a number: %d", &myData );
```

    c.
```
FILE    *fp;
char    *line;

fp = fopen( "My Data File", "r" );
fscanf( fp, "%s", &line );
```

    d.
```
FILE    *fp;
char    line[100];

fp = fopen( "My Data File", "w" );
fscanf( fp, "%s", line );
```

2. Write a program that reads in and prints a file with the following format:

    ■ The first line in the file contains a single int. Call it x.

    ■ All subsequent lines contain a list of x ints separated by tabs.

    For example, if the first number in the file is 6, all subsequent lines will have six ints per line. There is no limit to the number of lines in the file. Keep reading and printing lines until you hit the end of the file.

    You can print each int as you encounter it or, for extra credit, allocate an array of ints large enough to hold one line's worth of ints and then pass that array to a function that prints an int array.

3. Modify dvdFiler so memory for the title and comment lines is allocated as the lines are read in. First, you'll need to change the DVDInfo struct declaration as follows:

```
struct DVDInfo {
    char            rating;
    char            *title;
    char            *comment;
    struct DVDInfo  *next;
};
```

    Not only will you call malloc() to allocate a DVDInfo struct, you'll also call malloc() to allocate space for the title and comment strings. Don't forget to leave enough space for the terminating zero at the end of each string.

Chapter 11

Advanced Topics

Congratulations! By now you've mastered most of the fundamental C programming concepts. This chapter will fill you in on some useful C programming tips, tricks, and techniques that will enhance your programming skills. We'll start with a look at typecasting, C's mechanism for translating one data type to another.

Typecasting

Often, you will find yourself trying to convert a variable of one type to a variable of another type. For example, this code fragment:

```
float  f;
int    i;

f = 3.5;
i = f;

printf( "i is equal to %d", i );
```

causes the following line to appear in the console window:

```
i is equal to 3
```

Notice that the original value assigned to f was truncated from 3.5 to 3 when the value in f was assigned to i. This truncation was caused when the compiler saw an `int` on the left side and a `float` on the right side of this assignment statement:

```
i = f;
```

The compiler automatically translated the float to an int. **Typecasting** is a mechanism you can use to translate the value of an expression from one type to another. In general, the right side of an assignment statement is always translated to the type on the left side when the assignment occurs. In this case, the compiler handled the type conversion for you. Technically speaking, the compiler performed an **implicit cast** to convert one type (a float) to another (an int).

Another form of typecast is the explicit cast. An **explicit cast** always takes this form:

```
(type) expression
```

where type is any legal C type. In this code fragment, the variable f gets assigned a value of 1.5:

```
float f;

f = 1.5;
```

In this code fragment, the value of 1.5 is cast as an int before being assigned to f:

```
float f;

f = (int)1.5;
```

Just as you might imagine, casting a float as an int truncates the float, turning the value 1.5 into 1. In this example, two casts were performed. First, the float value 1.5 was explicitly cast to the int value 1. When this int value was assigned to the float f, the value was implicitly cast to the float value 1.0.

Cast with Care

Use caution when you cast from one type to another. Problems can arise when casting between types of a different size. Consider this example:

```
int  i;
char c;

i = 500;
c = i;
```

Here, the value 500 is assigned to the int i—so far, so good. Next, the value in i is cast to a char as it is assigned to the char c. See the problem? Since a char can only hold values between −128 and 127, assigning a value of 500 to c doesn't make sense.

CASTING A LARGER TYPE TO A SMALLER TYPE

What happens to the extra byte or bytes when a larger type is cast to a smaller type? The matching bytes are typecast, and the value of any extra bytes is lost.

For example, when a 2-byte `int` is cast to a 1-byte `char`, the leftmost byte of the `int` (the byte with the more significant bits, the bits valued 2^8 through 2^{15}) is dropped, and the rightmost byte (the bits valued 2^0 through 2^7) is copied into the `char`.

Consider the following example:

```
int i;

char c;

i = 500;

c = i;
```

The `int i` has a value of 0x01E4, which is hex for 500. After the second assignment, the `char` ends up with the value 0xE4, which has a value of 244 if the `char` was `unsigned` or −12 if the `char` is `signed`.

Casting with Pointers

Typecasting can also be used when working with pointers. This notation casts the variable `myPtr` as a pointer to an `int`:

```
(int *) myPtr
```

Casting with pointers allows you to link together `struct`s of different types. For example, suppose you declared two `struct` types, as follows:

```
struct Dog {
    struct Dog  *next;
} ;
```

```
struct Cat {
    struct Cat  *next;
} ;
```

By using typecasting, you could create a linked list that contains both Cats and Dogs. Figure 11-1 shows a Dog whose next field points to a Cat. Imagine the source code you'd need to implement such a linked list.

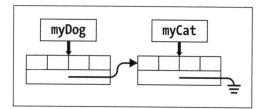

Figure 11-1. *This linked list contains structs of two different types. myDog.next points to myCat. myCat.next points to NULL.*

Consider this source code:

```
struct Dog   myDog;
struct Cat   myCat;

myDog.next = &myCat; /* <--Compiler complains */
myCat.next = NULL;
```

In the first assignment statement, a pointer of one type is assigned to a pointer of another type. &myCat is a pointer to a struct of type Cat. myDog.next is declared to be a pointer to a struct of type Dog. To make this code compile, we'll need a typecast:

```
struct Dog   myDog;
struct Cat   myCat;

myDog.next = (struct Dog *)(&myCat);
myCat.next = NULL;
```

If both sides of an assignment operator are arithmetic types (float, int, char, etc.), the compiler will automatically cast the right side of the assignment to the type of the left side. If both sides are pointers, you'll have to perform the typecast yourself.

There are a few exceptions to this rule. If the pointers on both sides of the assignment are the same type, no typecast is necessary. If the pointer on the right side is either NULL or of type (void *), no typecast is necessary. Finally, if the pointer on the left side is of type (void *), no typecast is necessary.

The type (void *) is sort of a wild card for pointers. It matches up with any pointer type. For example, here's a new version of the Dog and Cat code:

```
struct Dog {
    void  *next;
} ;

struct Cat {
    void  *next;
} ;

struct Dog   myDog;
struct Cat   myCat;

myDog.next = &myCat;
myCat.next = NULL;
```

This code lets Dog.next point to a Cat struct without a typecast. The void pointer should only be used as a last resort. An explicit type makes it quite clear what is going on. In our previous example, anyone looking over our code would easily be able to tell that we were forcing a Dog to point to a Cat. In the void pointer example, the difference in type is far less obvious. Use type and typecasting intentionally. Make both part of your program design.

Unions

C offers a special data type, known as a **union**, which allows a single variable to disguise itself as several different data types. unions are declared just like structs. Here's an example:

```
union Number {
    int  i;
    float f;
    char *s;
} myNumber;
```

This declaration creates a union type named Number. It also creates an individual Number named myNumber. If this were a struct declaration, you'd be able to store three different values in the three fields of the struct. A union, on the other hand, lets you store one and only one of the union's fields in the union. Here's how this works.

When a union is declared, the compiler allocates the space required by the largest of the union's fields, sharing that space with all of the union's fields. If an int requires 2 bytes, a float 4 bytes, and a pointer 4 bytes, myNumber is allocated exactly 4 bytes. You can store an int, a float, or a char pointer in myNumber. The compiler allows you to treat myNumber as any of these types. To refer to myNumber as an int, refer to

myNumber.i

To refer to myNumber as a float, refer to

myNumber.f

To refer to myNumber as a char pointer, refer to

myNumber.s

You are responsible for remembering which form the union is currently occupying.

CAUTION

If you store an `int` in myUnion by assigning a value to myUnion.i, you'd best remember that fact. If you proceed to store a `float` in myUnion.f, you've just trashed your `int`. Remember, there are only 4 bytes allocated to the entire union.

In addition, storing a value as one type and reading it as another can produce unpredictable results. For example, if you stored a `float` in myNumber.f, the field myNumber.i would *not* be the same as `(int)(myNumber.f)`.

One way to keep track of the current state of the union is to declare an `int` to go along with the union, as well as a #define for each of the union's fields:

```
#define kUnionContainsInt       1
#define kUnionContainsFloat     2
#define kUnionContainsPointer   3

union Number {
    int  i;
    float f;
    char *s;
} myNumber;

int    myUnionTag;
```

If you are currently using myUnion as a `float`, assign the value kUnionContainsFloat to myUnionTag. Later in your code, you can use myUnionTag when deciding which form of the union you are dealing with:

```
if ( myUnionTag == kUnionContainsInt )
    DoIntStuff( myUnion.i );
else if ( myUnionTag == kUnionContainsFloat )
    DoFloatStuff( myUnion.f );
else
    DoPointerStuff( myUnion.s );
```

Why Use Unions?

In general, unions are most useful when dealing with two data structures that share a set of common fields but differ in some small way. For example, consider these two `struct` declarations:

```
struct Pitcher {
    char    name[ 40 ];
    int         team;
```

```
    int         strikeouts;
    int         runsAllowed;
} ;

struct Batter {
    char    name[ 40 ];
    int         team;
    int         runsScored;
    int         homeRuns;
} ;
```

These structs might be useful if you were tracking the pitchers and batters on your favorite baseball team. Both structs share a set of common fields, the array of chars named name and the int named team. Both structs have their own unique fields as well. The Pitcher struct contains a pair of fields appropriate for a pitcher, strikeouts and runsAllowed. The Batter struct contains a pair of fields appropriate for a batter, runsScored and homeRuns.

One solution to your baseball-tracking program would be to maintain two types of structs, a Pitcher and a Batter. There is nothing wrong with this approach. As an alternative, however, you can declare a single struct that contains the fields common to Pitcher and Batter, with a union for the unique fields:

```
#define kMets    1
#define kReds    2

#define kPitcher   1
#define kBatter    2

struct Pitcher {
    int    strikeouts;
    int    runsAllowed;
} ;

struct Batter {
    int    runsScored;
    int    homeRuns;
} ;

struct Player {
    int    type;
    char   name[ 40 ];
    int    team;
    union {
        struct Pitcher    pStats;
        struct Batter     bStats;
    } u;
};
```

Here's an example of a `Player` declaration:

```
struct Player    myPlayer;
```

Once you created the `Player struct`, you would initialize the `type` field with one of either `kPitcher` or `kBatter`:

```
myPlayer.type = kBatter;
```

You would access the name and team fields like this:

```
myPlayer.team = kMets;
printf( "Stepping up to the plate:  %s", myPlayer.name );
```

Finally, you'd access the `union` fields like this:

```
if ( myPlayer.type == kPitcher )
    myPlayer.u.pStats.strikeouts = 20;
```

The u was the name given to the union in the declaration of the `Player` type. Every `Player` you declare will automatically have a `union` named u built into it. The `union` gives you access to either a `Pitcher struct` named `pStats` or a `Batter struct` named `bStats`. The previous example references the `strikeouts` field of the `pStats` field.

`union`s provide an interesting alternative to maintaining multiple data structures. Try them. Write your next program using a `union` or two. If you don't like them, you can return them for a full refund.

Function Recursion

Some programming problems are best solved by repeating a mathematical process. For example, to learn whether a number is prime (see Chapter 6) you might step through each of the even integers between 2 and the number's square root, one at a time, searching for a factor. If no factor is found, you have a prime. The process of stepping through the numbers between 2 and the number's square root is called **iteration**.

In programming, iterative solutions are fairly common. Almost every time you use a `for` loop, you are applying an iterative approach to a problem. An alternative to the iterative approach is known as **recursion**. In a recursive approach, instead of repeating a process in a loop, you embed the process in a function and have the function call itself until the process is complete. The key to recursion is a function calling itself.

Suppose you wanted to calculate 5 factorial (also known as 5!). The factorial of a number is the product of each integer from 1 up to the number, for example:

```
5! = 5 * 4 * 3 * 2 * 1 = 120
```

Using an iterative approach, you might write some code like this:

```c
#include <stdio.h>

int main (int argc, const char * argv[]) {
    int   i, num;
    long  fac;

    num = 5;
    fac = 1;

    for ( i=1; i<=num; i++ )
        fac *= i;

    printf( "%d factorial is %ld.", num, fac );

    return 0;
}
```

NOTE

If you are interested in trying this code, you'll find it in the *Learn C Projects* folder, under the subfolder named *11.01 - iterate*.

If you ran this program, you'd see this line printed in the console window:

```
5 factorial is 120.
```

As you can see from the source code, the algorithm steps through (iterates) the numbers 1 through 5, building the factorial with each successive multiplication.

A Recursive Approach

You can use a recursive approach to solve the same problem. For starters, you'll need a function to act as a base for the recursion, a function that will call itself. You'll need two things to build into your recursive function. First, you'll need a mechanism to keep track of the depth of the recursion. In other words, you'll need a variable or parameter that changes depending on the number of times the recursive function calls itself.

Second, you'll need a terminating condition, something that tells the recursive function when it's gone deep enough. Here's one version of a recursive function that calculates a factorial:

```
long    factorial( long num ) {
    if ( num > 1 )
        num *= factorial( num - 1 );

    return( num );
}
```

`factorial()` takes a single parameter, the number whose factorial you are trying to calculate. `factorial()` first checks to see whether the number passed to it is greater than 1. If so, `factorial()` calls itself, passing 1 less than the number passed into it. This strategy guarantees that, eventually, `factorial()` will get called with a value of 1.

Figure 11-2 shows this process in action.

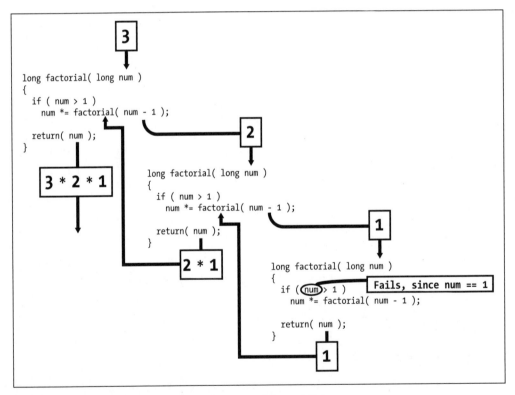

Figure 11-2. *The recursion process caused by the call factorial(3)*

The process starts with a call to `factorial()`:

```
result = factorial( 3 );
```

Take a look at the leftmost `factorial()` source code in Figure 11-2. `factorial()` is called with a parameter of 3. The `if` statement checks to see if the parameter is greater than 1. Since 3 is greater than 1, the following statement is executed:

```
num *= factorial( num - 1 );
```

This statement calls `factorial()` again, passing a value of n-1, or 2, as the parameter. This second call of `factorial()` is pictured in the center of Figure 11-2.

> **NOTE**
>
> It's important to understand that this second call to `factorial()` is treated just like any other function call that occurs in the middle of a function. The calling function's variables are preserved while the called function runs. In this case, the called function is just another copy of `factorial()`.

This second call of `factorial()` takes a value of 2 as a parameter. The `if` statement compares this value to 1 and, since 2 is greater than 1, executes the statement:

```
num *= factorial( num - 1 );
```

This statement calls `factorial()` yet again, passing num-1, or 1, as a parameter. The third call of `factorial()` is portrayed on the rightmost side of Figure 11-2.

The third call of `factorial()` starts with an `if` statement. Since the input parameter was 1, the `if` statement fails. Thus, the recursion termination condition is reached. Now, this third call of `factorial()` returns a value of 1.

At this point, the second call of `factorial()` resumes, completing the statement:

```
num *= factorial( num - 1 );
```

Since the call of `factorial()` returned a value of 1, this statement is equivalent to

```
num *= 1;
```

leaving num with the same value it came in with, namely 2. This second call of `factorial()` returns a value of 2.

At this point, the first call of `factorial()` resumes, completing the statement:

```
num *= factorial( num - 1 );
```

Since the second call of `factorial()` returned a value of 2, this statement is equivalent to

```
num *= 2;
```

Since the first call of factorial() started with the parameter num taking a value of 3, this statement sets num to a value of 6. Finally, the original call of factorial() returns a value of 6. This is as it should be, since 3 factorial = 3 * 2 * 1 = 6.

Do not use recursion lightly. It is expensive in terms of system resources, relative to its iterative cousin. That said, read on for some problems that are perfect for recursion.

Binary Trees

As you learn more about data structures, you'll discover new applications for recursion. For example, one of the most-often-used data structures in computer programming is the **binary tree** (see Figure 11-3). As you'll see later, binary trees were just made for recursion. The binary tree is similar to the linked list. Both consist of structs connected by pointers embedded in each struct.

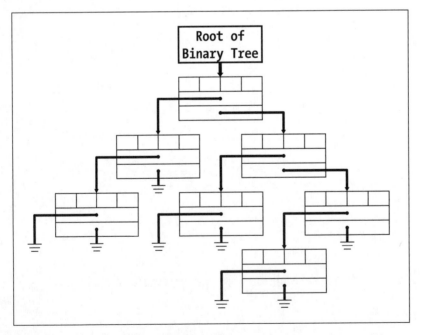

Figure 11-3. *A binary tree. Why "binary"? Each node in the tree contains two pointers.*

Linked lists are linear. Each `struct` in the list is linked by pointers to the `struct` behind it and in front of it in the list. Binary trees always start with a single `struct`, known as the root `struct` or **root node**. Where the linked list `struct`s we've been working with contain a single pointer, named `next`, binary tree `struct`s or nodes each have two pointers, usually known as `left` and `right`.

Check out the binary tree in Figure 11-3. Notice that the root node has a left **child** and a right child. The left child has its own left child but its `right` pointer is set to NULL. The left child's left child has two NULL pointers. A node with two NULL pointers is known as a **leaf node** or **terminal node**.

Binary trees are extremely useful. They work especially well when the data you are trying to sort has a **comparative relationship**. This means that if you compare one piece of data to another, you'll be able to judge the first piece as greater than, equal to, or less than the second piece. For example, numbers are comparative. Words in a dictionary can be comparative, if you consider their alphabetical order. The word *iguana* is greater than *aardvark*, but less than *xenophobe*.

Here's how you might store a sequence of words, one at a time, in a binary tree. We'll start with this list of words:

```
opulent
entropy
salubrious
ratchet
coulomb
yokel
tortuous
```

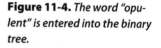

Figure 11-4 shows the word "opulent" added to the root node of the binary tree. Since it is the only word in the tree so far, both the left and right pointers are set to NULL.

Figure 11-4. *The word "opulent" is entered into the binary tree.*

Figure 11-5 shows the word "entropy" added to the binary tree. Since `entropy` is less than `opulent` (i.e., comes before it alphabetically), `entropy` is stored as `opulent`'s left child.

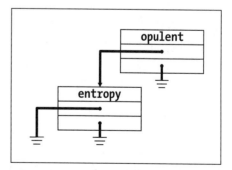

Figure 11-5. *The word "entropy" is less than the word "opulent" and is added as its left child in the binary tree.*

Next, Figure 11-6 shows the word "salubrious" added to the tree. Since salubrious is greater than opulent, it becomes opulent's right child.

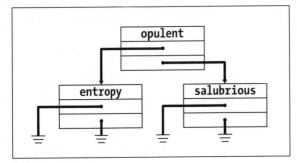

Figure 11-6. *The word "salubrious" is greater than the word "opulent" and is added to its right in the tree.*

Figure 11-7 shows the word "ratchet" added to the tree. First, ratchet is compared to opulent. Since ratchet is greater than opulent, we follow the right pointer. Since there's a word there already, we'll have to compare ratchet to this word. Since ratchet is less than salubrious, we'll store it as salubrious's left child.

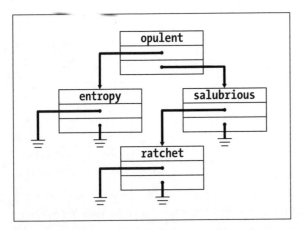

Figure 11-7. *The word "ratchet" is greater than "opulent" but less than "salubrious" and is placed in the tree accordingly.*

Figure 11-8 shows the binary tree after the remainder of the word list has been added. Do you understand how this scheme works? What would the binary tree look like if `coulomb` was the first word on the list? The tree would have no left children and would lean heavily to the right. What if `yokel` was the first word entered? As you can see, this particular use of binary trees depends on the order of the data. Randomized data that starts with a value close to the average produces a **balanced tree**. If the words had been entered in alphabetical order, you would have ended up with a binary tree that looked like a linked list.

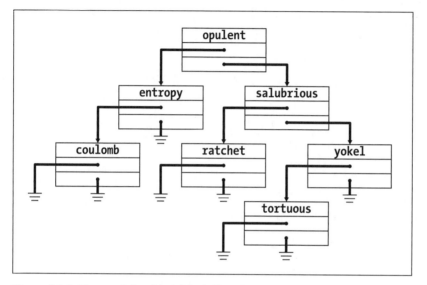

Figure 11-8. *The words "coulomb," "yokel," and "tortuous" are added to the tree.*

Searching Binary Trees

Now that your word list is stored in the binary tree, the next step is to look up a word in the tree. This is known as **searching** the tree. Suppose you wanted to look up the word "tortuous" in your tree. You'd start with the root node, comparing `tortuous` with `opulent`. Since `tortuous` is greater than `opulent`, you'd follow the right pointer to `salubrious`. You'd follow this algorithm down to `yokel` and finally `tortuous`.

Searching a binary tree is typically much faster than searching a linked list. In a linked list, you search through your list of nodes, one at a time, until you find the node you are looking for. On average, you'll end up searching half of the list. In a list of 100 nodes, you'll end up checking 50 nodes on average. In a list of 1,000 nodes, you'll end up checking 500 nodes on average. In the worst possible case, you'd end up searching all 1,000 nodes.

In a balanced binary tree, you reduce the search space in half each time you check a node. Without getting into the mathematics—check Donald Knuth's *The Art of Computer Programming, Volume 3: Sorting and Searching* (Addison-Wesley 1998) for more information—the maximum number of nodes searched is approximately $\log_2 n$, where n is the number of nodes in the tree. On average, you'll search $\log_2 n/2$ nodes. In a list of 100 nodes, you'll end up searching 3.32 nodes on average. In a list of 1,000 nodes, you'll end up checking about 5 nodes on average.

As you can see, a binary tree provides a significant performance advantage over a linked list.

A binary tree that contained just words may not be that interesting, but imagine that these words were names of great political leaders. Each node might contain a leader's name, biographical information, perhaps a pointer to another data structure containing great speeches. The value, name, or word that determines the order of the tree is said to be the **key**.

You don't always search a tree based on the key. Sometimes, you'll want to step through every node in the tree. For example, suppose your tree contained the name and birth date of each of the presidents of the United States. Suppose also that the tree was built using each president's last name as a key. Now suppose you wanted to compose a list of all presidents born in July. In this case, searching the tree alphabetically won't do you any good. You'll have to search every node in the tree. This is where recursion comes in.

Recursion and Binary Trees

Binary trees and recursion were made for each other. To search a tree recursively, the recursing function has to visit the current node, as well as call itself with each of its two child nodes. The child nodes will do the same thing with themselves and their child nodes. Each part of the recursion stops when a terminal node is encountered.

Check out this piece of code:

```
struct Node {
    int     value;
    struct Node    *left;
    struct Node    *right;
} myNode;
```

```
Searcher( struct Node *nodePtr ) {
    if ( nodePtr != NULL ) {
        VisitNode( nodePtr );
        Searcher( nodePtr->left );
        Searcher( nodePtr->right );
    }
}
```

The function Searcher() takes a pointer to a tree node as its parameter. If the pointer is NULL, we must be at a terminal node, so there's no need to recurse any deeper. If the pointer points to a Node, the function VisitNode() is called. VisitNode() performs whatever function you want performed for each node in the binary tree. In our current example, VisitNode() could check to see if the president associated with this node was born in July. If so, VisitNode() might print the president's name in the console window.

Once the node is visited, Searcher() calls itself twice, once passing a pointer to its left child and once passing a pointer to its right child. If this version of Searcher() were used to search the tree in Figure 11-8, the tree would be searched in the order described in Figure 11-9. This type of search is known as a **preorder search**, because the node is visited before the two recursive calls take place.

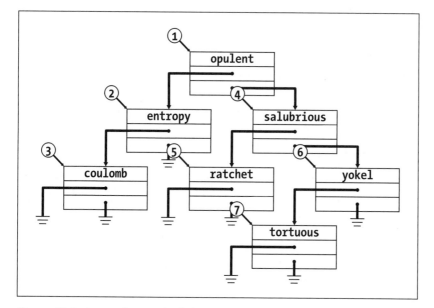

Figure 11-9. *A preorder search of a binary tree as produced by the first version of Searcher()*

Here's a slightly revised version of Searcher(). Without looking at Figure 11-10, can you predict the order in which the tree will be searched? This version of Searcher() performs an **inorder search** of the tree:

```
Searcher( struct Node *nodePtr ) {
    if ( nodePtr != NULL ) {
        Searcher( nodePtr->left );
        VisitNode( nodePtr );
        Searcher( nodePtr->right );
    }
}
```

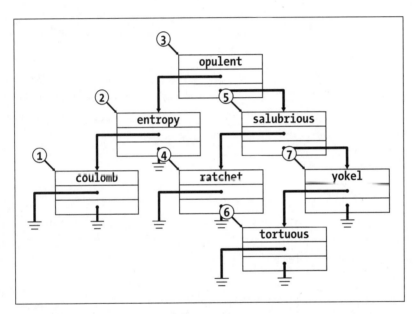

Figure 11-10. *An inorder search of the same tree*

Here's a final look at Searcher(). This version performs a **postorder search** of the tree (see Figure 11-11):

```
Searcher( struct Node *nodePtr ) {
    if ( nodePtr != NULL ) {
        Searcher( nodePtr->left );
        Searcher( nodePtr->right );
        VisitNode( nodePtr );
    }
}
```

Recursion and binary trees are two extremely powerful programming tools. Learn how to use them—they'll pay big dividends.

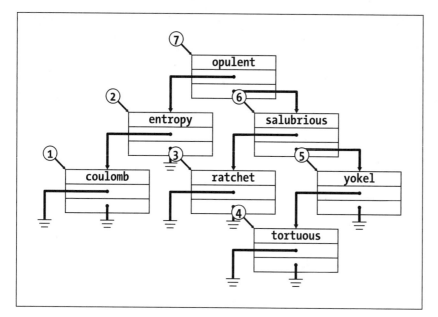

Figure 11-11. *A postorder search of the same tree*

Function Pointers

Next on the list is the subject of **function pointers**. Function pointers are exactly what they sound like: pointers that point to functions. Up to now, the only way to call a function was to place its name in the source code:

```
MyFunction();
```

Function pointers give you a new way to call a function. Function pointers allow you to say, "Execute the function pointed to by this variable." Here's an example:

```
int    (*myFuncPtr)( float );
```

This line of code declares a function pointer named myFuncPtr. myFuncPtr is a pointer to a function that takes a single parameter, a float, and returns an int. The parentheses in the declaration are all necessary. The first pair ties the * to myFuncPtr, ensuring that myFuncPtr is declared as a pointer. The second pair surrounds the parameter list and distinguishes myFuncPtr as a function pointer.

Suppose we had a function called DealTheCards() that took a float as a parameter and returned an int. This line of code assigns the address of DealTheCards() to the function pointer myFuncPtr:

```
myFuncPtr = DealTheCards;
```

Notice that the parentheses were left off the end of `DealTheCards()`. This omission is critical. If the parentheses were there, the code would have called `DealTheCards()`, returning a value to `myFuncPtr`. You may also have noticed that the & operator wasn't used. When you refer to a function without using the parentheses at the end, the compiler knows you are referring to the address of the function.

Now that you have the function's address in the function pointer, there's only one thing left to do—call the function. Here's how it's done:

```
int     result;

result = (*myFuncPtr)( 3.5 );
```

This line calls the function `DealTheCards()`, passing it the parameter `3.5` and returning the function value to the `int result`. You could also have called the function this way:

```
int     result;

result = myFuncPtr( 3.5 );
```

In my opinion, this latter form is a bit easier on the eye.

You can do a lot with function pointers. You can create an array of function pointers. How about a binary tree of function pointers? You can pass a function pointer as a parameter to another function. Taking this one step further, you can create a function that does nothing but call other functions!

For your enjoyment, there's a function-calling project in the *Learn C Projects* folder, inside the *11.03 - funcPtr* subfolder. The program is pretty simple, but it should serve as a useful reference when you start using function pointers in your own programs.

Initializers

When you declare a variable, you can also provide an initial value for the variable at the same time. The format for integer types, floating point types, and pointers is as follows:

```
type    variable = initializer;
```

In this case, the initializer is just an expression. Here are a few examples:

```
float   myFloat = 3.14159;
int     myInt = 9 * 27;
int     *intPtr = &myInt;
```

If you plan on initializing a more complex variable, like an array, struct, or union, you'll use a slightly different form of initializer, embedding the elements used to initialize the variable between pairs of curly braces. Consider these two array declarations:

```
int  myInts[] = { 10, 20, 30, 40 };
float myFloats[ 5 ] = { 1.0, 2.0, 3.0 };
```

The first line of code declares an array of four ints, setting myInts[0] to 10, myInts[1] to 20, myInts[2] to 30, and myInts[3] to 40. If you leave out the array dimension, the compiler makes it just large enough to contain the listed data.

The second line of code includes a dimension but not enough data to fill the array. The first three array elements are filled with the specified values, but myFloats[3] and myFloats[4] are initialized to 0.0.

Here's another example:

```
char s[ 20 ] = "Hello";
```

What a convenient way to initialize an array of chars! Here's another way to accomplish the same thing:

```
char s[ 20 ] = { 'H', 'e', 'l', 'l', 'o', '\0' };
```

Once again, if you leave out the dimension, the compiler will allocate just enough memory to hold your text string, including a byte to hold the zero terminator. If you include the dimension, the compiler will allocate that many array elements, and fill the array with whatever data you provide. If you provide more data than will fit in the array, your code won't compile.

Here's a struct example:

```
struct Numbers {
    int    i, j;
    float  f;
};

struct Numbers myNums = { 1, 2, 3.01 };
```

As you can see, the three initializing values were wrapped in a pair of curly braces. This leaves myNums.i with a value of 1, myNums.j with a value of 2, and myNums.f with a value of 3.01. If you have a struct, union, or array embedded in your struct, you can nest a curly-wrapped list of values inside another list, for example:

```
struct Numbers {
    int    i, j;
    float  f[ 4 ];
};

struct Numbers myNums1 = { 1, 2, {3.01, 4.01, 5.01, 6.01} };
```

An Initializion Example

Here's a bit of sample code. Before you read on, try to guess what the output will look like when this code runs:

```
#include <stdio.h>

#define kArraySize   10

int main (int argc, const char * argv[]) {
    int    i;
    char   s[ kArraySize ] = "Hello";

    printf( "i before it is initialized: %d\n\n", i );

    for ( i=0; i<kArraySize; i++ )
        printf( "s[ i ]: %d\n", s[ i ] );
    return 0;
}
```

This code defines an int, without initializing it, as well as a ten-element array of type char, initializing the array to the string "Hello". Here's the output:

```
i before it is initialized: -1881141193

s[ i ]: 72
s[ i ]: 101
s[ i ]: 108
s[ i ]: 108
s[ i ]: 111
s[ i ]: 0
s[ i ]: 0
s[ i ]: 0
s[ i ]: 0
s[ i ]: 0
```

One lesson to pull from this code is to always initialize your variables, preferably right where they are defined. In the previous example, no harm was done, since we initialized i in the for loop. But suppose we used i in a different way and simply forgot to initialize it. The random nature of uninitialized variables can make bugs very hard to track down. Take a look at this version of the same code:

```
#include <stdio.h>

#define kArraySize   10

int main (int argc, const char * argv[]) {
    int     i = 0;
    char    s[ kArraySize ] = "Hello";

    printf( "i before it is initialized: %d\n\n", i );

    for ( i=0; i<kArraySize; i++ )
        printf( "s[ i ]: %d\n", s[ i ] );
    return 0;
}
```

In this version, I initialized i to 0 even though I knew I was going to use it in a for loop. If you get in the habit of always initializing your variables at the point where they are defined, your program will be much more predictable and easier to debug.

The Remaining Operators

If you go back to Chapter 5 and review the list of operators shown in Figure 5.7, you'll likely find a few operators you are not yet familiar with. Most of the ones we've missed were designed specifically to set the individual bits within a byte. For example, the | operator (not to be confused with its comrade, the logical || operator) takes two values and ORs their bits together, resolving to a single value. This operator is frequently used to set a particular bit to 1.

Check out this code:

```
short    myShort;

myShort = 0x0001 | myShort;
```

This code **sets** the rightmost bit of myShort to 1, no matter what its current value. This line of code, based on the |= operator, does the exact same thing:

```
myShort |= 0x0001;
```

The & operator takes two values and ANDs their bits together, resolving to a single value. This operator is frequently used to **clear** a bit. Clearing a bit sets its value to 0.

Check out this code:

```
short        myShort;

myShort = 0xFFFE & myShort;
```

This code sets the rightmost bit of myShort to 0, no matter what its current value. It might help to think of 0xFFFE as 1111111111111110 in binary.

This line of code, based on the &= operator, does the exact same thing:

```
myShort &= 0xFFFE;
```

The ^ operator takes two values and XORs their values together. It goes along with the ^= operator. The ~ operator takes a single value and turns all the ones into zeros and all the zeros into ones. The &, |, ^, and ~ operators are summarized in Table 11-1.

Table 11-1. *The &, |, ^, and ~ Operators*

A	B	A & B	A	B	A ^ B	~A
1	1	1	1	0	0
1	0	0	1	1	0
0	1	0	1	1	1
0	0	0	0	0	1

The previous examples assumed that a short is 2 bytes (16 bits) long. Of course, this makes for some implementation-dependent code. Here's a more portable example.

This code sets the rightmost bit of myShort, no matter how many bytes are used to implement a short:

```
short  myShort;
myShort = (~1) & myShort;
```

You could also write this as follows:

```
myShort &= (~1);
```

The last of the binary operators, <<, >>, <<=, and >>= are used to **shift** bits within a variable, either to the left or to the right. The left operand is usually an unsigned variable, and the right operand is a positive integer specifying how far to shift the variable's bits.

For example, this code shifts the bits of myShort 2 bits to the right:

```
unsigned short    myShort = 0x0100;

myShort = myShort >> 2;     /* equal to myShort >>= 2; */
```

myShort starts off with a value of 0000000100000000 and ends up with a value of 0000000001000000 (in hex, that's 0x0040). Notice that zeros get shifted in to make up for the leftmost bits that are getting shifted over, and the rightmost bits are lost when they shift off the end.

CAUTION

These bit-shifting operators were designed to work with unsigned values only. Check with your compiler to see how it handles shifting of signed values.

The last two operators we need to cover are the , and :? operators. The , operator gives you a way to combine two expressions into a single expression. The , operator is binary, and both operands are expressions. The left expression is evaluated first, and the result is discarded. The right expression is then evaluated, and its value is returned.

Here's an example:

```
for ( i=0, j=0; i<20 && j<40; i++,j+=2 )
    DoSomething( i, j );
```

This for loop is based on two variables instead of one. Before the loop is entered, i and j are both set to 0. The loop continues as long as i is less than 20 and j is less than 40. Each time through the loop, i is incremented by 1 and j is incremented by 2.

The ? and : operators combine to create something called a **conditional expression**. A conditional expression consists of a logical expression (an expression that evaluates to either true or false), followed by the ? operator, followed by a second expression, followed by the : operator, followed by a third expression:

```
logical-expression ? expression2 : expression3
```

If the logical expression evaluates to true, expression2 gets evaluated, and the entire expression resolves to the value of expression2. If the logical expression evaluates to false, expression3 gets evaluated, and the entire expression resolves to the value of expression3.

Here's an example:

```
IsPrime( num ) ? DoPrimeStuff( num ) : DoNonPrimeStuff( num );
```

As you can see, a conditional expression is really a shorthand way of writing an if-else statement. Here's the if-else version of the previous example:

```
if ( IsPrime( num ) )
    DoPrimeStuff( num );
else
    DoNonPrimeStuff( num );
```

Some people like the brevity of the ?: operator combination. Others find it hard to read. As always, make your choice, and stick with it.

Here's a word of advice: don't overuse the ?: operator. For example, suppose you wanted to use ?: to generate a number's absolute value. You might write code like this:

```
int  value;
value = (value<0) ? (-value) : (value);
```

Though this code works, take a look at this code translated into its if-else form:

```
int  value;
if ( value<0 )
  value = (-value);
else
  value = (value);
```

As you can see, the ?: operator can lead you to write source code that you would otherwise consider pretty darn silly.

Creating Your Own Types

The typedef statement lets you use existing types to create brand-new types you can then use in your declarations. You'll declare this new type just as you would a variable, except you'll precede the declaration with the word typedef and the name you declare will be the name of a new type. Here's an example:

```
typedef  int  *IntPointer;

IntPointer    myIntPointer;
```

The first line of code creates a new type named IntPointer. The second line declares a variable named myIntPointer, which is a pointer to an int.

Here's another example:

```
typedef  float  (*FuncPtr)( int * );

FuncPtr  myFuncPtr;
```

The first line of code declares a new type named FuncPtr. The second line declares a variable named myFuncPtr, which is a pointer to a function that returns a float and takes a single int as a parameter.

Enumerated Types

In a similar vein, the enum statement lets you declare a new type known as an **enumerated type**. An enumerated type is a set of named integer constants, collected under a single type name. A series of examples will make this clear:

```
enum Weekdays {
    Monday,
    Tuesday,
    Wednesday,
    Thursday,
    Friday
};

enum Weekdays  whichDay;

whichDay = Thursday;
```

This code starts off with an enum declaration. The enum is given the name Weekdays and consists of the constants Monday, Tuesday, Wednesday, Thursday, and Friday. The second line of code uses this new enumerated type to declare a variable named whichDay. whichDay is an integer variable that can take on any of the Weekdays constants, as evidenced by the last line of code, which assigns the constant Thursday to whichDay.

Here's another example:

```
enum Colors {
    red,
    green = 5,
    blue,
    magenta,
    yellow = blue + 5
} myColor;

myColor = blue;
```

This code declares an enumerated type named `Colors`. Notice that some of the constants in the `Colors` list are accompanied by initializers. When the compiler creates the enumeration constants, it numbers them sequentially, starting with 0. In the previous example, `Monday` has a value of 0, `Tuesday` has a value of 1, and so on until we reach `Friday`, which has a value of 4.

In this case, the constant `red` has a value of 0. But the constant `green` has a value of 5. Things move along from there, with `blue` and `magenta` having values of 6 and 7, respectively. Next, `yellow` has a value of `blue+5`, which is 11.

This code also declares an enumeration variable named `myColor`, which is then assigned a value of `blue`.

You can declare an enumerated type without the type name:

```
enum {
    chocolate,
    strawberry,
    vanilla
};
int iceCreamFlavor = vanilla;
```

This code declares a series of enumeration constants with values of 0, 1, and 2. We can assign the constants to an `int`, as we did with `iceCreamFlavor`. This comes in handy when you need a set of integer constants but have no need for a tag name.

Static Variables

Normally, when a function exits, the storage for its variables is freed up, and their values are no longer available. By declaring a local variable as `static`, the variable's value is maintained across multiple calls of the same function.

Here's an example:

```
int    StaticFunc( void ) {
    static int  myStatic = 0;

    return myStatic++;
}
```

This function declares an `int` named `myStatic` and initializes it to a value of 0. The function returns the value of `myStatic` and increments `myStatic` after the return value is determined. The first time this function is called, it returns 0, and `myStatic` is left with a value of 1. The second time `StaticFunc()` is called, it returns 1, and `myStatic` is left with a value of 2.

NOTE

> Take a few minutes, and try this code out for yourself. You'll find it in the *Learn C Projects* folder in the subfolder *11.05 - static*.

One of the keys to this function is the manner in which `myStatic` received its initial value. Imagine if the function looked like this:

```
int    StaticFunc( void ) {
    static int    myStatic;

    myStatic = 0;    /* <-- Bad idea.... */

    return myStatic++;
}
```

Each time through the function, we'd be setting the value of `myStatic` back to 0. This function will always return a value of 0. Not what we want, eh?

The difference between the two functions? The first version sets the value of `myStatic` to 0 by initialization (the value is specified within the declaration). The second version sets the value of `myStatic` to 0 by assignment (the value is specified after the declaration). If a variable is marked as `static`, any initialization is done once and once only. Be sure you set the initial value of your `static` variable in the declaration and not in an assignment statement.

NOTE

> One way to think of `static` variables is as global variables that are limited in scope to a single function.

More on Strings

The last topic we'll tackle in this chapter is **string manipulation**. Although we've done some work with strings in previous chapters, there are a number of Standard Library functions that haven't been covered. Each of these functions requires that you include the file <string.h>. Here are a few examples.

strncpy()

strncpy() is declared as follows:

```
char *strncpy( char *dest, const char *source, size_t n );
```

strncpy() copies the string pointed to by source into the string pointed to by dest, copying a maximum of n bytes. strncpy() copies each of the characters in source, including the terminating zero byte. Any characters following a zero byte are not copied, which leaves dest as a properly terminated string. strncpy() returns the pointer dest.

An important thing to remember about strncpy() is that you are responsible for ensuring that source is properly terminated and that enough memory is allocated for the string returned in dest. Here's an example of strncpy() in action:

```
char name[ 20 ];

strncpy( name, "Dave Mark", 20 );
```

This example uses a string literal as the source string. The string is copied into the array name. The return value was ignored.

Note that there is also a Standard Library function named strcpy(). strcpy() is declared as follows:

```
char *strcpy( char *dest, const char *source );
```

strcpy() copies the string pointed to by source into the string pointed to by dest but does not feature the safeguard of a limited number of bytes to copy. This is bad and is subject to buffer overflow. Can you see why? Imagine what would happen if source was larger than dest. The extra bytes would flow off the end of dest, destroying whatever happened to be in its path in memory. Note that even with the protection, the programmer is still responsible for making sure that n is no larger than the number of bytes allocated for dest minus one (to save room for the terminating zero byte).

As always, when given a choice, use the Standard Library function that offers a safeguard against buffer overflow.

strncat()

strncat() is declared as follows:

```
char *strncat( char *dest, const char *source, size_t n );
```

strncat() appends a copy of the string pointed to by source onto the end of the string pointed to by dest, copying a maximum of n bytes. As was the case with strncpy(), strncat() returns the pointer dest. Here's an example of strncat() in action:

```
char name[ 20 ];

strncpy( name, "Dave ", 20 );
strncat( name, "Mark", 4 );
```

The call of strncpy() copies the string "Dave " into the array name. The call of strncat() copies the string "Mark" onto the end of dest, leaving dest with the properly terminated string "Dave Mark". Again, the return value was ignored.

As was the case with strcpy(), the Standard Library offers a matching function for strncat() called strcat(). It does not provide the safeguard against buffer overflow and should not be used.

strncmp()

strncmp() is declared as follows:

```
int strcmp( const char *s1, const char *s2, size_t n );
```

strncmp() compares the strings s1 and s2, comparing not more than n characters. strncmp() returns 0 if the strings are identical, a positive number if s1 is greater than s2, and a negative number if s2 is greater than s1. The strings are compared one byte at a time. If the strings are not equal, the first byte that is not identical determines the return value.

Here's a sample:

```
if ( 0 == strncmp( "Hello", "Goodbye", 5 ) )
    printf( "The strings are equal!" );
```

Notice that the if succeeds only when the strings are equal. The function strcmp() is the unsafe version of strncmp() and should not be used.

strlen()

strlen() is declared as follows:

```
size_t  strlen( const char *s );
```

`strlen()` returns the length of the string pointed to by s. As an example, this call

```
length = strlen( "Aardvark" );
```

returns a value of 8, the number of characters in the string, not counting the terminating zero.

More Standard Library Information

There is a lot more to the Standard Library than what we've covered in this book. Having made it this far, consider yourself an official C programmer. You now have a sworn duty to dig in to the C Standard Library page I've referred to throughout the book. In case you haven't bookmarked it yet, it's here:

```
http://www.infosys.utas.edu.au/info/documentation/C/CStdLib.html
```

A good place to start is with the functions declared in `<string.h>`. Read about the difference is between `strcmp()` and `strncmp()`. Wander around. Get to know the Standard Library very well. Whenever you need functionality, first turn to the Standard Library. Do not reinvent the wheel!

What's Next?

We've covered a variety of topics in this chapter. We started with typecasting and then moved on to unions. You learned about recursion, binary trees, and the inorder, preorder, and postorder techniques for searching binary trees. Next, we explored initializers and a final series of operators, and you learned how to create our own types and stepped through a series of string functions that reside in the Standard Library.

Chapter 12 answers the question, "Where do you go from here?" Do you want to learn to create programs with that special Mac look and feel? Would you like more information on data structures and C programming techniques? Chapter 12 offers some suggestions to help you find your programming direction.

CHAPTER 11 EXERCISES

1. What's wrong with each of the following code fragments?

a.
```
struct Dog {
    struct Dog *next;
} ;

struct Cat {
    struct Cat *next;
} ;

struct Dog    myDog;
struct Cat    myCat;

myDog.next = (struct Dog)&myCat;
myCat.next = NULL;
```

b.
```
int    *MyFunc( void );
typedef    int (*FuncPtr)();

FuncPtr    myFuncPtr = MyFunc;
```

c.
```
union Number {
    int    i;
    float    f;
    char    *s;
} ;

Number    myUnion;

myUnion.f = 3.5;
```

d.
```
struct Player {
    int    type;
    char    name[ 40 ];
    int    team;
    union {
        int    myInt;
        float  myFloat;
    } u;
} myPlayer;

myPlayer.team = 27;
myPlayer.myInt = -42;
myPlayer.myFloat = 5.7;
```

e. ```
int   *myFuncPtr(int);
```

```
myFuncPtr = main;
*myFuncPtr();
```

f. ```
char   s[20];
```

```
strncpy( s, "Hello", 5 );
```

```
if ( strcmp( s, "Hello" ) )
    printf( "The strings are the same!" );
```

g. ```
char *s;
```

```
s = malloc( 20 );
strcpy( "Heeeere's Johnny!", s );
```

h. ```
char *s;
```

```
strcpy( s, "Aardvark" );
```

i. ```
void DoSomeStuff(void) {
    /* stuff done here */
}
```

```
int main( void ) {
    int     ii;

    for ( ii = 0; ii < 10; ii++ )
        DoSomeStuff;

    return 0;
}
```

2. Write a program that reads in a series of integers from a file, storing the numbers in a binary tree in the same fashion that the words were stored earlier in the chapter. Store the first number as the root of the tree. Next, store the second number in the left branch if it is less than the first number and the right branch if it is greater than or equal to the first number. Continue this process until all the numbers are stored in the tree.

   Now write a series of functions that print the contents of the tree using preorder, inorder, and postorder recursive searches.
```

Where Do You Go from Here?

*n*ow that you've mastered the fundamentals of C, you're ready to dig into the specifics of Mac programming. As you've run the example programs in the previous chapters, you've probably noticed that none of the programs sport the look and feel that make a Mac program a Mac program.

For one thing, all of the interaction between you and your program focuses on the keyboard and the console window. None of the programs take advantage of the mouse. None offer color graphics, pull-down menus, buttons, check-boxes, scrolling windows or any of the thousand things that make Mac OS X applications so special. These things are all part of the Mac user interface.

The Mac User Interface

The user interface is the part of your program that interacts with the user. So far, your user interface skills have focused on writing to and reading from the console window, using functions such as `printf()`, `scanf()`, and `getchar()`. The advantage of this type of user interface is that each of the aforementioned functions is available on every machine that supports the C language. Programs written using the Standard C Library are extremely portable.

On the down side, console-based user interfaces tend to be limited. With a console-based interface, you can't use an elegant graphic to make a point. Text-based interfaces can't provide animation or digital sound. In a nutshell, the console-based interface is simple and, at the same time, simple to program. Mac OS X's **graphical user interface** (GUI) offers an elegant, more sophisticated method of working with a computer.

Objective-C and Cocoa

Your Mac just wouldn't be the same without windows, drop-down and pop-up menus, icons, buttons, and scroll bars. You can and should add these user interface elements to your programs. Fortunately, the set of Apple developer tools you downloaded and installed at the beginning of this book includes everything you need to build world-class applications with all the elements that make the Mac great!

The key to working with these elements is understanding Objective-C and Cocoa. The Objective-C language is a superset of C, developed by the same folks who designed and built Mac OS X. There are a number of excellent resources available for learning Objective-C. One of them is just a mouse click away.

Steer your browser to `http://developer.apple.com`, and log in using the same account you used when you downloaded the developer tools back in Chapter 2. Once you are logged in, click this link:

`https://developer.apple.com/referencelibrary/Cocoa/`

Look over the reference categories on this page, just to get a sense of what's available. Your first goal is to find the Objective-C reference materials. Click the link that says *Objective-C Language*. Here's the direct link:

`https://developer.apple.com/referencelibrary/Cocoa/`
`idxObjectiveCLanguage-date.html`

The item you are interested in is the document called *The Objective-C 2.0 Programming Language*. It is available as a PDF or in HTML.

I *love* this document. It is very well written and detailed, and best of all, it is free! Take a few minutes to read through the first few pages. If you feel comfortable with the language and the tone, you've found your path to learning Objective-C.

If this document makes your eyes glaze over and you start to feel a bit gassy, there are plenty of other ways to learn Objective-C. If you like the experience you had reading this book, check out the companion book from Apress, called *Learn Objective-C on the Mac* by Mark Dalrymple and Scott Knaster (2009). Mark and Scott are two of the smartest people I know, and they do an excellent job explaining the concepts behind the Objective-C language. Because that book was written as a sequel to this one, you should feel right at home.

What's Objective-C got that regular old C doesn't? In a word, objects. Just as a `struct` brings variables together under a single name, an object can bring together variables *as well as* functions, binding them together under a single class name.

Objects are incredibly powerful. Every part of the Mac user interface has a set of objects associated with it. Want to create a new window? Just create a new window object, and the object will take care of all the housekeeping associated with maintaining a window. The window object's functions will draw the contents of the window for you, perhaps communicating with other objects to get them to draw themselves within the window.

There are pull-down menu objects, icon objects, scrollbar objects, file objects, even objects that can organize other objects. Chances are, if you can imagine it, there's a set of objects that will help you build it.

Learning Cocoa

Learning Objective-C will teach you the mechanics of working with objects. Once you get that down, you'll turn your attention to Cocoa, Apple's object library. Cocoa is an extensive collection of objects that will allow you to implement pretty much every aspect of the Mac OS X experience.

As you might expect, Apple's developer tools contain some excellent Cocoa documentation. For starters, check out

```
https://developer.apple.com/referencelibrary/GettingStarted/GS_Cocoa/index.
html
```

Once again, you'll find some excellent documentation here, and you can't beat the price.

One Last Bit of Code

My editors are pounding on me to get this last chapter submitted, but I can't resist showing you a bit more—just two more projects, and then I'll let you go. These are just to give you a taste of where you're heading.

Fire up Xcode, and choose **New Project…** from the **File** menu. When the *New Project* window appears, select *Command Line Utility* on the left side of the window. Then, choose *Core Foundation Tool* from the list that appears (see Figure 12-1), and click the *Choose…* button. Name the project *tasteOfObjC*.

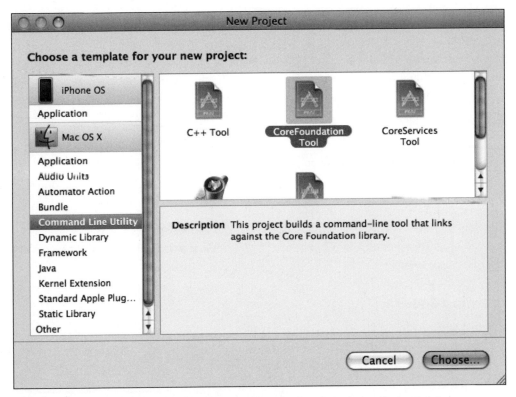

Figure 12-1. *Creating a new Objective-C project using the Core Foundation Tool template*

When the project appears, select **Build and Run** from the **Build** menu. Once the build is complete, bring up the console window. You should see this text:

```
Hello, World!
```

That's it. This project is the starting point for your next big adventure—mastering Objective-C. You'll find that your Objective-C output looks much the same as your C output. All your programs will run in the console window. The difference? You'll be building and using objects. Take the time to understand the mechanics of programming with Objective-C before you add Cocoa to the mix.

Speaking of Cocoa, let's build a Cocoa project, since we're here. Back in Xcode, choose **New Project...** from the **File** menu. When the *New Project* window appears, select *Application*, the very first item under the heading *Mac OS X*. Then, select *Cocoa Document-based Application* from the list that appears (see Figure 12-2), and click the *Choose...* button. Name the project *tasteOfCocoa*.

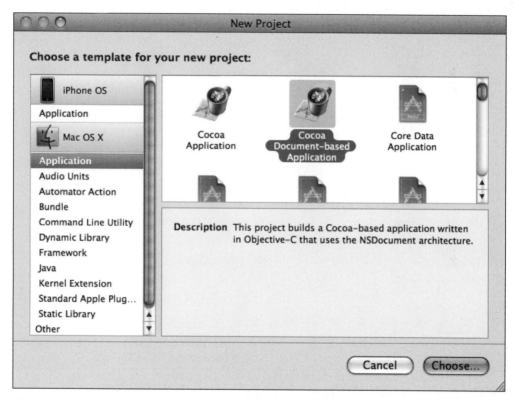

Figure 12-2. *Creating a new Cocoa project using the Cocoa Document-based Application template*

When the project appears, select **Build and Run** from the **Build** menu. After a few seconds of intense compiler action, a new application will launch. You'll be able to tell the new application is running because a window similar to the one shown in Figure 12-3 will appear. In addition, a new application icon with the name *tasteOfCocoa* will appear on the dock, toward the right side, and a menu named **tasteOfCocoa** will appear in the menu bar, just to the right of the Apple menu.

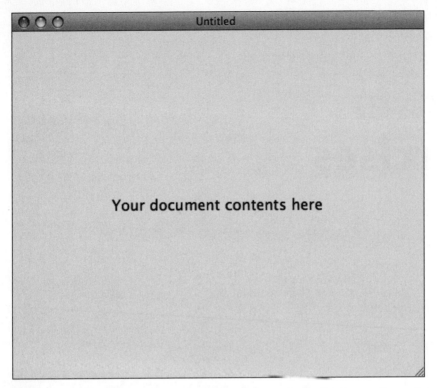

Figure 12-3. *This window tells you that your new Cocoa application is actually running.*

tasteOfCocoa is a real-life Cocoa application. Try resizing the window. Notice that the window redraws its text as you resize it. Select **New** from the **File** menu, and a new window will appear. You can open and close as many windows as you like. This is the "Hello, World!" of Cocoa applications.

Go Get 'Em

Well, that's about it. I hope you enjoyed reading this book as much as I enjoyed writing it. Above all, I hope you are excited about your newfound programming capabilities. By learning C, you've opened the door to an exciting new adventure. You can move on to Objective-C and Cocoa, tackle web programming with PHP, move into the Windows universe with C#, or explore the cross-platform capabilities of Java. There are so many choices out there. And they are all based on C.

Go on out there and write some code. And keep in touch!

Answers to Exercises

*t*his appendix features the answers to the exercises in the back of each chapter. Chapter 4 was the first chapter to feature exercises, so that's where we start.

Chapter 4

1. This screenshot shows the error we got when we changed SayHello(); to SayHello(;.

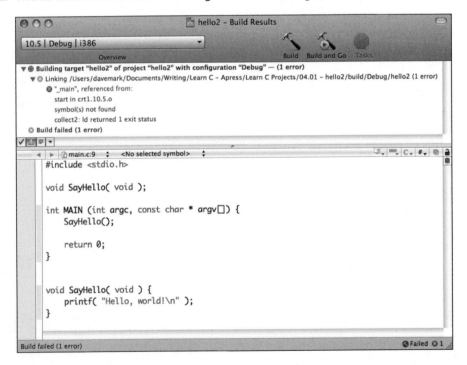

2. This screenshot shows the error we got when we changed main to MAIN.

3. This screenshot shows the error we got when we deleted the left curly brace that opens the main() function.

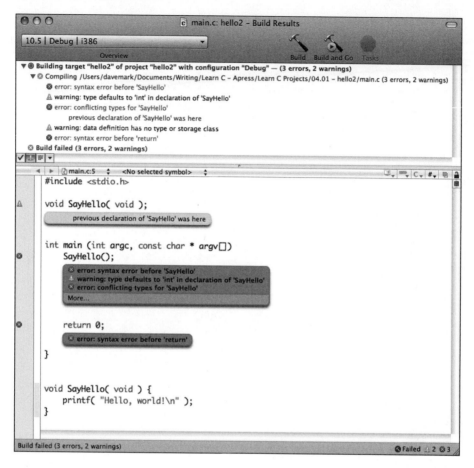

4. This screenshot shows the error we got when we deleted the semicolon at the end of the `printf()`.

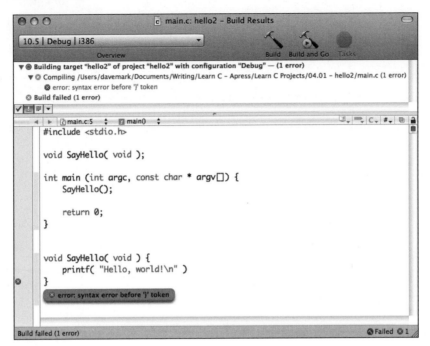

Chapter 5

1. Find the error in each of the following code fragments:

   a. The quotes around "Hello, World" are missing.

   b. The comma between the two variables (myInt and myOtherInt) is missing.

   c. =+ should be += (though =+ will compile with some older compilers).

   d. The second parameter to printf() is missing. Note that this error won't be caught by the compiler and is known as a run-time error.

   e. Here's another run-time error. This time, you are missing the %d in the first argument to printf().

   f. This time, you've either got an extra \ or are missing an n following the \ in the first printf() parameter.

   g. The left-hand and right-hand sides of the assignment are switched.

   h. The declaration of anotherInt is missing.

2. Compute the value of myInt after each code fragment is executed:

   a. 70

   b. −6

   c. −1

   d. 4

   e. −8

   f. 2

   g. 14

   h. 1

Chapter 6

1. What's wrong with each of the following code fragments?

   a. The if statement's expression should be surrounded by parentheses.

   b. We increment i inside the for loop's expression and then decrement it in the body of the loop. This loop will never end!

   c. The while loop has parentheses but is missing an expression.

   d. The do statement should follow this format:

   ```
   do
        statement
   while ( expression ) ;
   ```

   e. Each case in this switch statement contains a text string, which is illegal. Also, case default should read default.

   f. The printf() will never get called.

   g. This is probably the most common mistake made by C programmers. The assignment operator (=) is used instead of the logical equality operator (==). Since the assignment operator is perfectly legal inside an expression, the compiler won't find this error. This is an annoying little error you'll encounter again and again! Consider using 20==i instead of i==20.

   h. Once again, this code will compile, but it likely is not what you wanted. The third expression in the for loop is usually an assignment statement—something to move i toward its terminating condition. The expression i*20 is useless here, since it doesn't change anything.

2. Look in the folder *06.05 - nextPrime2*.

3. Look in the folder *06.06 - nextPrime3*.

Chapter 7

1. Predict the result of each of the following code fragments:

    a. The final value is 25.

    b. The final value is 512. Try changing the `for` loop from 2 to 3. Notice that this generates a number too large for a 2-byte `short` to hold. Now change the `for` loop from 3 to 4. This generates a number too large for even a 4-byte `int` to hold. Be aware of the size of your types!

    c. The final value is 1,024.

2. Look in the folder *07.06 - power2*.

3. Look in the folder *07.07 - nonPrimes*.

Chapter 8

1. What's wrong with each of the following code fragments?

a. If the char type defaults to signed (very likely), c can hold only values from –128 to 127. Even if your char does default to unsigned, this code is dangerous. At the very least, use an unsigned char. Even better, use a short, int, or long.

b. Use %f, %g, or %e to print the value of a float, not %d. Also, the variable being printed is f. It should be myFloat.

c. The text string "a" is composed of two characters, both 'a' and the terminating zero byte. The variable c is only a single byte in size. Even if c were 2 bytes long, you couldn't copy a text string this way. Try copying the text one byte at a time into a variable large enough to hold the text string and its terminating zero byte.

d. Once again, this code uses the wrong approach to copying a text string, and once again, not enough memory is allocated to hold the text string and its zero byte.

e. The #define of kMaxArraySize must come before the first non-#define reference to it.

f. This definition

```
char c[ kMaxArraySize ];
```

creates an array ranging from c[0] to c[kMaxArraySize-1]. The reference to c[kMaxArraySize] is out of bounds.

g. The problem occurs in the line:

```
cPtr++ = 0;
```

This line assigns the pointer variable cPtr a value of 0 (making it point to location 0 in memory) and then increments it to 1 (making it point to location 1 in memory). This code will not compile. Here's a more likely scenario:

```
*cPtr++ = 0;
```

This code sets the char that cPtr points to 0 and then increments cPtr to point to the next char in the array.

h. The problem here is with this statement:

```
c++;
```

You can't increment an array name. Even if you could, if you increment c, you no longer have a pointer to the beginning of the array! A more proper approach is to declare an extra char pointer, assign c to this char pointer, and then increment the copy of c, rather than c itself.

i. You don't need to terminate a #define with a semicolon. This statement defines kMaxArraySize to 200;, which is probably not what we had in mind.

2. Look in the folder *08.08 - dice2*.

3. Look in the folder *08.09 - wordCount2*.

Chapter 9

1. What's wrong with each of the following code fragments?

   a. The semicolon after `employeeNumber` is missing.

   b. This code is pretty useless. If the first character returned by `getchar()` is `'\n'`, the `;` will get executed; otherwise, the loop just exits. Try changing the `==` to `!=`, and see what happens. Also, if you are going to build a loop around a single semi-colon, put the semicolon on its own line. That will make it much easier to read.

   c. This code will actually work, since the double quotes around the header file name tell the compiler to search the local directory in addition to the places it normally searches for system header files. On the other hand, it is considered better form to place angle brackets around a system header file like `<stdio.h>`.

   d. The `name` field is missing its type!

   e. `next` and `prev` should be declared as pointers.

   f. This code has several problems. First, the `while` loop is completely useless. Also, the code should use `'\0'` instead of `0` (though that's really a question of style). Finally, by the time we get to the `printf()`, `line` points beyond the end of the string!

2. Look in the folder *09.06 - cdTracker2*.

3. Look in the folder *09.07 - cdTracker3*.

Chapter 10

1. What's wrong with each of the following code fragments?

   a. The arguments to `fopen()` appear in reverse order.

   b. Once again, the arguments to `fopen()` are reversed. In addition, the first parameter to `fscanf()` contains a prompt, as if you were calling `printf()`. Also, the second parameter to `fscanf()` is defined as a `char`, yet the `%d` format specifier is used, telling `fscanf()` to expect an `int`. This will cause `fscanf()` to store an `int`-sized value in the space allocated for a `char`. Not good! And last, but certainly not least, this code uses `fscanf()` instead of `fgets()`.

   c. `line` is declared as a `char` pointer instead of as an array of `char`s. No memory was allocated for the string being read in by `fscanf()`. Also, since `line` is a pointer, the `&` in the `fscanf()` call shouldn't be there. Once again, we should be using `fgets()`. You'd think we would have learned from the last example.

   d. This code is fine except for two problems. The file is opened for writing, yet we are trying to read from the file using `fscanf()`. Did you catch the fact that we once again did not use `fgets()`? Think about how you'd rewrite the last few snippets using `fgets()`.

2. Look in the folder *10.04 - fileReader*.

3. Look in the folder *10.05 - cdFiler2*.

Chapter 11

1. What's wrong with each of the following code fragments?

   a. In the next-to-last line, the address of `myCat` is cast to a `struct`. Instead, the address should be cast to a `(struct Dog *)`.

   b. The `typedef` defines `FuncPtr` to be a pointer to a function that returns an `int`. `MyFunc()` is declared to return a pointer to an `int`, not an `int`.

   c. The declaration of `myUnion` is missing the keyword `union`. Here's the corrected declaration:

      ```
      union    Number    myUnion;
      ```

   d. The `Player` union fields must be accessed using `u`. Instead of `myPlayer.myInt`, refer to `myPlayer.u.myInt`. Instead of `myPlayer.myFloat`, refer to `myPlayer.u.myFloat`.

   e. First, `myFuncPtr` is not a function pointer and not a legal l-value. As is, the declaration just declares a function named `myFuncPtr`. This declaration fixes that problem:

      ```
      int       (*myFuncPtr)( int );
      ```

      Next, `main()` doesn't take a single `int` as a parameter. Besides that, calling `main()` yourself is a questionable practice. Finally, to call the function pointed to by `myFuncPtr`, use either `myFuncPtr();` or `(*myFuncPtr)();`, instead of `*myFuncPtr();`.

   f. `strcmp()` returns 0 if the strings are equal. The `if` would fail if the strings were the same. The message passed to `printf()` is wrong. Finally, we should be calling `strncmp()` instead of `strcmp()`.

   g. The parameters passed to `strcpy()` should be reversed. And we should be calling `strncpy()` instead of `strcpy()`.

   h. No memory was allocated for s. When `strcpy()` copies the string, it will be writing over unintended memory. Once again, we should be calling `strncpy()`.

   i. Tons of people, including battle-scarred veterans, run into this problem. The function call in the loop is not actually a function call. Instead, the address of the function `DoSomeStuff` is evaluated. Because this address is not assigned to anything or used in any other way, the result of the evaluation is discarded. The expression `DoSomeStuff;` is effectively a no-op, making the entire loop a no-op.

In addition, note that the parameter list in `main()` is missing its usual `argc` and `argv`. Instead, it uses void, indicating that it has no parameters. This is actually quite legal. It tells the universe that you have no intention of ever taking advantage of `argc` and `argv`.

2. Look in the folder *11.05 - treePrinter*.

Index

You Need the Companion eBook

Your purchase of this book entitles you to buy the companion PDF-version eBook for only $10. Take the weightless companion with you anywhere.

We believe this Apress title will prove so indispensable that you'll want to carry it with you everywhere, which is why we are offering the companion eBook (in PDF format) for $10 to customers who purchase this book now. Convenient and fully searchable, the PDF version of any content-rich, page-heavy Apress book makes a valuable addition to your programming library. You can easily find and copy code—or perform examples by quickly toggling between instructions and the application. Even simultaneously tackling a donut, diet soda, and complex code becomes simplified with hands-free eBooks!

Once you purchase your book, getting the $10 companion eBook is simple:

❶ Visit **www.apress.com/promo/tendollars/**.

❷ Complete a basic registration form to receive a randomly generated question about this title.

❸ Answer the question correctly in 60 seconds, and you will receive a promotional code to redeem for the $10.00 eBook.

Apress®
THE EXPERT'S VOICE™

2855 TELEGRAPH AVENUE | SUITE 600 | BERKELEY, CA 94705

Offer valid through 6/09.